D0848322

TRANSITION TO PARENTHOOD

Volume 119, Sage Library of Social Research

RECENT VOLUMES IN
SAGE LIBRARY OF SOCIAL RESEARCH

TRANSITION TO PARENTHOOD

How Infants Change Families

Ralph LaRossa and
Maureen Mulligan LaRossa

Volume 119
SAGE LIBRARY OF
SOCIAL RESEARCH

SAGE PUBLICATIONS   Beverly Hills   London

For information address:

SAGE Publications, Inc.
275 South Beverly Drive
Beverly Hills, California 90212

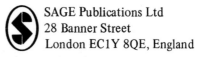

SAGE Publications Ltd
28 Banner Street
London EC1Y 8QE, England

Printed in the United States of America

Library of Congress Cataloging in Publication Data

LaRossa, Ralph.
  Transition to parenthood.

  (Sage library of social research ; 119)
  Bibliography: p.
  Includes indexes.
  1. Parenting–United States.   2. Parents
–United States–Interviews.   3. Parent and
child–United States.   I. LaRossa, Maureen
Mulligan, joint author.   II. Title.   III. Title:
How children shape parent's lives.
HQ755.8.L37   306.8'7   80-26766

ISBN 0-8039-1566-7
ISBN 0-8039-1567-5

FIRST PRINTING

CONTENTS

To Our Parents
and
To Brian

ACKNOWLEDGMENTS

Our principal debt is to the couples who so graciously gave of their time and their selves to be a part of the study. Their contribution is immeasurable.

Were it not for the financial support from Georgia State University, the study would not have been possible. We are especially grateful to the university review boards that voted to fund the project, and we hope that this book confirms the faith they had in us.

Our interviewer, Victor Wagner, deserves a tremendous amount of credit for his sensitivity and skill. There are not many people who could have done the job as well as he did.

No small factor in the successful completion of this book was the conscientious and competent administrative assistance we received. Our heartfelt thanks go to Cele G. Ouseley, Lanie Shaw, Pat Nodine, Jacquelyn J. Rosemond, Brenda A. Woodyard, and Sherry P. Hood.

We were very fortunate to have friends and colleagues who took a genuine interest in what we were doing. Michael L. Chernoff was always ready to listen, and even more ready to tell us straight out what he thought about our ideas, hypotheses, etc. Several chapters in this book were vastly improved thanks to his critical eye (and pen). Donald C. Reitzes, Joseph H. Pleck, Reuben Hill, Paula L. Dressel, Warren B. Miller, Jaymie Wolcott Chernoff, Barbara Dunbar, and Randall Stokes reviewed parts of the manuscript, often at record speed. We shall never forget their willingness to "make" time for us.

R. L. and M. M. L.

PREFACE

Numerous books have examined how parents shape the lives of their children, but how do children shape the lives of their parents? How, for example, does the presence of a baby in the home affect a couple's daily routine, the roles partners play, the feelings they have for each other?

This book is about these and other questions related to early parenthood. Based on conjoint, in-depth interviews with twenty couples during the third, sixth, and ninth months after the birth of each couple's first or second child, it attempts to penetrate the barrier that husbands and wives often create for outsiders, and provide a close-up look at one of the most important phases in the family life cycle.

A number of things make this book unique:

1. It takes a sociological rather than an individualistic approach. Up to now, researchers have primarily focused on the personal reactions of fathers and mothers to having a baby. What has been lacking, and what is seriously needed, is an examination of the social patterns, social processes, and socio-historical conditions underlying the transition to parenthood (Hill, 1978; Hobbs and Wimbish, 1977; Lamb, 1978; Mortimer and Simmons, 1978; Parke and Sawin, 1976).

2. It is a story about early parenthood as parents see it. Each interview was essentially open ended and free flowing; the couples were encouraged to talk about what was important to them, not what the interviewer presumed to be important.

3. It is a study of change. By scheduling not one but three interviews with each couple, we were able to monitor the shifts in the couples' marriages as well as the changing attitudes they developed toward their lives.

4. It examines both first- and second-time parenthood. Virtually all previous studies have assumed that the transition to parenthood is "over" with the birth of the first child. We do not make this assumption, but see the transition to parenthood as a "dynamic process of becoming" that theoretically can extend the whole length of the childbearing phase.

5. Finally, it is written from both an outsider's and an insider's perspective. Married in 1970, we had our first child in 1979, right in the middle of our analysis of the interview transcripts. Hence, we have had the unique opportunity of experiencing our own transition to parenthood at the same time that we were trying to understand the experiences of others.

We should make clear from the start that this is not a book on child development. Although the developmental stages of infants do, at times, figure into our analysis, they do not occupy center stage here, as they do, for example, in the work of Brazelton (1969) or Spock (1976). Our primary interest, in other words, is not the social world of children, but the social world of parents and, even more specifically, the social world of marriage during the transition to parenthood.

We should, perhaps, also make clear that, as do all studies, this study rests upon certain value judgments. One value judgment is especially central to the book, and should be made explicit from the beginning. We believe that sexual equality is morally right and, over the long run, in the best interest of men and women. We say "over the long run" because we know that instituting equality would mean some immediate sacrifices for a lot of people, particularly men. However, we think that men and women, as a group, would ultimately benefit from living in a society that gave all its members an equal chance to be whatever they wanted to be and to do whatever they wanted to do, a society that did not assume that certain individuals, by virtue of the fact that they were born male, should have more of a right or obligation to the marketplace, and that others, by virtue of the fact that they were born female, should have more of a right or obligation to nurture their children. Unfortunately, our study indicates that, contrary to what some people believe, sexual equality inside and outside the home is not a reality now, nor is it likely to become a reality in the very near future. Sexism is too firmly rooted in the taken-for-granted-world of family life for us to pretend otherwise. Our hope is that this book will, in some small way, help to change things for the better.

There are five parts to the book. Part One critically reviews the transition to parenthood literature, spells out what we mean by a sociological approach, and describes the sampling, interviewing, and analysis strategies in the study.

Part Two presents the major sociological orientations as well as the concepts and hypotheses that are the product of our analysis.

Part Three and Part Four detail the experiences of four of the couples in the sample, two of whom represent the breadwinner-homemaker family structure, and two of whom represent the two paycheck family structure. Within each of these classifications, the case studies are further divided according to first-versus second-time parenthood.

Part Five summarizes and extends the major thesis of the book by discussing variations in the basic pattern generated by the data and by comparing family systems with other social systems.

PART ONE: FOCUS

Chapter 1

TOWARD A SOCIOLOGY OF THE TRANSITION TO PARENTHOOD

There are few events that have more of an impact on a family than the birth of a child. Whether one focuses on the general consequences of adding members to a group, or looks more specifically at how the work and power structure of a marriage changes with the addition of a dependent infant, there is no denying that having a baby can radically alter a family's life.

Given the social structural significance of the transition to parenthood, one would expect an impressive body of sociological research dealing with the topic; however, this is not the case. Only about 1 percent of the family studies published in the most prestigious sociological journals deal with the question of how children affect parents (Atkinson and Gecas, 1978).[1]

Why has the transition to parenthood not been a popular topic among family sociologists? We think that the answer partially lies in the paradigm that currently dominates the field. We believe that this paradigm frames the transition to parenthood issue in ways that are uninteresting to sociologists, and that sociologists, perhaps not recognizing that it is the paradigm rather than the issue itself that is uninteresting, are underestimating the sociological significance of this research topic. If sociologists continue to overlook the transition to parenthood, they will miss the opportunity to examine what is, in our opinion, one of the most important social issues of the day.

The objective of this book, and particularly of this chapter, is to reframe the transition to parenthood issue, to put it squarely within "the sociological imagination" (Mills, 1959). In the next few pages, we will identify the paradigm which we feel has blinded sociologists to the potential in studying the transition to parenthood. We will then critically examine the major studies on the topic, and will show how, for the most part, they are nonsociological in both their conception and their design. Finally, we will describe the steps that we feel must be taken to move toward a sociology of the transition to parenthood.

THE INDIVIDUALISTIC PARADIGM
IN TRANSITION TO PARENTHOOD RESEARCH

The majority of studies on the transition to parenthood focus on how the quality of personal or marital life changes after the birth of a child. And perhaps because of their preoccupation with the quality of life, these studies suffer from the same problem that plagues many studies dealing with the quality of life issue, namely, the tendency to perceive and define the quality of life in individualistic terms.

An *individualistic* measure of the quality of life focuses on "the degree to which an individual succeeds in accomplishing his desires despite the constraints put upon him by a hostile or indifferent nature, God or social order." From this point of view, "the problem faced by people . . . is one of doing as well as possible" despite the situation (Gerson, 1976: 794, 796). For example, an individualistic measure of the quality of health care in a country would focus on how much individuals feel personally inconvenienced by having to be periodically hospitalized for one kind of illness or another; the fewer people who feel inconvenienced, the better the health care.

There are basically three flaws in this conceptualization. First, the individualistic approach stresses attitudes to such an extent that interaction patterns are often ignored altogether. In other words, researchers operating within this paradigm are so preoccupied with whether people are comfortable with a situation that they neglect to examine the situation itself. Second, the approach looks at health as a "status," and thus fails to seriously consider the reciprocal relationship between health and the other aspects of people's lives. Third, and last, the individualistic approach has a distinct administrative bias, which is to say that researchers using this paradigm seem to be more concerned with bureaucratic efficiency than with improving the quality of life ("As long as there are no complaints . . .") (Gerson, 1976: 802).

The empirical literature on the transition to parenthood generally suffers from these same three flaws; it too, in other words, exhibits a strong individualistic bent. To illustrate just how strong this bias is, we have put together an annotated bibliography (see Appendix A) summarizing the major studies on the transition to parenthood. The reader can thus see the extent to which researchers have tended to (1) examine attitudes rather than behavior, (2) rely on cross-sectional rather than longitudinal data, and (3) focus on personal coping rather than social-historical conditions. We estimate that approximately three-fourths of the findings in the bibliography can be classified as individualistic in scope.

Parenthood As Crisis Research

Probably the best known series of studies on the transition to parenthood is the "parenthood as crisis" series. Beginning with LeMasters's (1957) article and continuing through the work of Dyer (1963), Russell (1974), and all of Hobbs's reports (Hobbs, 1965, 1968; Hobbs and Cole, 1976; Hobbs and Wimbish, 1977), the principal question in this line of research has been, Does the transition to parenthood constitute a "crisis"? With the exception of the first two papers in this series, the sole criterion for answering this question has been a twenty-three-item checklist developed by Hobbs in 1965.[2]

On initial inspection, the checklist appears to be a measure that goes beyond an individualistic approach in that many of the items refer to patterns of family interaction. For example, subjects are asked about "interruption of routine habits of sleeping, going places, etc.," and "decreased sexual responsiveness of spouse." The individualistic assumptions underlying the instrument become apparent, however, when one recognizes that the subjects are not being asked whether there *has* been any interruption of routine or whether their sex life *has* changed in any way; they are being asked to "indicate the extent to which each one [one of the items] has *bothered* them." The options which the subjects have to choose from are "not at all," "somewhat," and "very much," which are scored 0, 1, and 2 respectively. Thus, if a husband or wife marks "not at all" for "decreased sexual responsiveness of spouse," we do not know whether there has been no change in the couple's sexual pattern or whether there has been a change but they are not bothered by such a change. The emphasis of the checklist, in other words, is not on patterns of interaction but on the coping abilities of the individual subjects. In the language of the individualistic approach, what Hobbs and others who have used the checklist have been mainly interested in is "how well" their subjects are doing despite the new constraints of parenthood.

The conceptual limitations in the crisis index were noted soon after Hobbs published his second article. In his review of the transition to parenthood studies published to date, Jacoby (1969: 722) indicated that:

Previous research has failed to differentiate between a behavioral change or adjustment and the (possibly negative) attitude taken toward this required change by the parents. It seems likely that some persons may view even minor role alterations as highly problematical, while others who are experiencing major changes accept them with equanimity. For example, many new mothers report having to quit a job with the arrival of the baby. Although this accommodation to parenthood probably represents a major change for the married couple, the change is likely to be viewed negatively by some, in a neutral way by others, and positively by still others. It would seem that "parenthood as crisis" research has allowed little opportunity or stimulus for the reporting of affectively positive or neutral attitudes toward the adjustments required by parenthood.

Although Hobbs did not change his approach in any of his studies published after Jacoby's article (Hobbs and Cole, 1976, and Hobbs and Wimbish, 1977, essentially replicate the earlier studies), one "parenthood as crisis" researcher did consider Jacoby's critique and designed her study accordingly. When Russell (1974) carried out her research, she attempted to counteract the "negative" element in previous studies by "fashioning after Hobbs's crisis checklist" a twelve-item gratification checklist. It should be noted, however, that using a positively oriented checklist in addition to the Hobbs index only responds to Jacoby's second point. His first, and more important, point— that previous research has failed to distinguish between behavioral and attitudinal changes—is ignored.

Russell's gratification checklist asks "new parents what things they enjoyed about their newly acquired role" (1974: 295).[3] Given the way the instructions are worded, it is possible that some subjects reported their behavior while others reported their attitudes (their enjoyment with the items listed), which seems to be what Russell wanted them to do. Assuming the purpose and consequence of the new checklist is to tap personal attitudes, then it too must be considered individualistic. Again, the principal concern is "how well" the subjects are doing.

Marital Satisfaction Research

Interestingly enough, although the parenthood as crisis issue is probably better known, there is a second question which has been asked more often by transition to parenthood researchers. That question is, How does the transition to parenthood impact on marital satisfaction (or marital adjustment, happiness, stress, etc.)? All but one of Hobbs's studies (Hobbs, 1968) included "marriage ratings" reflecting how his subjects perceived their relationships before (retrospectively) and after birth. And Feldman (1974), Meyerowitz and Feldman (1966), Miller and Sollie (1980), Russell (1974), Ryder (1973), and Sollie and Miller (1980) all examined how parenthood affects marital satisfaction. That marital satisfaction is the most frequently studied dependent variable is actually not surprising, since conjugal satisfaction/adjustment is one of the most popular topics in the family life literature (Atkinson and Gecas, 1978).

On initial inspection, marital satisfaction measures also appear to go beyond an individualistic approach in that the reference point for these measures is often a variety of marital patterns. But like the crisis index, the main focus in virtually all marital satisfaction questionnaires is not marital patterns per se but the personal attitudes of husbands and wives. As Hawkins (1968: 648) notes:

> Marital satisfaction is clearly an *attitudinal variable* and, thus, is a *property of individual spouses.* . . . It is a global measurement in the sense that the respondent is asked to express his feelings of satisfaction or dissatisfaction regarding large numbers of specific facets [our italics].

For example, the subjects in Miller and Sollie's (1980) study were asked to indicate "the degree to which they felt bothered, bored, tense, frustrated, unhappy, worried, and neglected in their day to day marriage relationship" (1980: 5). Although the phrase "marital relationship" denotes a group-level phenomenon, the purpose of using the measure (which was developed by Pearlin, 1975) is to determine, in the vernacular of the individualistic approach, "how well" Miller and Sollie's subjects are personally coping with the new constraints of parenthood.

SHIFT IN EMPHASIS:
FROM INDIVIDUAL EVALUATIONS
TO SOCIAL INTERACTION

We want to make clear that we are not taking the position that attitudes (or feelings, beliefs, etc.) are irrelevant variables in transition to parenthood research. We do not want to give the impression that we think that the "parenthood as crisis" and "marital satisfaction" studies have been wasted efforts. Rather, we are simply concerned about the extent to which individual evaluations have become the principal focus of the field, and would like to see more attention being given to (1) social patterns, (2) social processes, and (3) sociohistorical linkages. These three items are essentially the alternatives to the three flaws underlying the individualistic approach, and they consti- tute the core elements of a *sociological* approach to the transi- tion to parenthood. To best show the difference between the individualistic and the sociological approaches, we will review, once again, the three major flaws of the individualistic approach to the quality of life issue, but this time we will directly apply the flaws to the transition to parenthood studies.

Social Patterns

Because studies of the transition to parenthood have relied so extensively (and in many cases exclusively) on evaluative mea- sures such as the crisis index and marital satisfaction scales, the question of "normal activity" during the transition to parent- hood remains vague. For example, we do not know very much about how family routines change after birth. Nor do we have a good sense of how sexual interaction (and by "interaction" we mean more than simply the frequency of intercourse) changes with a newborn in the family. If there is one particular topic that should intrigue even the most committed "satisfaction researchers," it is sex after birth. Yet postpartum sexual activity has been largely ignored by family scholars.

The potential payoff of shifting from individualistic to sociological concerns can be seen by examining the studies that have not taken a crisis/satisfaction approach to the transition to parenthood. Sociologically oriented researchers have been building a body of evidence that suggests a very strong and very definite shift toward traditional marital patterns after the birth of a child. Whether the variable in question is patterns of communication (as in Meyerowitz and Feldman, 1966, and Raush et al., 1970) or patterns of housework and baby care (as in Cowan et al., 1978, and Entwisle and Doering, 1980), couples seem to become more differentiated (segregated, specialized, etc.) when they become parents. This structural transformation is theoretically significant. Since social systems become more transparent during transition periods (cf. Lewis, 1959; also Garfinkel, 1967), researchers should be able to learn a great deal about the sometimes subtle patterns underlying traditional marital systems if they focus their attention on the early postpartum phase in the marital life cycle. The practical implications of traditionalization following birth should also not be ignored. Traditionalization may, in fact, be the key to the one consistent finding in the crisis/satisfaction studies; that is to say, a traditional role structure may be the primary cause behind middle-class mothers experiencing significantly more difficulty during the transition to parenthood than middle-class fathers.

Social Processes

The second major flaw underlying the majority of studies on the transition to parenthood is the tendency to conceptualize the quality of life after birth as a "status" or "condition" rather than as a "process." The individualistic approach of these studies has encouraged a quasi-medical orientation whereby one's attitude to the transition to parenthood is seen as something that one "has," in the same sense that one "has" a cold.

This quasi-medical orientation has probably played a significant part in determining the methodological designs which are popular in transition to parenthood research. All but one of the crisis/satisfaction studies employ cross-sectional (versus longitudinal) designs. (That one study is the research on which Miller and Sollie, 1980, and Sollie and Miller, 1980, are based.) Thus, the major focus of this body of research has been to try to determine whether (not how) relatively fixed variables (such as age, gender, length of time married, socioeconomic status) "put someone *in* crisis or distress." What these researchers have failed to capture is the complex way in which postpartum health reciprocally interacts over time with the emergent aspects of people's lives.

We are not suggesting that researchers drop demographic variables from their analyses. On the contrary, we are very interested in how gender and socioeconomic status impact on the quality of postpartum life. However, we recognize that we will never grasp the dynamics of male-female relationships or the plight of the various social classes during the transition to parenthood unless we empirically examine how interaction variables (e.g., marital power, the division of labor) and attitude variables (e.g., distress, but also values, beliefs, and norms) are related.

The best example of the point we are trying to make is provided by Entwisle and Doering (1980). In our opinion, their short-term longitudinal study of lower- and middle-class couples is, by far, the most impressive study to date on the transition to parenthood. Using multivariate analysis, they uncover an interesting interaction effect between social class, gender, previous baby experience, and present division of infant care. Whereas previous baby care experience was found to be positively related to the amount of infant care that middle-class fathers contributed, previous baby experience was negatively related to the amount of fathering that the lower-class men did. As we see it, this suggests a complex reciprocal relationship between parent-infant interaction and attitude toward parent-infant interaction. The lower-class men's negative conception of a

baby's interpersonal competence may have resulted in a self-ful-
filling prophesy whereby their experiences with infants rein-
forced and strengthened their beliefs that "kids are not much
fun." These beliefs would then serve to discourage the men
from further interaction (or "not any more than we have to
do"). In contrast, the middle-class men may have, from the
start, attributed higher interpersonal competence to infants
than their lower-class counterparts, and thus may have found
their initial experiences with babies generally more rewarding,
which served to encourage their future interaction with their
sons or daughters. (The general connection between perceived
interpersonal competence and satisfaction with a relationship is
discussed by Burr et al., 1979a.)

The essentially static orientation underlying the individualistic approach to the transition to parenthood has also influenced one other methodological decision. With a single exception, all of the transition to parenthood studies focus exclusively on the first birth. (The exception is the research on which
Feldman, 1974, and Meyerowitz and Feldman, 1966, are based.
This research included parents who just had their second child.)
Selecting the first birth not only implies that one sees the initial
step into parenthood as the most important transition, it also
suggests that one views the process of becoming a parent as
"over" with the first birth. This is a weak assumption, one that
reflects a psychologistic conception of personality/social system
development. A better approach would be to view the transition
to parenthood as a *"dynamic process of becoming* rather than a
static state of being" (Olsen, 1968: 4). Such an approach would
encourage studies of second- (or third-, fourth-, etc.) time
parenthood which collectively would form an overall picture of
the process of becoming a parent and an overall picture of the
process of becoming a larger family system.

Sociohistorical Linkages

The third major drawback of the individualistic approach is
that it takes a remedial rather than a preventative stance to

whatever troubles couples seem to be having with the transition to parenthood. Assuming that these troubles stem from a lack of interpersonal support, individualistically oriented researchers (as well as individualistically oriented writers and therapists) see the problem as an administrative one: the key, to them, is putting couples who are having problems in touch with various agents of change, such as group or individual counseling, or some program of continuing education. Thus, in the past few years, a number of self-help organizations, such as C.O.P.E. (Coping with the Overall Pregnancy/Parenting Experience), and how-to courses, such as those which are regularly offered by C.E.A. (the Childbirth Education Association) have become part of the American scene. While we applaud the introduction of these programs, we believe it is imperative to recognize that they are not enough.

The difficulties which many couples are experiencing are not simply "personal troubles" to be dealt with only on a couple-by-couple basis; they are "public issues" with deep sociohistorical roots (see Mills, 1959: 8). To mistake societal problems for individual troubles not only impedes the discovery of solutions to the social problem, but may in fact add to the social problem itself. A case in point is the tendency for many self-help groups to be limited to women. In some instances, this is the choice of the mothers, whereas in others it is a function of the fathers' unwillingness to get involved. As helpful as these women-only groups are to many individuals, the groups, by their structure, implicitly define the difficulties of early parenthood as falling under the heading of "women's troubles." Furthermore, by excluding fathers (either by choice or by circumstance), the onus of responsibility for dealing with the difficulties of early parenthood falls on the mother. This is true even if the collective opinion of the group is that the burden of guilt lies with the father. It is not uncommon, in fact, for many of these group discussions to center on "what is to be done about Dad's refusal to 'help' with the baby." Whatever solutions are proposed, however, have been formed without Dad's imprimatur, which means he can reject them out of hand, or worse, reply with anger over his wife's supposed attempt to "run his life." These unintended but very real consequences of individualistically oriented support groups perpetuate and amplify the larger problem.

Although having men-only and couples' groups in addition to the women-only groups would be a vast improvement, the groups are still only remedial in that they can do nothing about the structural inequality that is built into the society. The fact that, as Entwisle and Doering (1980) note, the "lion's share" of baby care is shouldered by the mother is not something that will change through individual/group counseling. The most that the group movement can hope for is that fathers will do more than they are doing now, or that they will do enough to "give their wives a break every once in a while." The group movement cannot, however, change the sociohistorical conditions which underlie the difficulties that many men and women are experiencing with the transition to parenthood. Only by attacking the division of labor at its roots, in the larger society, can we ever hope to change the inequalities in the home. This means that we must concern ourselves with more than simply whether people are willing to admit that they are "bothered," or "distressed," or "gratified" with parenthood. We must begin to examine the macro- and micro-social organizational processes which are the "stuff" in the transition to parenthood issue.

CONCLUSION

The principal message of this chapter is in its title: we must move toward a sociological understanding of the transition to parenthood; we must begin to study, over time and within sociohistorical boundaries, the patterns of interaction in families with infants. Focusing not only on child socialization or development, but also on parent socialization, marital communication, conflict, power, the division of labor, etc., we must channel our efforts toward achieving a better understanding of how family systems are affected by the birth of a child.

This book is intended as but a first (or perhaps, more accurately, a second or third) step in this direction. We do not pretend to have perfectly met the three criteria by which previous studies have been judged, but we do believe that we have progressed far beyond an individualistic approach and that the concepts and hypotheses developed from our analysis can serve as a map in designing studies that will bring us closer to a sociological understanding of the transition to parenthood.

NOTES

1. Atkinson and Gecas (1978) content analyzed articles published between 1968 and 1977 in the *Journal of Marriage and the Family* and family related articles published in the *American Sociological Review* and the *American Journal of Sociology,* and found that nine of the eight hundred seventy-nine articles in their sample could be classified under the topic, "effect of child on parent." All nine were in *JMF.* By way of contrast, forty-four of the articles dealt with "effect of parent on child," and thirty-four of the articles dealt with "parent-child interaction." In their discussion of their coding procedures and category definitions for topics, it is clear that transition to parenthood studies were coded under the first topic heading.

2. The Hobbs Index: "Below are listed some things which other persons have said bothered them following the birth of their first child. Please indicate the extent to which each one has bothered you by a check mark in the appropriate column. Not at all (Score 0). Somewhat (Score 1). Very much (Score 2). This has bothered me—(1) My husband (or wife) showing too little attention to baby. (2) Interference from in-laws. (3) Worry about wife's personal appearance in general. (4) Decreased contact with friends. (5) Interruption of routine habits of sleeping, going places, etc. (6) My husband (or wife) showing too much attention to baby. (7) Additional amount of work. (8) Disturbed about feelings I have toward baby. (9) Housekeeping not as neat as it should be. (10) Decreased sexual responsiveness of self. (11) Feeling more 'distant' from my husband (or wife). (12) Being unable to sleep after going to bed. (13) Having to change plans we had before baby's birth. (14) Decreased sexual responsiveness of husband (or wife). (15) Meals being off schedule. (16) My husband (or wife) showing too little attention to me and too much to the baby. (17) Increased money problems. (18) Reduced feelings of privacy. (19) Doubting my worth as a parent. (20) Worry about wife's 'loss of figure.' (21) Decreased contact with persons at work, etc. (22) Physical tiredness or fatigue. (23) Feeling 'edgy' or emotionally upset."

3. The Russell Index: "Below are listed some things which persons have enjoyed since the birth of their first child. Please indicate the extent to which each one has been true for you. Not at all (Score 0). Somewhat (Score 1). Very much (Score 2). (1) Pride in my baby's development. (2) Fewer periods of boredom. (3) Relationship with relatives closer. (4) Increased appreciation for family and religious tradition. (5) Increased contact with neighbors. (6) More things to talk with spouse about. (7) Feeling 'closer' to spouse. (8) Feeling of 'fulfillment.' (9) New appreciation of my own parents. (10) Baby fun to play with. (11) A purpose for living. (12) Enjoy baby's company."

Chapter 2

THE STUDY

From the start, we intended to conduct an *exploratory* study of the transition to parenthood. The existing literature in the field (annotated in Appendix A, and analyzed in Chapter 1) suggested that there was a need for a study that would have as its purpose the discovery of concepts and hypotheses relevant to the transition to parenthood. From the start, we also intended to design a study that would take a *sociological* versus an individualistic approach to the topic. Thus, following through on points made in Chapter 1, we were determined to: first, study behavior as well as attitudes and their relationship to each other; second, examine the transition to parenthood as a longitudinal process; and third, look at how sociohistorical and biographical factors are interrelated in families in which a birth has recently occurred. A *qualitative* design was chosen because this style of research is one of the best ways, if not the best way, to carry out an exploratory study of social interaction.[1]

SAMPLE

While reviewing past studies, it was discovered that, with a single exception (the project on which Feldman, 1974, and Meyerowitz and Feldman, 1966, are based), research on the transition to parenthood has focused exclusively on the first birth. Believing that this might be a mistake both conceptually and methodologically, we decided to split our sample in half, and interview ten couples who just had their first child and ten couples who just had their second.

We also decided to limit the sample to white, middle-class couples because, for one thing, we felt that a sample of twenty was just too small to validly support more than a few "comparison groups." The first- versus second-time comparison was seen as more important, given our objectives, than either racial or socioeconomic comparisons. As it turned out, the differences between breadwinner-homemaker families and two-paycheck families also became significant during the analysis, so in retrospect it is a good thing that we did not try initially to divide the sample in any way other than the first versus the second birth. Another reason why the sample includes only white, middle-class couples is because, being white and middle class ourselves, we knew that this was the group with whom we would be able to establish the most rapport and with whom we could best empathize.

Two sampling plans were employed. The first entailed contacting pediatricians in the surrounding area and asking them if they would be willing to help us locate subjects. Nine different practices (some individual, some group) agreed to try, and they were sent letters of introduction to give to their patients and referral forms through which we would learn the names and phone numbers of people who had expressed an interest. For reasons unknown to us, this plan did not work well. In the span of a month, only two couples were referred. (Both agreed to be in the study.)

The second plan, put into effect when the first one failed, entailed drawing couples from a list of recent births.[2] After circling the names of people who lived in predominantly white, middle-class neighborhoods, we mailed out sixty letters explaining the nature and purpose of the study and saying that our research assistant would be calling in a few days to ask if they would be interested in participating. To obtain the eighteen families needed to supplement the two who had been referred by the pediatricians, forty-five couples had to be called. Fifteen of these did not qualify for the study because they would have been moving away during the data-collection period, or because they had given birth to a third, fourth, fifth, or sixth child. Couples were also disqualified if they had twins, even if the children were firstborns. Thus, only twelve couples declined outright, an acceptance rate of 60% (18/30), which is typical for qualitative family research.[3]

The twenty couples who compose the sample are a relatively privileged group. Eight of the first-time parents and five of the second-time parents hold graduate degrees. Their family incomes range from $12,000 to $65,000 for the first-time parents (Mean = $30,000) and $12,000 to $40,000 for the second-time parents (Mean = $25,000). Thus, our middle-class sample is actually an *upper* middle-class sample. Also noteworthy is the similarity between the first- and second-time parents with respect to age and length of time married. The first-time fathers range in age from 23 to 37 (Mean = 30), the first-time mothers 26 to 32 (Mean = 29). The second-time fathers range in age from 26 to 41 (Mean = 33), the second-time mothers 25 to 36 (Mean = 29). The number of years married in the first-time group ranges from 1 to 8 (Mean = 6), the second-time group 2 to 14 (Mean = 7). Thus, it would perhaps be more appropriate to view the second-time parents as people who, in the same amount of time, "accomplished" twice as much as the first-time parents rather than seeing them as "a later stage" of the first-timers. (A complete description of the sample is provided in Appendix B.)

Relying only on middle-class couples means that we will not be able to discuss how social class impacts on the transition to parenthood, and that many of our points will be slanted toward middle-class life. However, the essentials of our argument, presented in subsequent chapters, are not class bound, but cut across the entire socioeconomic spectrum. In other words, we would hypothesize that if a similar study with different social classes were done, the basic pattern discovered in this study would be seen again, but that significant variations in the pattern would be unearthed. We also think that, given the interesting social class variations found by other researchers (especially Entwisle and Doering, 1980), such a follow-up study would be worthwhile indeed.

DATA COLLECTION

A variety of qualitative designs were considered. For example, we contemplated studying a large sample of new fathers and mothers who would each be interviewed privately — that is, without their spouses present (cf. Cuber and Harroff, 1965). We also thought about observing, over time, the day-to-day activities of a small sample of new-parent families (cf. Kantor and Lehr, 1975). In the end, however, we selected a strategy that was essentially a synthesis of these two designs: a conjoint-interview, longitudinal study.

Conjoint interviews are not a popular method in qualitative family research, so some justification for our choice may be in order. Generally speaking, family researchers prefer private interviews to conjoint interviews because they feel that conjoint interviews fail to uncover "the true story" of a family's life. First, it is argued that husbands and wives interviewed together will not share their secret thoughts with the researcher—the thoughts that they keep from their spouses—whereas in a private interview they will. And second, the point is made that when spouses are interviewed together, there is the risk that one will dominate the conversation to such a degree that only one side of the story is presented. Both of these arguments raise potential problems, but they do not, in our opinion, necessarily mean that private interviews are the best possible strategy for all research situations. For one thing, asking spouses to reveal their secrets and then publishing these secrets in articles and books for their partners to see raises serious ethical problems (LaRossa et al., forthcoming). For another, the risk of a one-sided interview, though genuine, can be minimized to some degree by a skilled and perceptive interviewer, one who consciously tries to insure that both spouses have an opportunity to speak their minds. Most importantly, there are the advantages of conjoint interviewing: (1) the atmosphere of friendliness and trust which is so crucial to the success of a family study ("We are not here to pry into your closely guarded secrets"); (2) the tendency for spouses to help the researcher by noting things that their partners forgot (perhaps conveniently) or, in their opinions, misinterpreted; and (3) most important of all, the opportunity to see for oneself, either directly during the interview or indirectly through the tapes and transcripts, the couple's inter-action pattern (admittedly influenced by their knowing that they are being watched).[4]

Because of funding limitations, data collection had to be restricted to an eight-month period. Working within this time limit, we considered several schedules and eventually concluded that our purposes would best be served if the couples were interviewed during their third, sixth, and ninth months post-partum.

When the time came to hire an interviewer, age and sex factors were not as important as the ability to do the job. "The job" entailed conducting interviews which would be essentially open ended and conversational. Although we would instruct the interviewer as to how we wanted the sessions to flow, there would be no interview guide with a set list of questions to ask. The direction and content of the interviews would be princi-pally determined by each individual couple. This, of course, is not the only way to conduct qualitative interviews, and in fact it probably represents a "looser" strategy than is typically employed in qualitative family research. But the transition to parenthood affords the researcher a unique opportunity to conduct what appears to the subjects to be nothing more than a friendly visit but which, because of the transition they are experiencing, is actually a contextually structured interview session. As Rapoport et al. (1977: 151) note, "Pregnancy and childbirth are times when people tend to be especially open with information about their feelings, and are often eager to talk about their experiences and concerns." In other words, a simple question such as "What is happening now?" will sometimes generate a discussion that will last the entire length of the interview. Since the sessions would be so unstructured, the interviewer had to be someone who could be comfortable without a guide.

The interviewer also had to be someone who could make a commitment to do *all* the interviews. We did not want to switch interviewers midstream because we felt that the rapport gained by having the same interviewer visit with the couple each time outweighed the multiple perspectives resulting from having, say, three different interviewers for three different interview sessions.

After considering several candidates, we selected a twenty-nine-year-old, white, male, psychology graduate student who had experience conducting open-ended interviews (though only with clinical couples).

We are aware of the implications of having a male interviewer versus a female or a female-male team. One of the most important implications—one that we think is an asset—is that a male interviewer probably increased the input of the husbands. Not only did the husbands probably speak more during the interview sessions than they might have with a female interviewer, but they also probably found it more difficult to define the study as "my wife's thing." Given the paucity of research on fathers, if the study had to lean toward either men or women, it is perhaps best that it leaned toward men. A female-male team would have, of course, been the best strategy, but our funding precluded having more than one interviewer at a time on the staff.

We should also note that the interviewer was both single and childless. This, we feel, also worked to our advantage. As a nonparent, he could assume the role of the "ignorant-student-who-has-to-be-taught" (Lofland, 1971: 101), and legitimately ask "naive" questions. In an exploratory study, these are often the questions that yield the most important findings.

Before each of the three waves of interviews, the field worker was given instructions on the form and general content of the interviews (see Appendix C). As expected, the character of the interviews changed to some degree as the study progressed. For example, originally we thought that we would get a lot of information on the couples' relationships with their own parents, but it soon became apparent that, by the couples' own design, the focus of the study was to be the household. In contrast to this change, one key variable in the analysis—time— was seen as important after only a few interviews. So often was it mentioned in the discussions that after the first wave of interviews we were tempted to shift our focus to this topic alone. However, we bridled our enthusiasm for temporal life and instructed the interviewer to continue pretty much as he had been doing, covering very general areas. With the benefit of hindsight, we are glad that we proceeded in this manner, for as important as time proved to be, the study clearly benefited from a general approach.

Each interview lasted from an hour to an hour and a half, with the last interview generally being the longest of the three. A tape recorder was used to allow the interviewer to concentrate on what the couple was saying rather than to have to take notes, and to give us the opportunity to hear as well as transcribe what was said. We would have preferred to have had our secretary transcribe each interview session immediately afterward, so that we could review the typed copy before the couple would be visited again, but this was not possible. Thus, in most cases, the interviewer would conduct subsequent interviews with only his memory of the previous visit to go on. Although one might expect that this would seriously undermine the research, we found that there were only a few instances where we wished the interviewer had followed up on a line of questioning that had been initiated in a previous session. More often than not, the continuity of the interviews was successfully orchestrated from memory by the interviewer and the couple. In one sense, not having transcripts from previous interviews to go on was a plus in that it forced the interviewer to concentrate on the immediate interview and let the couple provide the context, rather than predetermine the direction of an interview because of what had come before. As noted previously, we were deliberately avoiding a funneling technique in order to be receptive to changes across the three interviews.

ANALYSIS

When all the tapes were finally transcribed, there were 1701 pages of typed conversation available for analysis. The physical characteristics of the transcripts are worth mentioning. The major difficulty with analyzing qualitative data is that one cannot easily shuffle and sort the data. Though some people might argue that this problem is not unique to qualitative research, that shuffling and sorting data in a computer is no simple chore either, there is no denying that the computer's ability to reliably remember where an item of data is or to quickly rearrange masses of data in an almost infinite variety of ways does give the quantitative researcher a certain administrative advantage. In order to achieve some flexibility with the data, we had our secretary type the transcripts on cards as well as paper. She would simply put both a card (measuring 8½ X 11) and four sheets of paper (a four-color carbonless set) in the typewriter, and simultaneously produce a chronology of events and the backbone of our analytical file. The cards gave us a data deck that was durable enough not to tear and crumble under the abuse of constant shuffling and sorting. With the cards to "play with," we then set to work devising a coding system that would allow us to quickly find different topics. Using color-coded stick-on labels, we began to identify common issues in the transcripts by placing the labels in the lefthand margin. When the cards were on their sides, left side up, we thus had a reasonably easy way to locate and sort the cards into various topics.

In addition to this 8½ X 11 card file, we also had a 5 X 8 card file in which we kept a running account of musings, hypotheses, theories, etc. By the end of our analysis, close to six hundred cards had been used.

It was while we were in the middle of coding the transcripts that we learned that our own efforts to become parents had been successful; our first child would arrive in January 1979. Initially, we thought that it was only "cute" that we would be analyzing the couples' experiences at the same time that we would be having a baby ourselves. We soon realized, however, that the opportunity to participate in the very transition which our subjects had been through would clearly lend unexpected strength to our analysis. We decided that we would try as much as we could to step up our analysis during the first nine months of our transition to parenthood, and that we would consciously relate what we felt about the transition with what the couples felt, and vice versa. Although we entertained the idea of keeping detailed notes of our own attitudes and behaviors, or at least taping our thoughts on a more-or-less daily basis, we eventually decided that we would not subject our own lives to this kind of scrutiny (which, of course, would entail far more self-exposure than any of our sample couples had been asked to endure); we simply did not want our personal and professional lives fused to that extent. Thus, this is not a participant observation study in the sense that our own activities constitute a significant portion of the data. Rather, it is more appropriately called a *participant informed* study, by which we mean that our participation in the transition to parenthood informed our analysis of the interviews. In sociological terms, becoming parents in the middle of our analysis increased our role-taking ability, which gave us a greater understanding (*Verstehen*) of the couples' thoughts, feelings, and actions.[5]

The fact that two of us were poring over the data also enhances the validity of the study. Not only did our team approach increase the study's "memory bank"—what one of us would forget about a couple, the other often remembered—but working together also served as a good "checks and balances system," reducing the problem of seeing things in the data that were not "really" there.[6]

A critical step in the analysis was preparing the first drafts of the case studies. As important as a comparative coding system is for mapping out key issues, there is nothing like "the agony and the ecstasy" of case analysis to force the investigator to "get serious" about the research. The significance of the case studies in this book is twofold. First, each detailed examination of a specific couple is a systemic form of analysis (Weiss, 1966) that perhaps captures best "the sociological imagination" (Mills, 1959), the interconnection of biography and history in a particular social structure (Wellman, 1977). Second, case analysis "suggests lines of thoughts, urges reexamination of contemporary theory, reveals areas of behavior in which our knowledge is sparse, and stimulates hypotheses that may be tested in other research formats" (Hess and Handel, 1959: ix). In short, case studies are an excellent method and medium for exploratory sociological research.

For close to a year we debated how many couples should be selected for case studies and who these couples should be. We had decided from the beginning to include an equal number of first- and second-time parents, but beyond this rule we found it difficult to agree on a set of criteria. The main problem was that there were so many interesting couples in the sample that it was hard to exclude anyone. About midway through the year, it became apparent that in addition to the first- versus second-time comparison, there was another sociodemographic breakdown that was equally if not more relevant, namely, unemployed versus employed mothers. The combined importance of time availability and role conflict during the transition to parenthood made comparing breadwinner-homemaker families and two-paycheck families essential. Thus, at this point, we decided that whoever was chosen would have to represent a balance of the following four categories of couples: first-time/mother unemployed (N = 5), first-time/mother employed (N = 5), second-time/mother unemployed (N = 7), second-time/mother employed (N = 3). About midway through the year, it also became apparent that each couple could be classified according to several basic themes: connectedness, flexibility, conflict, power, ambivalance, and communication. We decided that whoever was chosen would also have to somehow represent the thematic contours of the entire sample. Considering both the sociodemographic and the thematic criteria, we eventually selected four "representative" couples.

We cannot emphasize enough the fact that although only four couples have starring roles in the book, the other sixteen couples, serving as a supporting cast, were just as important in the analysis. Our efforts to make sense of the four case-study couples absolutely depended on absorbing and reflecting on the lives of all the couples in the sample (cf. Wellman, 1977: 67).

CONCLUSION

What follows is "an integrated set of hypotheses, not findings" (Glaser, 1978: 134). Although we do not, for the sake of readability, constantly use the phrase, "we hypothesize," this is implicit in every statement made about the data. Also, although we rely heavily on transcript material to illustrate and support our arguments, our main goal is to discuss the conceptual insights gleaned from the interviews. In other words, we are more interested in making "theoretical statements about the relationship between concepts" than we are in making "descriptive statements about people" (Glaser, 1978: 133).

NOTES

1. We do not intend to offer a defense of qualitative research. There are numerous books and articles that discuss the philosophical foundations, methodological assumptions, and general operating procedures involved in a study such as ours. See, for example, Bruyn (1966), Filstead (1970), Glaser (1978), Glaser and Strauss (1967), Lofland (1971), and McCall and Simmons (1969).

2. Credit for locating the list of births goes to our research assistant, Victor Wagner.

3. The acceptance rate in our first study (LaRossa, 1977) was 57%. Bott's (1971) acceptance rate in her qualitative study of London families was 56%.

4. There is quite a bit of testimony from therapists, and recently from researchers, praising the assessment/measurement value of conjoint (or group) interviewing. See Allan (1980), Belville et al. (1969), Bennett et al. (1978), Collins and Nelson (1966), Couch (1969), LaRossa (1978), Leslie (1964), Lofland (1971), O'Connor (1975), Sager (1967), Satir (1964), Sjoberg and Nett (1968), Skidmore and Garrett (1955), Smith and Anderson (1963), Watson (1963), and Weisberg (1964).

5. Participant observation is difficult (and typically impossible) in family research, if by "participant" we mean that the field worker actually joins the group

under study. One cannot join a family as one can join a gang (Whyte, 1955) or a religious cult (Lofland, 1966). Hence, *participant informed* family research is often the closest that qualitative family researchers can come to a true insider's view of family life. Kantor and Lehr's (1975) study, though entitled *Inside the Family,* is based on outsiders' observations of nineteen families in their homes. Of course, as Weber (1947) noted, the difference here is a matter of degree, not kind. We are all insiders to the worlds of other humans, because we all know and can understand what it is like to think like a human.

6. The advantages of team research are generally recognized. See, for example, Douglas (1976) and Laslett and Rapoport (1975).

PART TWO: FRAMEWORK

Chapter 3

BABY CARE: FATHERS VERSUS MOTHERS

This chapter begins the second part of the book. Up to this point, we have presented the reasons why we embarked on a study of the transition to parenthood, and the decisions made to see the study through. Now we begin to present the principal "findings" generated by our approach.

In our efforts to make sense of the data, we discovered that we increasingly relied on three sociological theories or, more accurately, orientations: the conflict orientation, the choice and exchange orientation, and the symbolic interactionist orientation.

The *conflict orientation* serves as our overarching orientation. Throughout the book, we assume that "when confronted with a choice under conditions of real or perceived scarcity, humans will be inclined to choose themselves over others" (Sprey, 1979: 132). The reason why this orientation is so central to our argument is related to what we see as the starting point in a sociological understanding of the transition to parenthood–the helplessness of the human infant at birth. A newborn child cannot survive on its own, but is dependent on adults to feed it, protect it from the elements, and teach it to use symbols (most importantly, language) so that it can become a functioning member of society. In fact, the human infant at birth is more poorly equipped to deal with the world than any other mammal in the animal kingdom. Whereas other mammals have a reasonably developed instinctual structure to program their responses to the world, humans are principally dependent on an external structure, namely, culture, to organize their responses to the environment. No other mammal at birth needs adult caretakers as intensively and as long (years as opposed to months or days) as human beings do. It is this fact of life (literally) that confronts all new parents. Faced with the reality of having to care for a helpless child (or children), how do parents interact, and what kinds of social organizations do they build? The task of finding answers to these questions is what this book is all about.

The helplessness of the human infant places a family that is in the midst of a transition to parenthood within the class of social arrangements that have as their primary function "coverage." For example, a medical hospital in the United States is a *continuous-coverage* system; there is always someone who is on call, ready to respond to the needs of the patients at a moment's notice (Zerubavel, 1979b). The same kind of coverage characterizes new parenthood. Having a baby launches a couple into the responsibilities of continuous coverage for that baby; someone, either the couple themselves or their representative (e.g., a babysitter), must always be on call. The obligation of having to be ready and able to care for their infant son or daughter tends to reduce the couple's free time, the time when they can do what they want to do rather than what someone else (the baby) wants them to do. Indeed, it is the loss of free time accompanying parenthood that surprises and bothers new parents more than anything else (see, for example, Hobbs, 1965, and Hobbs and Wimbish, 1977). The scarcity of this valued resource creates a conflict of interest between husbands and wives. No matter how much they may try to avoid it, periodically there will arise zero-sum, game like situations in which one partner's "winning" (being free to pursue his or her own interests) means that the other must "lose" (forego his or her own interests for the sake of the baby). Conflicts of interest generally result in conflict behavior, tactics and strategies which theoretically extend from verbal persuasion to the use of force as both parties in the encounter pursue their own short-term and long-term interests, often at the expense of the other. It is this basic pattern—child dependency resulting in continuous coverage, which means a scarcity of free time, which leads to conflicts of interest and often conflict behavior—that cuts across the experiences of all the couples in our sample and explains why the conflict orientation is the central framework in this book. The remainder of this book is, in fact, simply the explication of this basic pattern.

Critical to this explication are two other conceptual orientations. Closely tied to the conflict orientation is the *choice and exchange orientation,* the basic assumption of which is that "humans avoid costly behavior and seek rewarding statuses, relationships, interaction, and feeling states to the end that their profits are maximized" (Nye, 1979: 2). This orientation will be useful in explaining the organization of a couple's commitments to various activities. It will also be instrumental in drawing a distinction, made in the next chapter, between equality (parity of activities) and equity (parity of opportunities and constraints).

Not as often associated with the conflict orientation but just as important to our argument is the *symbolic interactionist orientation.* The basic insight derived from this orientation is that "humans live in a symbolic [conventional sign] environment as well as a physical environment," and that "the best way to understand humans is to deal with the mentalistic meanings and values [the symbols] that occur in the minds of people, because that is the most direct cause of their behavior" (Burr et al., 1979a: 46, 49). Qualitative research is based, in large part, on the symbolic interactionist orientation; the idea of getting "inside" people's lives, which is what a qualitative researcher tries to do, essentially entails understanding their world as they see it. Since this is a qualitative study, the symbolic interactionist orientation cannot help but be instrumental to our analysis. Its methodological contribution is, however, only part of why it is one of the three orientations used here. The symbolic interactionist orientation is also indispensable to the conflict perspective that runs through the book. The inability of infants at birth to use symbols, the different levels of value that fathers and mothers attribute to free time, the definitions of social structures as legitimate or illegitimate, and, finally, the symbolic aspects of conflict behavior are all crucial to our presentation and, indirectly, to the utility of the conflict perspective.

Thus, on a theoretical plane, our goal is to attempt a synthesis of three orientations. We believe, as others do (e.g., Hays, 1977), that an eclectic approach to family life is necessary, if by "eclectic" it is meant that the researcher goes beyond using individual orientations on an ad hoc basis, like a carpenter choosing the best single tool for the job at hand, to the utilization of several orientations, interwoven with each other, to unravel the complexities of family life.

In our examination of early parenthood as a continuous coverage system, we will proceed as follows. First, in this chapter, we will describe the character of parental coverage—its range and composition—and compare the obligations of fathers and mothers to provide that coverage. It will become clear that, for a variety of reasons, fathers are less likely than mothers to sacrifice their free time for the baby. In the next chapter, we will move from a quantitative to a qualitative conception of time, and discuss how the division of baby care is a subjective reality that husbands and wives socially construct through bargaining, debating, and influencing. We then move on to the four major case studies, which are intended to illustrate the systemic relationship of the concepts as well as specify important variations in the basic conflict pattern. Following the case studies, we will return to our starting point—the helplessness of the human infant—to present a conflict sociological model of the transition to parenthood that puts the experiences of the couples within a comparative perspective.

WORK AND PLAY

The continuous coverage of infants is somewhat unique in that it entails both work and play. Not only is it important to feed, clothe, and carry the baby, it is also important to play with the baby, since it is through play (and especially games) that the child develops a concept of self, which is indispensable to becoming a full-fledged member of society (Mead, 1934).[1]

In his 1965-66 study, entitled *How Americans Use Time,* Robinson (1977) discovered several things about child work and child play that we think are highly significant. First of all, he found that not only did housewives spend seven times as much time as employed men in child-care activities, and employed women twice as much time, but that while less than a tenth of women's child care was play, half of all men's child care was play (1977: 64-65).[2] When one considers the range of activities that constitute "baby care," it is indeed remarkable that fathers are able to limit their own activities to such a degree. In their study of the content and organization of housework, Berk and Berk (1979) identify approximately sixty discrete tasks that can be categorized as baby care (1979: 265-275). However, only six of these tasks fall under the heading of play. Combining Robinson's and the Berks' surveys thus suggests that fathers are devoting 50 percent of their baby care time to 10 percent of the baby care. We also found that it was not uncommon for new fathers to define short bursts of play with their infants (often immediately upon coming home from work, or after dinner) as efforts which made up for the fact that they were absent all day or which balanced out their inability or unwillingness to take a more active part in the so-called "dirty work" (e.g., diaper changing, feeding). The fact that playing is generally "cleaner" than other kinds of baby care and thus more desirable may only partially explain why fathers tend to prefer this form of contact with their children. The other, perhaps more important, factor in the equation is that play requires less attention than custodial responsibilities.

With the express purpose of measuring different levels of attention, Robinson's research was based on having families keep a log or a diary of their activities over a specified time, usually a twenty-four-hour period. Looking somewhat like a bookkeeper's ledger sheet, a time-diary lists the hours of the day down the left-hand side of the page, and the following seven questions across the top (thus creating seven columns): "What did you do [at this time]? Time began? Time ended? Where? With whom? Doing anything else? Remarks?" (Robinson, 1977: 7). The first question ("What did you do [at this time]?") tapped into the subject's *primary* or main activity. The next-to-last question ("Doing anything else?") recorded the subject's *secondary* activity, which by definition was anything done secondarily and in addition to the primary activity. Robinson found that the comparisons between men and women with respect to primary child care were exactly the same as the comparisons for child care in general; that is, housewives spend seven times as much time in primary child care, and employed women spend twice as much time in primary child care than men (1977: 72). The principal reason for the similar figures can be traced to the correlation between the kind of child-care activity and the amount of attention devoted to that activity. In a footnote, Robinson reports that (1977: 70):

> While over two-thirds of primary activity child care in the 1965-1966 study was "custodial" (feeding, clothing, chauffeuring, etc.) rather than "interactional" (reading, playing, etc.) in nature, the bulk of secondary activity child care consisted of international activities.

It is unfortunate that Robinson relegates this finding to a footnote without additional discussion. Our data suggest that the propensity for play activities to be secondary-level activities is significant in that it may provide the key to understanding why fathers are more prone to play with their infants. Not only is play cleaner than many other forms of child care activity, but play also has the advantage of being less demanding in terms of the amount of attention that one must give to that activity. Fathers, in other words, may choose play over work because play "eats" less into their own free time.

Perhaps the best way to conceptualize the differences between play and nonplay is to think of play and work as ideal-typical poles of a hypothetical continuum. Toward the play end of the continuum one would include activities such as piggy-back riding, tickling, and hide-and-seek. Toward the work end of the continuum one would include feeding, diaper changing, putting to sleep, etc. In the middle would be those activities that fall between play and work, the borderline cases: reading a story, giving a bath (with toys, of course), going on nature walks. Generally speaking, activities that are toward the play end of the continuum require less parental attention than the other activities. First, these activities are often shorter in duration. A piggy-back ride, for example, may last only two or three minutes. Yet at the end of the ride, the parent can legitimately terminate contact with the baby, often with the assistance of the other parent (e.g., "Come on now, give Daddy a break, you tired him out"). Second, play activities are typically not as scheduled or as urgently required as work activities. The parent can usually decide when and how long to play ("Not now, later, but only for a few minutes"), whereas activities such as feeding and diaper changing are more on demand; letting one's child go hungry or remain dirty is frowned upon. Third, play activities are less bounded spatially than work activities. Roughhousing can take place anywhere in the house—in front of the television, in the backyard—which means that the parent can more easily integrate personal activities with play. Feeding and diaper changing, on the other hand, are usually done in specific locales, severely restricting the kinds of activities that a parent can perform in addition to child work.[3]

The play-work continuum does not only apply to baby care; it can apply to adult "care" too. Adult-centered activities can also be plotted along the continuum with the more "mindless" activities at the play end and the "thinking" activities at the work end. Generally speaking, new parents discover that with an infant in the house and awake, it is difficult to "get any work done" or to pursue leisure activities which typically require concentration and separation from the baby (e.g., sex).

Thus, many parents will shift their adult-centered activities toward the play end when the baby is present. For example, one mother who was an avid reader decided that it was too difficult to read a book or newspaper when the baby was up, so she started to watch television during the day, something which she felt guilty about.

The age of the child can be a significant variable when it comes to parental attention levels. Robinson (1977: 80-81) found that women's primary activity time with their children is related more to the age of their children than to the number of children they had; the younger the children, the more primary activity time with the children. Men's primary child-care activity time, on the other hand, was found not to be related either to the age or the number of children (1977: 82). We suspect, however, that men's activity time is related to the age of their *preschool* children. As toddlers get older, and especially when they begin to talk and "ask so many questions," low parental attention play activities are harder to carry out. In other words, some activities which formerly were toward the play end of the play-work continuum may shift to the right, becoming more like work.

GETTING "DOWN TIME"

Primary and secondary are not the only levels of attention. There is logically a third level of activity, *tertiary* activity, which can be defined as time during which there is no social contact whatsoever. Of course, as with primary and secondary activity, tertiary activity must be operationalized in terms of some referent or referents. Thus, for example, a mother at work would be at a tertiary level with respect to her children, while being primarily and secondarily involved with her job. If, on the other hand, her child happens to call her at her office, then during the phone call she would be primarily attending to her child, and secondarily attending to her work.

Rather than think of attention, one may think of social accessibility (Zerubavel, 1979a). In the primary mode one is most accessible to a referent, and in the tertiary mode least accessible to a referent. Hence, primary, secondary, and tertiary time actually represent points on a continuum that extends from being totally attuned or accessible to a referent (total connection) to being totally neglectful or inaccessible to a referent (total separation).

When adults interact with each other, they generally have the freedom to move, within specified parameters and rules, across all three levels. A husband and wife can, for example, be involved in a very intense conversation one moment (primary status), then shift their attention to the television while still maintaining contact with each other (secondary status), and finally move to separate corners of their house to work on their individual hobbies (tertiary status). (Some husbands and wives might define this third move as secondary status because, as far as they are concerned, being in the same house means that they are *with* each other. But let us assume, for the sake of simplicity, that the husband and wife do not define their situation in this way, but believe that any time that they are not in face-to-face contact with each other, they are in a no-contact status.) The advantage of being able to move across all three levels is that husbands and wives can give each other their undivided attention at one moment, and then withdraw completely from each other the next. They can, in other words, coordinate a system of connectedness and separateness such that at one moment they are concentrating on each other, and the next they are essentially removed from each other.[4]

This is very different from what it is like to interact with an infant. If a mother, for example, is alone with an infant at home, she can never move to a tertiary level, but must always be "up" or "ready" to attend to her child's needs. This is indeed one of the biggest surprises for new parents. They soon learn that infants are not only very dependent on them, but that the demands of infants are also nonnegotiable. The simple phrase "I'll be with you in a moment," which works so well in the adult world to delay moving to a primary or secondary level, is useless with someone who does not understand language. ("Infant" is derived from the French word *enfant* which means incapable of speech.) Infants also do not like to be alone. Expectant parents who think that as long as their children are provided with enough toys, they will be content to amuse themselves soon discover that the attention span of infants is extremely brief. Babies who will occupy themselves without interruption for twenty or thirty minutes are truly unique, and will often be talked about as "great kids." Even so, these children will still expect to be allowed to keep their parents within sight, which is why no matter how "great" an infant is, if a parent is left alone with that infant, the chances are fairly good that the child will be accompanying the parent to the bathroom, formerly perhaps the only private place in the house. Parents who refuse to surrender their bathroom time, insisting that this one room should remain "private" no matter what, may resort to planning their "visits." As one wife said, "I feel like I have this schedule [as to] when I can go to the bathroom."

We do not mean to suggest that primary contact with one's child is unrewarding, or that some parents do not find pleasure in having an individual who is totally dependent on them. What can be unrewarding and unpleasant, however, is the *repetitiveness* of that level of contact. No matter how much we love someone or something, satiation (too much of a good thing) reduces the reward value of that person or object (Homans, 1974: 29). Also the *pace* of parent-infant interaction can take its toll. As with assembly-line work (see Blauner, 1964) and air traffic control work, the most alienating and most distressing aspect of baby care is its pace. It is the baby and not the parent who generally controls when shifts from one level to the next will occur. The parents' job is to "keep track" of the child, who, if mobile (walking), must be "plotted" in terms of direction, speed, and altitude (height).

It is perhaps worth noting that people who work in situations from which they cannot voluntarily withdraw, from which they cannot take "time-outs" when they want to but must wait to be relieved, have been found to be more prone to "burn-out," the symptoms of which include not only physical and emotional exhaustion, but social exhaustion as well, involving "the loss of concern for the people with whom one is working," taking a "very cynical and dehumanized perception of these people," and treating them accordingly (Maslach and Pines, 1977: 101; also Maslach, 1976). Thus, we suspect that there are parents who develop dehumanized views of their own children as a result of the constant attention they are giving to them, and that the parents who are probably most likely to undergo this experience are those who "cannot do enough for their kids," the supermoms and superdads.

Even when the baby is sleeping, an adult left alone in the house cannot move to a tertiary level. Although the parent will probably not be in the same room as the baby during nap time, the parent is still monitoring the infant, still standing watch. This is not to say that the parent will not feel restored by having an hour or two "off." In reality, however, the "ah" feeling experienced by the parent when he or she carefully closes the door to the nursery after having just rocked the baby to sleep is because now there is time to be primarily involved in his or her own needs while secondarily involved with the baby's needs, rather than vice versa. In short, after a hectic morning of being "up" for the baby—feeding, changing, amusing, watching, consoling, etc.—the parent can now enjoy a long awaited *semi-*attentiveness.

If there are two adults in the house, the picture can change dramatically. Now each adult can slip into periodic "down times" while the other remains on a secondary level. Sometimes responsibility for the baby is formally arranged, as in those cases where fathers and mothers alternate who gets up in the morning with the baby and who sleeps late. However, more often than not, we suspect, the movement from one level to the next is informal and emergent, a procedure which can sometimes court disaster (He: "I thought *you* were watching the baby!" She: "And I thought *you* were watching the baby!").

If one of the adults refuses to share responsibility for the baby, then the other must always be "up" or "ready." Thus, while one parent watches television, reads a book, works in the den—essentially oblivious to the needs of the baby—the other must be continuously on guard. Again the formal/informal distinction applies. One husband (who will be introduced in the next chapter) formally announced to his wife that, as far as he was concerned, she was always on duty—seven days a week, twenty-four hours a day. With other husbands, the results were still the same—the wife always attending to the baby—but the means were more subtle and more informal. Thus, a husband may claim that he, too, is in a secondary status with respect to the baby, but in reality he is technically in second while functionally in third; if the baby starts to cry or moves too close to the house plants, he will not feel any compulsion to intervene, but will let his wife take care of it. Even more subtle is the strategy of arranging his activities so that he precludes his having to share in the baby work. The father who decides to pay the bills or perhaps clean the kitchen just when the baby needs to be fed or changed has effectively preserved a tertiary level of contact with his child.

The significance of negotiating protectiveness becomes clear at this point. It is quite common for fathers and mothers to debate over how protective they should be with their babies (e.g., "Should we let her cry?"). Although the manifest function of these discussions is to decide what is best for the child, the hidden agenda is often what is best for the husband and wife. Should a father conclude that his wife is too protective ("You are spoiling her"), he can then justify his refusal to respond to the baby's demands. However sincere he may be, the results are still the same—"down time" for the father, often at the expense of his wife. For example, one of the case-study fathers went out virtually every night of the week, despite his wife's protests that he should stay home with her and the baby. One of his responses to her protests was that if she were willing to hire a babysitter, she could join him. Since she refused (she felt that as a working mother it was bad enough that she had to leave her baby during the day; she was not going to leave her at night too), it was, in his opinion, basically *her* fault that the two of them did not spend more time together.

HELPING VERSUS SHARING

The father who refuses, either formally or informally, to do anything is the exception, not the rule. What is the rule—as suggested by our data and other studies—is that fathers will periodically move to a primary or secondary attention level with their infants, thus enabling their wives to get tertiary ("down") time, but that when they do take over, they almost always assume that they are "helping" their wives rather than "sharing" the parental responsibilities.

Mothers are also likely to see fathers as surrogate parents, and, like their husbands, will use words such as "helping" and "babysitting" to denote the father's contribution. It is interesting to note that in the 1701 pages of transcripts, *every* couple would, at least once in their interviews, refer to the husband as "helping" the wife with the baby, whereas not a single couple defined the wife's parental responsibilities in these terms.

There are a variety of ways that a "helping" role can be performed. The first signs that the father will be less involved than the mother in child care can be seen before the baby arrives, during the pregnancy. More often than not, the wife will be the one to think first about and eventually buy several of the how-to books on parenting. If the father does read any of the books, either in whole or in part, it is likely to be as a result of the mother's coaxing. Clearly, from the start, the mother is the one who is "in charge" of the baby. Her purchase of the books reflects what is generally accepted: babies are "women's work." The fact that she will read the books more thoroughly than her husband directs what is to come: since the father is not as informed about what it means to be a parent, both parents will assume that Mom is the one to orchestrate and implement the child's care. When and if the father does participate, it is presumed to be under the mother's direction.

After the baby is born, performances which reflect and direct the father and mother's separate roles become more sophisticated. Perhaps the most easily recognized is the behavior that ensues the first few times the father holds the baby. Upon being handed his infant son or daughter, he will often say something to the effect that he hopes he does not drop the baby. Then, while he is cradling the baby in his arms, the father will stiffen up, demonstrating both to himself and to everyone in the room (including the baby) that this is not his accustomed role. Often, the coactors in this drama will reinforce the father's definition of the situation by standing very close, as if to be ready to catch the baby should he or she actually fall out of the father's arms. Another typical manuever is to encourage the father to sit down, preferably in a stuffed chair, so that his arms can be supported. Throughout the scene, the father will ask for and the other performers will readily offer instructions on how to position the arms, where to hold the baby's head, etc. Additional touches may include having someone gather everyone in the house so that they can see Daddy holding Junior or, even better, grabbing a camera to capture a "rare" moment for posterity.

In sociological terms, this scene is a perfect example of what Goffman (1961) refers to as *role distance*. The mock or comedic aspects of the performance indicate an attempt by the father to deny "not the role but the virtual self that is implied in the role" (1961: 108). In other words, the father is distancing or disassociating his self from the parental role.

The father's performance stands in stark contrast to the mother's actions when she holds the baby. Even if she does fear that she will drop the baby during those first few days of parenthood, it is considered poor form for her to display that fear. Rather, she is likely to try to appear as if holding the baby is well within her abilities. And the other performers in the room are likely to communicate to the mother that she does indeed look "natural" for the job.

The mother's performance is the flip side of role distance. What she is doing is *embracing* the parental role—disappearing, as it were, "into the virtual self available in the situation," confirming "expressively [her] acceptance of it" (Goffman, 1961: 106).

The role distance/role embracement distinction is actually a continuum, one that may be useful for understanding a puzzling set of findings. Studies indicate that most husbands and wives do not believe that men should do more family work than they are doing now. And among the minority who do feel that men should contribute more, a greater proportion of men than women express an interest in expanding the man's family role (Pleck, 1976). Women, in other words, generally "want" to remain chiefly responsible for the house and for the children.

One explanation—perhaps the most popular—is that women have a psychological investment in their family roles, and become threatened if they cannot count on housework and baby care as their domain. For example, one of the case-study wives was very proud to be a full-time housewife and mother, feeling that these roles constituted her "career" in life. If her husband had decided one day that from then on he would take over a substantial part of the homemaking duties, we have no doubt that this particular woman would have indeed felt threatened.

In terms of what we have been saying, the psychological investment explanation focuses on the role embracement of the mother. Because her self is so closely tied to motherhood, reducing her role performances would undermine her identity. This is probably true for many women, but it does not seem to us to be the whole story. Also operating, we suspect, are the consequences of the father's role distance. To continue our discussion of the variety of ways that helping behavior may manifest itself once the baby comes, consider these role-distancing performances disclosed by the couples: A father "forgets" to change the baby's diaper for the whole time (about six hours) that he is "babysitting" while his wife has gone shopping; he claimed that he was just about to do it. A father just "gives up" trying to feed his infant son and concludes that he is just not "as good at it" as his wife is. A mother reports that her husband did such a terrible job of cleaning their daughter that she finally decided that it was easier for her if she just did it herself. And finally, a mother notes that when her husband did care for the baby he would always ask for her assistance, which meant that she ended up doing most of the work anyway. Thus, another explanation for why mothers do not want more cooperation is that they may not trust their husbands to do a good job or they have learned that their husband's assistance is more trouble than it is worth.

What about the fathers? Although fathers are more inclined to "want" to increase their participation more than mothers "want" them to, the number of fathers who advocate change is still small. Role embracement and role distance can still apply. While the mother embraces parenthood, the father is embracing the traditional male role, which means he sees himself more as the breadwinner than the caretaker. His job, as some of our husbands said, is to "put the food on the table and pay for the kid's college education." Thus, many fathers take exception to the claim that they do not care for or about their children. They point out that although they may not be involved in the day-to-day feeding and cleaning of the baby, they are very much involved in the day-to-day responsibility of providing financial support. Indeed, they argue, because their responsibilities in this realm are so time consuming and energy exhausting, they cannot possibly help their wives more, nor should they be expected to. Even if the wives themselves are employed, many fathers still insist that their jobs are more pressure-laden than their wives' jobs are, and that they still, therefore, should not be expected to help more around the house. (Studies have found that the wife's employment has a negligible impact on the husband's housework and child care responsibilities [Berk and Berk, 1979; Pleck and Rustad, 1980; Robinson, 1977].) One father in the sample resented the whole idea that men in this society must hold a job, while women can presumably take off when they like to have a baby. The implication was that although men may be "helpers" at home, women are "helpers" in the economic world.

Related, of course, to the father's embracement of the traditional male role is the fact that some men have a psychological investment in *not* helping more at home. In their minds, husbands who do too much housework and baby care are not "real men."

The fact that fewer mothers than fathers advocate change is, however, the real puzzle, the solution to which may be linked to the use of the word "help" to denote the father's parental performances. If the wife believes that her husband's contribution to child care is an act of charity, a "gift" from him to her, then each time the husband helps with the baby, he alters the social exchange balance in the marriage. Having done his wife a "favor," both he and she expect that the favor will be returned (quid pro quo). The form of the repayment may not be known. It can, itself, be an act of charity (e.g., helping the husband pay the bills), or simply an immediate response to a request (e.g., sex even though she is tired). The norm of reciprocity (Gouldner, 1960), nevertheless, dictates that over time role partners will strive for a balanced exchange (Blau, 1964).

Thus, the reason that more mothers than fathers may not be too keen on the idea of having men help more (and significantly, it is in terms of "help" that the surveys are sometimes phrased; see Robinson, 1977, for example) is that mothers may not want to "pay the price." They may not be comfortable with the deferential stance they are expected to take to offset their husband's gratuities (cf. Bell and Newby, 1976).

Of course, the choice may not be theirs to make. The few studies that have examined whether the marital power structure changes after the birth of a child have found that marriages typically become more patriarchal during the transition to parenthood (Cowan et al., 1978; Meyerowitz and Feldman, 1966). Speculation on why this shift occurs has generally centered on the fact that many women quit work when they have their first baby (see Hoffman, 1978, for example). Since power is inversely related to dependency (Emerson, 1962), the increased financial reliance of the wife on the husband is presumed to decrease her power in the relationship, all other things being equal (cf. Blood and Wolfe, 1960). We would hypothesize that the wife's power will typically decrease, regardless of whether there is a change in her employment status. The unrelenting demands of an infant increase the wife's dependency on the husband for "down time." Though she may not like the fact that when she does get relief from her husband it is defined as a gift for which she will be beholden, she is not likely to cut herself off from his aid. Nor is the husband likely to stop contributing care, particularly if he begins to sense that his wife is indeed grateful for his support. Some husbands in our sample, in fact, tried to increase their wives' dependency not by doing more baby work, but by demanding that their wives acknowledge that since they did a lot more than most of their male friends, they should be appreciated more than they are now. In short, we suspect that marriages tend to become more patriarchal after the birth of the first child because of the socially defined character of baby care.

As might be expected, there are always exceptions to the rule. Women can and do increase their power in a relationship by using their children to increase their demands on their husbands (LaRossa, 1977: 45-46). Also, husbands and wives who do not see the husband's contribution as "helping" are less likely to have the power-dependency balance in their marriages dramatically altered.

One final point on helping: the only study to examine how (rather than whether) the marital power structure changes after the first birth found that couples use more "coercive tactics" (power plays, guilt induction, disparagement) with each other when they become parents (Raush et al., 1974). These tactics may very well be related to the power-dependence imbalances that are created by helping behavior during the transition to parenthood. If so, then having a baby could, for some couples, precipitate a cycle of mutual coercion escalating ultimately to the use of physical force. The existence of a relationship between parenthood and marital violence is not unheard of. Gelles (1975) found that a disproportionate number of women are hit by their husbands while they are pregnant. And Straus et al. (1980) recently reported that the most likely conflict to lead to blows between a husband and wife is conflict over children.

THE REIFICATION OF INFANTS

After reading the transcripts only once, we realized that the value of parenthood was different for the fathers and mothers in our sample. What we did not immediately realize, but what became more apparent with each successive reading, was the way in which the fathers' and mothers' value differences influenced their interactions with their children. In a nutshell, because of the configuration of the fathers' values, they were more likely to act toward their infants as if they, the infants, were *things* (reifications).

One of the fathers, for example, said that his mind would often wander while he was talking with people. His wife, in particular, would become annoyed when, in the middle of a conversation, she would sense that he had "left." The father said that he was working very hard to break this habit with his wife, but that when he did it with his new son, he did not feel that guilty. Since his son was too young to sense that he was not getting his undivided attention, he could, as he put it, "fink [out]" on his kid. Critical to this father's attitude was his disappointment with very young babies. As far as he was concerned, they could not "interact." When the father made this remark, his wife immediately disagreed, saying that their son, and indeed all infants, could interact, but on a different level. The mother, in other words, seemed more sensitive to the fact that infants may not be able to use symbols, but they can communicate through signs (e.g., crying means "I want something"). In general, the mothers in the sample were more sensitive to their infant's abilities than the fathers were.

Another way of describing the different attributions that fathers and mothers gave to their infants is to say that mothers were likely to see their infants as more "interpersonally competent" than fathers saw them. The more interpersonal competence that one imputes to other actors in a relationship, the more satisfied one is with that relationship (Burr et al., 1979a). Thus, we would hypothesize that mothers generally enjoy the relationship with their infants more than fathers do.

All of this is not to say that fathers do not want their children, that they do not think they are rewarding. Nor do we mean to suggest that there are not moments when mothers would just as soon hide from their kids, or that mothers do not have other reasons, besides simple enjoyment, for wanting to be mothers. Rather, the point is that the socially determined configuration of values for fathers and mothers is different. To explain what we mean by this, we will apply the often used intrinsic/extrinsic distinction to parental values.

A *value* "is the position of anything in a preference ordering" (Kuhn, 1974: 107). All social objects, including people, have some value—and often a complex of values—attached to them by others. Essentially, there are two kinds of values—intrinsic and extrinsic. The *intrinsic value* of something or someone is the amount of sheer pleasure or enjoyment that one gets from experiencing that object or person. The *extrinsic value* of something or someone is the amount of social rewards (e.g., money, power, prestige, approval, positive self-image, avoidance of stigma or physical pain) associated with having or being with that object or person.

If, for the sake of simplicity, we divide both intrinsic value and extrinsic value into "high" and "low," we arrive at the following ideal types:[5]

A. High Intrinsic Value, High Extrinsic Value
B. High Intrinsic Value, Low Extrinsic Value
C. Low Intrinsic Value, High Extrinsic Value
D. Low Intrinsic Value, Low Extrinsic Value

Configurations "A" and "D" in their most extreme forms would include "love" and "hate" respectively. Thinking in interpersonal terms, an "A" type would be the parent who very much enjoys interacting with his or her child, and who derives prestige and social approval from being a parent. An example of a "D" type would be the parent who has decided not to keep his or her baby because of the lack of both enjoyment and perceived social rewards accompanying the transition to parenthood. Category "B" would, in its extreme form, include fathers and mothers who get a thrill just from being in contact with their kids but who have never seen their children as assets to be displayed or bartered. And finally, category "C" would, in its extreme form, include fathers and mothers who see their children only in utilitarian terms, as commodities in the interpersonal marketplace. Though presented here as dichotomous variables (high/low), intrinsic value and extrinsic value are, in reality, continuous variables (highest . . . mid-point . . . lowest). Hence, whereas it may be difficult to conceive of the four types in their most extreme forms, the chances are that all of us have directly or indirectly known people who more or less conform to one type or another. We may not know, for example, a parent who derives only intrinsic benefits from being a parent, but we can perhaps think of fathers and mothers who just seem to get "a charge" out of being parents, and who seem to be relatively uninterested in the extrinsic payoffs.

The relevance of the typology to understanding the reification of infants is that category "C" is a reified relationship. To see a baby largely in terms of the social rewards which he or she provides is to dehumanize the baby. We recognize that this statement is itself a value judgment, but we believe that "thing-like relationships" is an accurate description of some of the interactions that were described during the interviews. To be more specific, and to return to the central point about father-child relationships, our data suggest that there are 'many fathers who could be said to, more or less, fall into category "C," many fathers who certainly want and treasure their children, but who do not really enjoy being with their kids. Sure, they will roughhouse with their toddlers on the living-room floor, and will blush when hugged or kissed by their one-year-olds, but when you really get down to it, they just do not have that much fun when they are with their children. If they had their druthers, they would be working at the office or drinking at the local pub—and quite often they are doing precisely that either in fact or in fantasy—but they commit themselves to their kids out of a sense of responsibility.

Relationships which are perceived as primarily obligatory take on a very different character than intrinsically valued relationships. First, obligatory relationships operate at lower levels of attention than intrinsically valued relationships, which is to say that there would be more divided attention, more secondary activity in these relationships. Also, obligatory relationships are generally more routinized, so as to facilitate the addition of other activities (and other people) when enacting the obligatory relationship. Thus, we would hypothesize that Low Intrinsic/High Extrinsic parent-child relationships would be marked by more multiple activities and, because they can be easily routinized, more play activities than High Intrinsic/High Extrinsic parent-child relationships.

The best example of this was provided by the father who complained that his son could not interact and who said that he had developed a series of "tricks" which helped him get through any extended contact with his son. Basically, the tricks were toys and events which kept the baby distracted, and which thus decreased the father's level of attention. The father had also learned what particular sequence of introducing the tricks worked best for distracting the baby the longest. Thus, the father would initiate a routinized series of distractions when his son started to get too demanding.

Reification of children can spiral. Parents who, from the start, assume that their infants are not interpersonally competent may conclude that they do not enjoy being with their children, which can result in a lowering of their attention and routinization of their interaction with their kids. This strategy can prevent the parents from effectively discovering that their children (1) may be more interpersonally competent than they originally thought they were, and (2) are becoming more interpersonally competent with each passing day (because of developmental changes). Not being receptive to these changes may contribute further to the parents' low level of enjoyment when they are with their children, which may mean that they will withdraw even more, and so on. The significance of this hypothetical pattern is that it suggests that child-care differences between couples and between fathers and mothers are not simply a function of internalized value differences being "played out," but are a consequence of *interactional processes* that take place during the transition to parenthood itself.

PUBLIC VERSUS PRIVATE BEHAVIOR

The distinction between intrinsic and extrinsic values under-scores the serious mistake that can be made if one fails to recognize a basic truth, namely, that people act differently in public than they do in private.

In contrast to what we have been saying, a recent cross-cult-ural study of adult male-child interaction concluded that "American men do associate with children in large numbers when the societal norms allow them access to the children and that American men interact with children at levels consonant with adult female-child dyads" (Mackey and Day, 1979: 287). These conclusions were based on more than 24,000 (thirty-second) observations in five countries (United States, Mexico, Japan, Spain, and Ireland) during a variety of time periods (specifically, time intervals when adult males may normally be expected to be exempted from associating with children be-cause of cultural norms—for example, when they would be at work—and time intervals when they would be expected to be available to children—for example, on holidays). This is truly an impressive endeavor. There is, however, a flaw in the study's design which seriously limits the researchers' conclusions. All observations were conducted in public settings.

To give fathers equal credit for "interacting" with their children because they can be observed pushing or carrying their children in a shopping mall ignores the intrinsic/extrinsic value distinction. If fathers value their children in extrinsic terms, if they enjoy the social approval and the prestige that go along with fatherhood, then we would expect them to take the opportunity to publicly display their children, and we would expect them to look good when their extrinsic benefits were on the line. Pushing a stroller in public requires only a secondary level of attention toward the child in the stroller. In fact, the umbrella stroller is popular among parents precisely because it serves as a portable and socially acceptable child restrainer. If the baby is in the stroller, the parent can more easily shop, take lunch breaks, talk with other adults, while the baby is amused (distracted) by quick changes in scenery.

Of course, one of the methodological problems of studying family groups is that most family interaction takes place "behind closed doors." Conducting an observation study similar to the one above *inside* the home would be much more difficult, and even then the researcher would be getting the families' public behavior, since the families would, of course, know that they were being observed. This is one reason why so much family research is based on interviews and questionnaires (Atkinson and Gecas, 1978; Hodgson and Lewis, 1979; Nye and Bayer, 1963, Ruano et al., 1969). Unable to see private family behavior for themselves, investigators hope that family members will tell them what "really" goes on.

Our study, and others like it, strongly suggest, however, that we must develop alternative ways to uncover the private reality of family life, especially during the transition to parenthood. The institution of the family is too central to the structure of society for us to be satisfied with measures that only scratch the surface.

CONCLUSION

The purpose of this chapter has been to lay out the three sociological orientations used in the study—the conflict orientation, the choice and exchange orientation, and the symbolic interactionist orientation—and to discuss the division of baby care between fathers and mothers. Several substantive distinctions were made: play/work, primary/secondary/tertiary attention, helping/sharing, role distance/role embracement, intrinsic/extrinsic values, and public/private behavior. Each of these will, to varying degrees, be used throughout the book. We have tried to deal not only with outcomes, but also with processes in describing the experiences of the couples because we feel that one of the major contributions that sociology can offer is a dynamic view of social life. In the next chapter, we will attempt to press even further toward a sociological conception of the transition to parenthood, as we move closer in our analysis to the symbolic world of new fathers and mothers.

NOTES

1. We say that the continuous coverage of infants is "somewhat" unique, entailing both work and play, because there are other continuous coverage systems that also define play as an element of coverage. For example, nursing homes are more or less continuous coverage systems in which play is an important aspect.

2. Although Robinson's data are not current, having been collected in 1965-66, we rely on his study more than on other time-use studies because of his distinction between play and work, and because of his distinction, yet to be discussed, between primary and secondary activity. Both of these proved to be especially important in our analysis. Comparisons across studies are difficult to make, but the reader may be interested in the following set of findings from a more recent (1975-76) time-use survey. Pleck and Rustad (1980) report that in their study, housewives spent about five times as much time as their husbands in child-care activities (486.9 versus 103.4 minutes per week), and that employed women spent about three times as much time (269.3 versus 99.2). Note that the difference in terms of the absolute amount of time is negligible between husbands of housewives and husbands of working wives (103.4 versus 99.2). This coincides with what other researchers have found (Berk and Berk, 1979; Robinson, 1977).

3. One does not have to be ostensibly involved in other activities in order to reduce the amount of attention one is giving to a task. To an observer, a parent playing with an infant in the living room can appear to be a conscientious model. If there is nothing apparently distracting the parent (no television, newspaper, etc.), an observer can be quite impressed with the parent's concern. And if the observer and the parent are the same person, the parent can use the activity as evidence for and confirmation of a positive self-image. But suppose that in addition to playing with the baby, the parent is also *thinking* about work of tennis or the interesting conversation he or she just had. Then, although the parent appears to be giving the baby undivided attention, in truth his or her attention is divided. Moreover, in the course of a very short time (minutes, even seconds), the parent can shift these activities to and fro in his or her consciousness, so that at one moment the parent is giving the baby undivided attention (nothing else on his or her mind), the next moment the parent is thinking, though only secondarily, about work, and then the next he or she is primarily absorbed in the financial deal that has just been closed or the article waiting to be written, while only secondarily involved with the baby. We mention the cognitive aspects of attention because we think they are important and worthy of research. However, in this study we will focus on the *behavioral* aspects of primary, secondary, and tertiary time. We simply do not have enough information in the transcripts on "daydreaming" to say anything more (save for the point we will make later in the chapter when we introduce the section on the reification of infants).

4. Connectedness and separateness are, of course, central to all human groups, especially the family. For a recent discussion of these concepts, see Olson et al. (1979).

5. These ideal types and their relationship to reification were suggested by Israel (1971: 317) in his discussion of Karl Marx's theory of alienation. We have substituted "intrinsic value" for "use value" and "extrinsic value" for "exchange value" because intrinsic and extrinsic are more descriptive for our purposes than use and exchange.

Chapter 4

NEGOTIATING A DIVISION OF
LABOR AFTER BIRTH

The last chapter described the transition to parenthood as a transition to a continuous-coverage family system. It was noted then that during this transition, husbands and wives are more likely to experience a scarcity of free time, and more likely to conflict with each other over the allocation of that time. This chapter examines marriage during the transition to parenthood by focusing on the negotiations that husbands and wives engage in to initiate and maintain the necessary coverage for their children while insuring a fair distribution of "down time" for themselves.[1]

The chapter hinges on an important but sometimes overlooked fact, namely, that there is a difference between the quantitative aspects of time and the qualitative aspects of time, and that the sociotemporal order of all social systems is based as much on the latter as on the former. For example, the negotiation of the division of labor in a particular work setting is affected not only by the time on the clock (the quantity of time) but also by the common understanding that there are desirable and undesirable times to work, and that there are desirable and undesirable tasks (the quality of time). The *meaning* that people attribute to various times and tasks makes it possible for them "to unequalize mathematically equal durations . . . as well as to equalize mathematically unequal ones" (Zerubavel, 1979a: 56). Were it not for this social ability, the practice of paying time-and-a-half for working overtime, as well as the phenomenon of giving more credit (e.g., money, time off, recognition) for hazardous duty, would make no sense.

The negotiation of the division of labor in a family operates under the same quantitative and qualitative rules. However, unlike the situation in most work settings, where the rules of the clock are rigidly applied (e.g., punching in and out) and where the values of certain times and tasks are formally defined (e.g., a doctor's work is more valued than a nurse's work), in most family settings the rules of the clock are relatively flexible and the values of certain times and tasks are informally defined and often ambiguous. The result is that the negotiations in most families over who does what are generally more problematic than the negotiations in most work settings. By "more problematic" we mean that the negotiations are generally more overt, more conscious, and more intense (sometimes violent).[2]

During periods of transition—either on the job or in a family—negotiations become even more problematic. Hence, we would expect that a family in the midst of a transition to parenthood would find itself involved in more "labor disputes." The focus of this chapter is the character and process of these disputes.

Our analysis of the division of labor after birth begins with an examination of the qualitative aspects of paid work, housework, and baby care. The desirability of various times and tasks will be operationalized in terms of the relative opportunities and constraints associated with those times and tasks. We will then discuss the negotiation process itself, giving special attention to the verbal tactics and strategies used by husbands and wives to excuse and justify their conduct. Of particular importance here is our attempt to offer a sociological explanation for a phenomenon reported by other researchers and exhibited by the couples in this study, namely, the tendency of husbands and wives to drift toward a traditional division of labor during the transition to parenthood.

Before we jump into these issues, however, we want to present a brief case study to bring what may seem to be an abstract argument down to earth. The transcript analysis that follows will also be a good warm-up for the four full-length case studies in Chapters 5 through 8.

FLO AND FRED

When Flo and Fred were asked why they decided to become parents, they said that they had always known that they would have children at some point in their marriage, but that they had been waiting for a time when they could afford to lose Flo's income and still be able to "give the kid what it should have." That Flo would become a full-time mother once the baby arrived was just assumed. Having been stuck in a boring, low-paying job, she was more than happy to give it up. On the other hand, even if she had enjoyed her work, it is doubtful that she would have been given the opportunity to juggle a career and motherhood. Since Fred's job afforded no flexibility whatsoever, if Flo worked, the baby would have had to be left with someone during the day, an arrangement which they perceived in negative terms (Fred: "I don't trust putting a dog in a kennel, let alone putting a baby in a nursery").

Generally speaking, Flo was responsible for housework and baby care, while Fred was responsible for being the breadwinner. Fred was unwilling to share in the housework and baby care because he said that: (1) housework and baby care were "women's work"; (2) when he was home he needed to "rest" from the "pressures" of his job; and (3) staying home all day with the baby was a "mindless" activity which essentially constituted a vacation for Flo, so why should he make it any easier for her.

No other segment of the interviews better captures the flavor of Flo and Fred's relationship than the following one from their last interview. We pick up the conversation just after the couple has been asked to describe their division of baby care.

FLO: He [Fred] thinks because you're a housewife—

FRED: That you're a housewife twenty-four hours a day. [slight pause] Right? That's it. She's going to not work. Yeah, I play with her [the baby] and hold her and mess around with her, you know. But as far as just, you know, doing all this other stuff, man, I ain't got, I don't feel like it. Right?

FLO: Right. . . .

INTERVIEWER: Does it surprise you, his attitude, or were you expecting this before the child was born?

FLO: I expected it. [Fred laughs] That's why I was thinking I wouldn't go back to work for a while.

FRED: She knows me by now. She knows me by now. [laughing]

INTERVIEWER: What about yourself? Did you [Fred] think you would be doing more stuff for the child or doing pretty much what you . . . [are] doing?

FRED: Well, I knew I wasn't going to do none of that stuff. I mean, I'm talking about—

FLO: Changing diapers, fixing bottles.

FRED: Yeh, that's right. I guess that's what you're talking about. Yeh, making bottles, changing diapers, well, I just know that's not for men to do. That's women's work. Right?

FLO: He should be able to help, right?

FRED: I do help occasionally. I change her diapers some. As a matter of fact, the first few months . . . from the time I got home I changed her almost 90 percent of the time till she went to bed. Yes sir. But [now] . . . I might change her once during the night, maybe. That's it, you know.

FLO: Why did you change?

FRED: Well, 'cause . . . I've just been working longer and been tireder and I didn't feel like it. That's right. Now maybe when I start working less and coming home earlier, I'll feel better, right? That's right. It has a lot to do with your mental status, that's what it is. You gotta give your mind a break. That's right. See, yours is in neutral all the time.

FLO: Ha! Ha! Ha!

FRED: You're just going around here at the house when you know I got, how much brains does it take to wash dishes?

FLO: You think I wash dishes all day?

FRED: Vacuum, change diapers, do all that stuff. See, you don't have pressures, not to think, and that's why you can go—

FLO: Oh. [laughing] . . . You don't think a kid gives you any trouble during the daytime, huh?

FRED: Not that much. No.

FLO: They have their good days and their bad days just like you do.

FRED: I know that, I already said that earlier, but I'm just saying—

FLO: So then it has pressure on me. Right?

FRED: Yeh, but it's not the same kind, Flo.

FLO: It's still pressure.

FRED: You are just talking about that—

FLO: It's just a different type.

FRED: Yelling and screaming and whining and crying; that's easy to put up with.

FLO: But you don't want to put up with it, okay?

FRED: Not in conjunction with what else I have to put up with, no. See, it's different—

FLO: Even on weekends, right?

FRED: On the weekends I'm resting.

FLO: Housewives don't get rest.

FRED: Un-un [meaning no].

FLO: Not even on the weekend.

FRED: Uh-hum [meaning yes]. Seven days a week, twenty-four hours a day, you're a housewife. And you do rest. I do help you some on the weekends. I do, don't I? Some?

FLO: Some.

FRED: Give me a break.

FLO: I think most husbands feel the same way about housewives. . . .

INTERVIEWER: Do you feel that what he says is true about, your staying home, [that] it's like a mindless kind of thing?

FLO: No.

FRED: [laughing] You didn't really think she would agree with that, did you? That would be admitting defeat right there. . . .

INTERVIEWER: Do you think it's good for her to be in . . . a situation where she doesn't have to think? Do you think that's good?

FRED: Good for her?

INTERVIEWER: Yeh.

FRED: Well, I don't know if it's necessarily good for her, but that's what she wants. And I guess everybody needs a break, whether it's for six months, nine months, a year, two years, you know, as far as working women are concerned. A lot of them like to, you know, work and make careers out of it. But Flo, she never has liked to work. She's always looked for an excuse or reason to quit.

EQUITY VERSUS EQUALITY

What exactly are Flo and Fred arguing about? Basically, Flo is saying that Fred is not contributing enough to the care of the baby, while Fred is contending that what he does with the baby is quite sufficient. What is "enough" or "sufficient" is a function of some standard implicit in their remarks. It is clear that they are not arguing over whether they should set up a role-sharing or androgynous system. Neither, in other words, seems to be suggesting that both should devote equal amounts of time to baby care, or that their contributions should be similar (that is, that both should be equally responsible for changing, feeding, and playing with the baby.) Hence, the central issue for them is not task equality. In this respect, they parallel all the other couples in the sample. Not one couple in the study was, in the strictest sense, striving to set up a role-sharing arrangement. This is not to say that the couples were not concerned about creating a division of labor that was impartial. Just the opposite; all the couples were striving for what they saw as a just or fair arrangement. Herein lies the key to the standard being applied by Flo and Fred: the crux of their argument is whether they have an "equitable" arrangement.

Equity is not the same as equality. Whereas *equality* refers to parity of activities, *equity* refers to parity of opportunities and constraints (Rapoport and Rapoport, 1975). Translating this distinction in terms of our introductory remarks, equality is based on a quantitative conception of time, equity on a qualitative conception of time.

In Flo's mind, what is wrong with their present arrangement is that when she looks at their total situation (their division of paid work, housework, and baby care), she sees herself with fewer opportunities and with more constraints than Fred. Fred's definition of the situation is, however, different. As he sees it, Flo is the one who is better off.

COMPUTING EQUITY

In their evaluation of whether they have an equitable arrangement, Flo and Fred need some criteria against which to judge their relative opportunities and constraints. At least two different kinds of criteria can be identified, the comparison level and the comparison level for alternatives, which refer respectively to the satisfaction and stability levels of a course of action (Thibaut and Kelley, 1959).

The *comparison level* (CL) is "the modal value of all out-comes of persons within the categories with which the person identifies" (Nye, 1979: 3). For example, couples who have just had a first child are more likely to compare themselves with other brand-new parents than with parents of a second child or with parents in general. Also, new mothers are likely to com-pare themselves with other new mothers, whereas new fathers are likely to compare themselves with other new fathers. There is one exception to this second rule, and that is, husbands and wives are likely to use each other as points of comparison, which means simply that contemporary husbands and wives generally identify with each other. The way the comparison level operates is this: persons will decide what their opportun-ities and constraints are in a course of action by first computing their payoffs in the situation. "Payoffs" are equal to opportun-ities (rewards, benefits, resources, etc.) minus constraints (costs, risks, losses, etc.). Then they will compute the average level of payoffs of all other persons within the categories with which they identify. Having done this, they will then compare their payoffs with the average. If their assessments of their positions are greater than the average, they are satisfied with their posi-tions. If their assessments of their positions are below this average, they are dissatisfied.

In contrast to the comparison level, the *comparison level for alternatives* (CLalt) is "the comparison of the outcomes in a given relationship, position, or milieu to those of the alterna-tives to the relationship, position, or milieu" (Nye, 1979: 3). For example, in making the decision whether or not to have a baby, couples will compare their payoffs in their present child-free situation with the anticipated payoffs of a parental status. If a couple decides that the CLalt is lower (that is, the antici-pated payoffs of having children are lower than the existing payoffs of not having children), then their current position is stable; they are not likely to conceive. Couples who have children cannot use the childfree position as an alternative, unless they believe that giving their children away is a viable option (not likely), or they are anticipating what life will be like when their children move out of the house. However, a couple with children can compare the payoffs that they are getting from their day-to-day contact with their children with the payoffs that they receive from their contacts with their friends, relatives, and each other, as well as the payoffs that they receive from being alone. If the payoffs for these specified alternatives are generally lower than the payoffs for interacting with their children, then the relationship that the couple has with their children is stable, which is to say that the couple is likely to "make" time for their children. If, on the other hand, the payoffs for these specified alternatives are generally higher than the payoffs for interacting with their children, then the relationship that the couple has with their children is unstable, which is to say that the couple is likely not to "make" time for their kids.[3]

Note that what is being said here is that the availability of *time* and, implicitly, *energy* for a relationship (a complex of actions) is a function of the payoffs associated with that relationship. This is in contrast to saying that the amount of time and energy available for a given relationship is a function of the amount of time and energy that has been "allotted" or "expended" to other relationships. This latter approach uses an essentially economic conception of human time and energy to explain what is commonly called role overload or role strain, and fails to take into account the fact that in a person's repertoire of activities (relationships, roles, etc.), there are typically a select few that can always be "fit in" to one's schedule, and that seem to be energy producing rather than taxing. Someone who loves his or her job, for example, can always find time to do that job (even if it means working evenings and weekends) and will generally experience exhilaration during the performance (and in the anticipation of the performance) of that job. Someone who loathes his or her job, on the other hand, is likely to feel that his work "cuts into" other things he or she would like to do, and will experience exhaustion during the performance (and in the anticipation of the performance) of that job. Thus, *commitment* to an activity (the payoffs associated with that activity) determines the amount of time and energy for that activity (Marks, 1977). Within the context of our introductory remarks, the economic approach to role overload or role strain assumes a quantitative conception of time, while the commitment approach assumes a qualitative conception of time.

Although Flo and Fred are not aware of the concepts, comparison level and comparison level for alternatives, their pattern of behavior can be described in these terms. The fact that they do not always rationally choose courses of action based on their own notions of what is valued does not diminish the theoretical leverage gained from these concepts (Emerson, 1976). Take, for example, Flo and Fred's differences over how much "pressure" each has in his or her life. This is a theme that cuts across the entire sample. While the words may differ—with some couples arguing over who "slaves" more and others debating over who "gave up" more—the issue is still the same, namely, equity, and it can always be better understood if it is examined in terms of comparison levels and comparison levels for alternatives.

Fred introduces the pressure idea to justify why he is doing less baby care than before. He is not, as he sees it, shirking his responsibilities. Rather, his decision not to be as involved is based on the greater pressure he has begun to experience in his job and on his assessment of how much pressure Flo is experiencing. Compared to what he has to put up with, the pressures of Flo's job (as full-time mother and homemaker) are negligible ("God, it's nothing"). And compared to what she had before, her situation is a vacation from "real" work ("She's always looked for an excuse or reason to quit"). Fred's first comparison is an application of the comparison level; he sees himself as "worse off" than Flo. His second comparison is an application of the comparison level for alternatives; he sees her as "better off" than before. The combination of the two comparisons leads him to conclude that the only way that he can achieve equity is to completely disassociate himself from baby care, which suggests that his comparison level for alternatives to interaction with his daughter is relatively high. If it were low, then he would find it difficult to limit his interaction with his child, even if it meant that Flo would be getting "the break" he is so ardently fighting against.

What about Flo's definition of the situation? She says that in anticipation of Fred's refusal to share the load, she decided that the only way that she could preserve equity would be to quit her job. She also disagrees with Fred's assessment of what it means to be a parent, and contends that being a full-time mother is a pressure cooker in its own right ("You sit here and let her scream"). Her anticipation of what life would be like and her assessment of what it is like after the birth is an application of the first comparison level; she anticipated being "worse off" than Fred if she continued to work, and she figures that she is no "worse off" than other housewives now that she is solely responsible for the baby's care ("I think most husbands feel the same way about housewives"). Her point about how difficult it is to take care of an infant is her attempt to refute Fred's assessment of *her* comparison level for alternatives; she does not believe that she is on an extended vacation, that her mind "is in neutral all the time." Flo's comparison level for alternatives to her job was relatively high. If it were low, then she would find it difficult to cut herself off from that job, even if doing so meant that Fred would be getting "the break" she insists he does not deserve.

As complex as this analysis may seem, it is really quite simple when one considers the manifold consequences of shifting from counting tasks (quantity) to computing opportunities and constraints (quality). Three things, in particular, complicate the picture even more.

First, although the comparison level and the comparison level for alternatives are typically correlated with each other, there are situations in which the two are not sychronized. Thus, there are not two but four different ideal typical combinations of the CL and the CLalt (Swensen, 1973: 228-229):

A. Higher CL, Higher CLalt
B. Higher CL, Lower CLalt
C. Lower CL, Higher CLalt
D. Lower CL, Lower CLalt

Configurations "A" and "D" are satisfying/stable and unsatisfying/unstable situations respectively. "A" situations involve parents who consider themselves relatively better off than others in their position, and who value parenting more than any other activity. "D" situations involve parents who feel just the opposite; they consider themselves relatively worse off than others in their position, and value parenting less than any other activity. Configuration "B" is a satisfying/unstable situations. People who consider themselves fortunate as parents but who, because of economic constraints, rarely see their children would be one example of this type. Configuration "C" is an unsatisfying/stable situation, and would include parents who think, as one of our couples put it, that being a full-time parent is "the pits" (compared to being a part-time parent who is employed) but who believe that their options are closed and thus conclude that one of them must stay home full-time with the baby. The complication in terms of computing equity is trying to decide which is worse—"B" or "C"? Is a mother who must go to work each day and leave the maternal role she loves more than any other (situation "B") relatively deprived compared to the father who must go to work each day and assume the career role he hates more than any other (situation "C")?

The second reason why focusing on equity complicates the division of labor is that the different perceptions of the husband and wife must be taken into account. A husband and wife are not only estimating their own comparison level and comparison level for alternatives, they are also computing each other's. This means that there are eight potentially different realities: the husband's perception of his CL and CLalt and his wife's CL and CLalt, and the wife's perception of her CL and CLalt and her husband's CL and CLalt. Take Flo and Fred. Working against Flo in their negotiations is Fred's perception of her CL and CLalt. Unfortunately, his perception of her situation is not based on personal experience, but on what he imagines she is experiencing. He does not directly know what it is like to be a full-time mother because he has not spent more than a few hours alone with his daughter. Many of the husbands in the sample either chose or were "forced" by their wives to get an inkling of what it meant to stay home all day with an infant when, on the weekends or in the evening, they would "babysit" to "give" their wives some time off. But Fred does not change diapers or feed the baby, let alone take full responsibility while Flo goes out, because on the weekends he is supposedly resting from the increased pressure of his job. Of course, even if Fred did spend one Saturday a month alone with his daughter, his perception of what it means to be a full-time parent would not coincide with Flo's. The inability of fathers to fully appreciate the everyday life of their wives makes the equity issue especially problematic. Of course, the screw turns both ways. Although there are more women full-time in the labor force than there are men full-time in the "child force," it is difficult for women to understand the "pressures" of "the job" which men experience. Flo assumes that she knows the pressures that Fred is under because she used to work. But the societal expectations for men with respect to the work role are far more intense and far more confining than they are for women. Even career-oriented women are generally allowed the break from work that Fred begrudges Flo. There are, of course, exceptions to the rule. Also, in the past ten years, the rule has become less applicable, as more and more women choose to or are compelled (by inflation) to take their jobs more seriously.

A third and final reason why focusing on equity results in a more complex view of the division of labor is that when husbands and wives are negotiating over equity, they are operating within the overall organization of their CL and CLalt. That organization has both horizontal and vertical structures which are continuously changing. A new boss, for example, may change the CL and CLalt picture at work, which means that the whole equity structure may be rearranged. To capture the social interactive character of the division of labor, we must actually "freeze" the picture in time. In sum then, equity means that:

Participation in a particular social setting . . . provides some distribution of constraints and resources. Although this distribution will usually be changing constantly, at any given moment we can assume an overall position for each individual consisting of: (a) the cumulative net balances in resources and constraints which obtain in all situations in which he participates; (b) the effects of simultaneous participation in a number of different settings; (c) the anticipated outcomes of negotiations not yet completed [Gerson, 1976: 797].

Thus, when husbands and wives negotiate over the division of labor during the transition to parenthood, they are essentially concerned with the distribution of resources and constraints emerging from their interactions in a variety of settings. To put it another way, the division of labor after birth is not simply task differentiation, but the "patterns of commitment organization, as expressed in flows of resources and constraints upon" a couple (Gerson, 1976: 799).

MISALIGNMENTS

It is clear from the above analysis (and from the previous chapter) that during the transition to parenthood, the probability of misunderstandings, screw-ups, snafus, conflicts of interest, and unplanned consequences is quite high. In a word, things can "get out of line" quite easily. Generally, these misalignments take two forms. *Interpersonal misalignments* are those situations in which there is a misunderstanding or basic conflict of interest between people. *Culture-conduct misalignments* are those situations in which there is a perceived discrepancy between the cultural ideals and expectations of the participants in a social system and their actual or intended conduct; they say one thing and do another (Stokes and Hewitt, 1976).

The two forms of misalignments are closely related. Interpersonal misalignments are often based on one person accusing the other of acting "improperly" (suggesting a culture-conduct misalignment), and culture-conduct misalignments will generally result in a "run-in" with somebody (suggesting an interpersonal misalignment). It is important, however, to keep the two forms separate for several reasons (Stokes and Hewitt, 1976: 844). First, many misalignments "have little to do with cultural ideals. They are focused instead on a great variety of more particular difficulties people have in dealing with the environment and with each other." For example, a wife may have told her husband to give the baby some aspirin, but for one reason or another the husband did not hear her. Second, if there exists a culture-conduct misalignment, "the nature and degree of the misalignment is by no means an obvious, objective or easily established fact. The way in which cultural standards apply to a particular fact is a matter of negotiation among people interacting with one another and not simply a question of applying rules or principles to conduct." For example, parents have a general sense that they should be sensitive to their children's needs, but exactly how sensitive they should be and in what way that sensitivity should be translated into conduct is not clear. The ongoing debates between fathers and mothers over protectiveness, permissiveness, etc., is but one example of this simple fact. Finally, in situations in which there is both an interpersonal misalignment and a culture-conduct misalignment, the participants very often will focus on the former and conveniently ignore the latter. "People typically want to square what they are doing with their conception of what is culturally appropriate, but such an alignment does not always, and perhaps does not often, take the form of a dedicated effort to *do* what is culturally required. Rather, alignment may take the form of paying ritual to cultural expectations so that the business of getting done what has to be done can proceed." For example, a middle-class egalitarian-oriented couple may overlook the fact that their child-care arrangement is sexist, no matter how you look at it. But in the interest of "getting the job done," they may focus their energies on coordinating with each other a traditional baby-care arrangement. This is, in fact, the problem for most couples who think they can create androgynous parenting situations. The larger system (the inavailability of flex-time work and adequate day care, for example) is at odds with their personal goals. In the interest of not making their children political pawns, these parents often must be satisfied with a traditional (but perceived equitable) baby-care arrangement.

ALIGNING ACTIONS

When people are confronted with either an interpersonal misalignment or a culture-conduct misalignment, they will engage in what are called (reasonably enough) aligning actions (Stokes and Hewitt, 1976). *Aligning actions* are principally verbal activities and include, among other things, *motives* ("answers to questions interrupting acts or programs" [Mills, 1940: 473]), *remedial interchanges* ("corrective readings calculated to show that a possible offender actually had a right relationship to the rules, or if he seemed not to a moment ago, he can be counted on to have such a relationship henceforth" [Goffman, 1971: 108]), and *accounts* ("a statement made by a social actor to explain unanticipated or untoward behavior" [Scott and Lyman, 1968: 46]).

There are several typologies of aligning actions that have been proposed, each focusing on a different set of criteria. Three of these typologies are especially useful to our analysis and, in our opinion, hold particular promise in terms of the development of a sociological theory of the transition to parenthood. The three are excuses versus justifications, emergence appeals versus relativity appeals, and appeals to positional coorientations versus appeals to personal coorientations.

Excuses are aligning actions (more specifically, accounts) "in which one admits that the act in question is bad, wrong, or inappropriate but denies full responsibility." Conversely, *justifications* are aligning actions (more specifically, accounts) "in which one accepts responsibility for the act in question, but denies the pejorative quality associated with it" (Scott and Lyman, 1968: 47). Suppose, for example, that a father who spends virtually no time with his child is called on the carpet by his wife. If he attempts to correct the misalignment by saying that he realizes that he has been negligent, but that his job has been demanding a lot of his time lately, then he is offering an excuse. If he says that he is deliberately avoiding his child because he does not want to upset the balance of labor (equity) in the home, then he is offering a justification. Both of these aligning actions were, of course, used by Fred toward Flo.

Each, however, signifies a different tack. We suspect that the ratio of excuses to justifications in a given argument is significant. Since justifications embody the idea that one is in control (responsible), a heavy reliance on justifications rather than excuses may signify less alienation in the situation. Self-control has been found to be an important factor in pregnancy/child-bearing adjustment (Breen, 1975; Davenport-Slack and Boylan, 1974); the more self-control, the better one seems able to cope with the transition. Hence, the proportion of justifications versus excuses used during misalignments could be a measure of adjustment (cf. LaRossa, 1979).

Emergence appeals are aligning actions in which "the individual tends to define his or her present activity not by describing the immediate moment itself, but by describing that moment in relation to other moments past and present." Conversely, *relativity appeals* are aligning actions in which "the individual's attention turns more closely to his or her immediate locale" (Hansen and Johnson, 1979: 591). For example, when Fred remarks that just after the baby was born he changed the baby's diaper "almost 90 percent of the time till she went to bed," he is putting his current refusal to change diapers within a past-present context, and thus is offering an emergence appeal. He is implying that he already did "his share" of baby care. This was a very popular aligning action of fathers who "came on strong" in the beginning of the transition to parenthood, but who tapered off their baby care as time wore one. An example of a relativity appeal is Fred's attempt to cast their disagreement as but one more attempt by Flo to outmaneuver him into doing her work ("You didn't think she would agree with that, did you? That would be admitting defeat right there"). It has been hypothesized that emergence appeals are used more in fairly stable situations, while relativity appeals are used more in times of heightened uncertainty (Hansen and Johnson, 1979: 591). This would suggest that during the transition to parenthood, couples experiencing minor misalignments would rely more on emergence appeals, while couples experiencing major misalignments would rely more on relativity appeals.

Appeals to positional coorientations are aligning actions in which the individual emphasizes "specific normative prescriptions which do not depend on his or her own individual personal characteristics. Focus is generally on manifest behaviors and on the consequences of actions." Conversely, *appeals to personal coorientations* are aligning actions in which the individual focuses on "feelings" and "the personal qualities and meanings of the participants" (Hansen and Johnson, 1979: 595). When Fred says that he does not make bottles and change diapers because "that's women's work," he is appealing to the social positional differences between him and Flo. Needless to say, this was also a popular aligning action used by the husbands in our sample. It was also a very popular aligning action used by the wives. People generally are more comfortable if they can assure themselves that the division of labor in their home is part of some grand societal scheme; it makes them feel in tune with the world. Fred resorts to an appeal to personal coorientations when, at the end of the dialogue, he says that Flo has "always looked for an excuse or reason to quit" her job. He is insinuating that his wife is lazy, and that *that* is why he does not intend to do more baby work. It is hypothesized that "conditions of heightened ambiguity pose a more serious threat to families strong in positional coorientations; yet they are more likely to induce changes in interaction patterns in families that are strong in personal coorientations" (Hansen and Johnson, 1979: 595). If this is indeed the case, then traditional families may be more likely to experience a crisis during "abnormal" transitions to parenthood (e.g., when a premature or deformed baby is born), while nontraditional families may be more likely to undergo a major structural change.

ALIGNING ACTIONS AND
TRADITIONAL DIVISIONS OF LABOR

Aligning actions are central to a sociological perspective because they help us to understand a central sociological problem, namely, the existence of continuity and change in social life. Given instances of culture-conduct misalignment (the second of the two forms of misalignment), the major functions of aligning actions are to (1) "maintain culture in the face of conduct that is at variance with it," and (2) "provide a social lubricant that simultaneously permits social change and yet allows conduct to be linked to recognized cultural boundaries" (Stokes and Hewitt, 1976: 848).

With respect to the first function, aligning actions explain how a couple can believe that they have a role-sharing (nontraditional) system when their conduct clearly indicates that they have a role-segregated (traditional) system. The aligning actions in this case define role-segregated conduct as nothing more than a legitimate exception to the rule. Thus, for example, the couple who very much wants to institute an androgynous parental arrangement but who finds it virtually impossible to carry out, given the existing societal constraints, may conduct themselves on a traditional plane but continue to believe that they are "into androgyny" by defining their deviance from their beliefs as "excusable," "justifiable," etc. In other words, aligning actions are a form of situational ethics which allows people to hold on to their absolute standards. Of course, aligning actions need not be used conjointly by a couple. A husband may, through aligning actions, continue to genuinely believe that he is sharing the load despite evidence to the contrary. A wife may, through aligning actions, continue to honestly believe that she wants to be with her kids more than anything else in the world despite her efforts to disassociate from them.

The continuity function of aligning actions points to their significance in reducing stress. Whether they are called motives, remedial interchanges, or accounts, aligning actions are essentially collective or individual rationalizations which permit people to cope with the problematic. Their existence may explain why Hobbs's (1965) twenty-three-item checklist has failed to uncover any major "crisis" during the transition to parenthood. As noted in Chapter 1, the major focus of the "parenthood as crisis" research is not on behavioral changes but on attitudes toward behavioral changes. It would seem logical to argue that misalignments probably increase during the transition to parenthood. And yet, according to the checklist studies, couples are not generally "bothered" by these misalignments. The fact that the checklist indicates no crisis should not, however, be considered the end of the story. On the contrary, the relatively smooth way in which couples presumably deal with misalignments during the transition to parenthood should be the subject of inquiry. New parents may not complain of problems because they have developed a complex set of aligning actions to "make sense" of a confusing and threatening situation.

The second function of aligning actions—the change function—is perhaps even more important than the continuity function, in that the change function provides a sociological explanation for traditionalization during the transition to parenthood. You will recall that, in Chapter 1, we reported that several studies found that traditional marital behavior *increased* during the months following the birth of a first child (Cowan et al., 1978; Entwisle and Doering, 1980; Meyerowitz and Feldman, 1966; Raush et al., 1974). Explanations for why these changes occur have typically centered on either physiological or personality factors which are supposedly triggered by parenthood. Our data suggest, however, that there are other factors, more sociological in scope, that may also contribute to the traditionalization process after birth. But before we discuss what these sociological factors are and how they operate, we will first, for the sake of comparison, provide a brief review of the physiological and personality theories of traditionalization.

A Physiological Theory of Traditionalization

In a controversial article entitled "A Biosocial Perspective on Parenting," Alice Rossi (1977) argues that hormonal changes in women during pregnancy, birth, and nursing establish "a clear link between sexuality and maternalism." New mothers receive "erotogenic pleasure" from nursing their infants, which means, according to Rossi, that "there may be a biologically based potential for heightened maternal investment in the child, at least through the first months of life, that exceeds the potential for investment by men in fatherhood." Implicitly answering the traditionalization question, Rossi goes on to say that "significant residues of greater maternal than paternal attachment may then persist into later stages of the parent-child relationship." In short, Rossi is arguing that physiological forces create an affective relationship between mother and child that is stronger than the relationship between father and child, and that this closer affective bond results in mothers taking a greater interest than fathers in the care of their children. So strong is this force, says Rossi, that "family life and parent education in youth, even when available to both boys and girls, may not be sufficient to override the contribution of pregnancy and birth" (1977: 17, 24).

The significance of hormonal factors during the transition to parenthood is a hotly debated topic. If hormones are as strong as Rossi contends they are, then, at least with respect to the traditionalization issue, anatomy is destiny. Attempts to establish role-sharing parental arrangements would be going "against the natural grain," and would inevitably fail.

A Personality Theory of Traditionalization

Critics of the physiological perspective have mainly argued that Rossi is wrong when she says that family life and parent education in youth are inconsequential in the establishment of traditional role behaviors. In their opinion, child socialization is indeed an important variable, and may in fact be the most important variable operating on parents in the early months following the birth of a child.

Interestingly, one of the representatives of this point of view was, at one time, Rossi herself. In a paper published eight years before the biosocial perspective article, Rossi takes a psychological approach to traditionalization, proposing that personality rather than hormonal factors explain gender differentiation in the marital system after birth (1969: 4):

Sex role expectations tend to remain a stubborn part of our impulse lives. This is often not visible among young men and women until they become parents. Many young people have egalitarian peers in school, courtship, and early marriage. With the birth of a child, deeper layers of their personalities come into play. Since there is little or no formal education for parenthood in our society, only a thin veneer of Spock-reading hides the acting out of old parental models that have been observed and internalized in childhood, triggering a regression to traditional sex roles that gradually spreads from the parental role to the marriage and the self definition of both sexes.

If personality factors are as strong a force as Rossi contends here, then instead of anatomy being destiny, child socialization is destiny. Again, attempts to establish role-sharing parental arrangements would be going "against the grain," and would inevitably fail, only now the culprit would be nurture rather than nature.

A Sociological Theory of Traditionalization

The physiological and personality theories of traditionalization during the transition to parenthood are both deterministic explanations. Both essentially argue that traditional behavior is "epiphenomenal and derivative," a product of "a programmed routine" which is "blindly" acted out. The only difference between the two is the "source of control" (cf. Stokes and Hewitt, 1976: 839). We cannot test the relative validity of the physiological and personality explanations with our data. And this is not the place to embark on a review of studies which have attempted to test these two theories. We can, however, say this: the existing evidence indicates that physiological and personality factors are *not* sufficient to explain traditionalization after birth. As important as these variables may be, no one has yet conclusively demonstrated that physiology or personality, or some combination of the two, is all that is needed to understand why couples shift to a traditional family system during the transition to parenthood.

The inability of physiological and personality theories to explain everything points to the importance of including sociological variables in models of traditionalization. But we must be careful here; in principle, a sociological approach does not mean simply paying homage to societal factors impacting on couples after they become parents. Contending that society "forces" couples into traditional roles is to conceive of a society that is separate from, rather than integrated with, individuals. This approach is nothing more than deterministic reasoning disguised as sociological reasoning. Substituting societal determinism for physiological or personality determinism is *not* in keeping with a sociological perspective.

Thus, for example, when Michael Lamb, a psychologist by training, attempts to explain traditionalization by arguing that "the insistent and undeniable dependency of the baby makes equivocation or ambiguity about role demands more difficult to sustain than in the preparental phase, and our society's expectations regarding nurturant maternal roles are more clearly defined than any other" (Lamb, 1978: 146), he falls short of offering a truly sociological explanation because he leaves open the question of exactly how societal expectations translate into marital behavior. Where Lamb's proposition actually fails is in his implicit assertion that traditional behavior is nothing more than cultural programming. As noted earlier, however, the relationship between culture and conduct is not as smooth as Lamb suggests. Whereas in earlier times traditionalization may indeed have been a puppetlike process, postindustrial society does not provide couples with a "clearly defined" script for how to act when a baby arrives. To the contrary, parental expectations in modern society are extremely complex and highly ambiguous (LeMasters, 1970). Ironically, however, Lamb the psychologist does come closer to a sociological explanation than Rossi the sociologist underscoring the fact that when we use the term "sociology," we are referring not to what sociologists do but to a perspective, which may be used by anyone.

The part of Lamb's statement that, in our opinion, should have been developed more is the beginning, where he says that "the insistent and undeniable dependency of the baby" poses special problems for new parents. Here he is suggesting some social interactional process operating to move the couple toward traditional role behavior. Our data suggest that the dependency of the baby on the parents is indeed an important factor in traditionalization, but that it is not simply a matter of making "equivocation or ambiguity about role demands more difficult to sustain." Rather, it is the dependency of the baby which creates a scarcity of free time, and which places the couple in a more competitive stance toward the other.

Before the transition to parenthood, it is relatively easy for couples (and especially men) to believe that they are nontraditional in the same way that it is easy, during times of economic growth and prosperity, for the middle class to believe that it is not racist. In both situations, valued resources (time in one case, money in the other) are not immediately threatened. However, history has shown that when it becomes apparent that strict adherence to sexual or racial equality can mean personal losses, then the basic axiom of the conflict orientation applies: when resources are scarce, people tend to choose themselves over others. Put simply, under conditions of scarcity, whites become more racist and men become more sexist. But in choosing themselves over others, both the middle-class white and the husband-father are faced with their own culture-conduct misalignments. In all likelihood, their behavior in the economic or temporal "squeeze" is at odds with their stated beliefs before the scarcity. This is where aligning actions come into play. By blaming others (their parents, their bosses, the government, and even the people they are competing with—blacks or women) and/or by justifying their conduct on grounds that run the gamut from the biological (e.g., the physiological explanation) to the ethical (e.g., the equity argument), they try their best to symbolically (but not behaviorally) mend their broken promises. Initially, these aligning actions serve as stopgap measures, helping the people in the system (both the "haves" and the "have-nots") cope with the transition, helping them maintain a consistent and orderly reality to their lives. Over time, the aligning actions help to transform the reality of the system itself.

In order to make our point clear, we should more precisely define what we mean by "traditionalization." Up to now, we have used the term to refer to increases in traditional behavior. This is because the existing studies on the transition to parenthood have employed the term in this way, and because it would not have been meaningful to question their approach until after we had introduced the change function of aligning actions. In truth, limiting traditionalization to behavioral shifts is theoretically vacuous. To know simply that a couple exhibits traditional behavior tells us nothing about whether the husband and wife "have their hearts in it" (role embracement), or whether they are mechanically "going through the motions." In other words, the meaning which the couple imputes to their activity is lost. We are not talking about whether the couple is "bothered" or "gratified" by their behavior. Rather, we are referring to the couple's total way of looking at what they are doing, their world view, their *Weltanschauung.* Although the studies which have focused on the transition to parenthood have equated traditionalization with behavioral change, there are other studies which have attempted to assess the impact of parenthood by comparing couples with the without children, and which indicate that, in addition to changing their behavior, couples may also shift to traditional ways of thinking (Hoffman and Manis, 1978). If both the culture and the conduct of a marriage traditionalize, then *traditionalization is an organizational transformation rather than simply a behavioral change.* This is how we prefer to use the term, and for good reason. Our data suggest that, more often than not, the transition to parenthood initiates a systemic level change in marriage toward a more traditional social organization.

The key to the difference between the continuity and the change function of aligning actions is time. On a short-term basis, aligning actions serve a preservative function, allowing beliefs to persist despite contradictory evidence. But on a long-term basis, aligning actions serve a morphogenic function, allowing beliefs to drift, ever so gradually, in the direction of the misaligned conduct. The presumption being made here is that over extended periods of time "culture follows conduct" (Stokes and Hewitt, 1976: 848). Thus, on a short-term basis, the couple whose conduct after the birth of their child is more traditional than their beliefs can use aligning actions to preserve those beliefs. But on a long-term basis, their willingness to excuse and justify their behavior rather than actually make it conform to their beliefs will result in an adjustment of their beliefs to their conduct. They will, in other words, begin to develop a marital culture that is closer to (but not necessarily in exact correspondence with) their actual conduct. Thus, aligning actions serve as a "social lubricant" for traditionalization in that they allow misalignments to be explained away rather than seriously examined.

The typology of aligning actions can also be brought to bear here. If, for example, excuses mean that the actor admits that the misalignment is wrong, while justifications signify a refusal to see the misalignment in pejorative terms, we might find couples relying more on justifications (e.g., equity) than on excuses. Thinking of traditionalization as a transformation that occurs over time, we might also want to know whether different types of aligning actions are used in the beginning and end of the transformation. For example, if emergence appeals are used in fairly stable situations, while relativity appeals are used in times of heightened uncertainty (Hansen and Johnson, 1979: 591), we might find that emergence appeals would be typically used in the beginning of traditionalization, while relativity appeals would be used toward the end. Finally, since appeals to positional coorientations (e.g., "Women are cut out to be parents") are generally more sociohistorically grounded than appeals to personal coorientations (e.g., "I'm too tired to take care of the baby"), we might find couples using the former more often than the latter because doing so makes their argument more legitimate in the eyes of society.

This last point about the legitimacy of aligning actions is especially important. Not all aligning actions are honored—that is, accepted—by the "offended" party as a legitimate explanation for the misalignment. Whether or not an aligning action is deemed legitimate is a function of the social structural and symbolic universe of the people in the interaction. For example, while it is generally considered socially acceptable for a father to say that his career is keeping him from his children, it is not as acceptable for mothers to use this excuse. It is also not as acceptable for mothers to say that they have less patience with their newborns than their husbands do, or that they are not as skilled in feeding, changing, or quieting the baby. If any of these aligning actions were offered by a mother, there is a fairly good chance that they would be disallowed by her husband, her family, her friends, etc. Thus, crucial to the traditionalization process is the availability of aligning actions that legitimate the father's withdrawal from baby care, and the corresponding absence of aligning actions that legitimate the mother's withdrawal from baby care.

The legitimacy of an aligning action is, however, not a given, which is to say that social actors cannot assume that an aligning action will be accepted when it is offered. The critical stage in the "life" of an aligning action is when the aligning action is presented and accepted or not accepted by the other party. Up until this point, the validity of an aligning action for any particular relationship is an open question. Only after the aligning action is presented *and* accepted does it become part of the social reality of the relationship. For example, when a husband says for the first time (perhaps just after he has had difficulty giving the baby breakfast) that he feels that he is inept at feeding his son or daughter, the wife's immediate response to the husband's assertion is critical. If at this point she does not challenge her husband's definition of the situation, or if she takes over responsibility for feeding the baby because of what he has just said, she has effectively endorsed the aligning action, accepting it, at least for the moment, as part of their consensual world. Thus, the theory proposed here for the traditionalization process is both sociohistorical and interactional. As much as the aligning actions may appear to the husband and wife as realities that are "out there," programming their every move, the fact is that they are part and parcel of the negotiation process itself, intrinsic to the whole idea of social interaction.

We should emphasize that this theory of traditionalization focuses only on the first nine months after birth, and is not meant to serve as a general theory of sexual inequality.

Although our data strongly suggest that the key sociological variable in the traditionalization process during the transition to parenthood is the husband's perception of his own free time and his decision to withdraw or not withdraw from baby care based on that perception, we cannot generalize beyond this and assert that conflict over time is the story of sexism in a nutshell. In our opinion, sex stratification is too complex for us to make such a claim. On the other hand, our research has convinced us that more attention should be given to the relationship between time and the sexual division of labor. The fact is that "down time" from children means more than simply having time to play tennis or go to the bathroom; it also means time to make money, time to pursue a career, and time to gain power (Polatnick, 1973). Thus, while the negotiation over time may not tell the whole story, it certainly appears to be a significant part of the issue. And, while the traditionalization process just described may not explain all gender-role behavior, it certainly appears to be an important cog in the machine.

CONCLUSION

We have tried in this chapter to present a sociological approach to the division of labor during the transition to parenthood. The heart of this approach is the recognition that, in the minds of the participants, the division of labor is a problem of equity, based on a qualitative conception of time, and that the character and form of the division of labor is interactive, emergent, and processual (cf. Friedson, 1976).

Our analysis stands in sharp contrast not only to most research on the transition to parenthood, but to most research on the division of labor as well. The standard strategy of family researchers interested in studying work patterns has been to reduce these patterns to task differentiation. Typically, subjects are given a list of jobs and then asked to indicate how, in their families, the jobs are divided: husband always, husband more than wife, husband and wife exactly the same, wife more than husband, wife always (see, for example, Blood and Wolfe, 1960: 282). Although there is nothing essentially wrong with this approach, one thing should be made clear: measures such as these focus only on the outcomes of the division of labor; the processes underlying it are basically ignored. The tendency to study outcomes rather than processes is common in family research. We are just now, for example, beginning to recognize how simplistic it is to reduce the power variable to outcomes. Asking people "who makes the final decision on issue A, B, and C?" ignores power processes (Cromwell and Olson, 1975). The same is true with respect to the division of labor.

This completes Part Two of the book, the purpose of which was to lay out the general framework developed from our analysis. The remainder of the book is basically an elaboration of this framework. Zeroing in on four of the couples in the study, we will show how such things as aligning actions and primary, secondary, and tertiary time operate together to form a systemic picture of the transition to parenthood. After the case studies, we will return again to a more abstract level of analysis, and discuss how the issues can be studied within a comparative perspective.

NOTES

1. Following Druckman (1977) but in contrast to Strauss (1978), *negotiation* is meant to include all acts of bargaining, debating, and influencing (powering).

2. Note that we did not say that family members negotiate a division of labor, whereas workers do not. Nor did we say that the negotiation of a division of labor is problematic in families and nonproblematic in work settings. The negotiation of a division of labor is endemic to all social organizations, and it is always problematic. What is a variable, however, is how overt, how conscious, and how intense the negotiations are.

3. It should be apparent that the comparison level and the comparison level for alternatives offer a general approach to a qualitative conception of time. For example, the reason that weekend duty in a work setting is typically "worse" than weekday duty is because the workers see themselves as relatively deprived compared to their friends who are off (an application of the comparison level), and because they know that if they were not working they could be taking advantage of the leisure activities that often are scheduled only on weekends (an application of the comparison level for alternatives). Of course, the situation changes depending on one's reference group and nonwork activities.

*PART THREE: CLOSE-UPS OF
BREADWINNER-HOMEMAKER FAMILIES*

Chapter 5

CAROL AND CHESTER

This chapter presents the first of four case studies intended to provide a glimpse of the transition to parenthood at close range. In this part of the book, we present two families in which the wife is not employed; and in the next, two families in which the wife is employed.[1]

According to our data, the most important sociodemographic variable qualifying the relationship between parenthood and family interaction (generally speaking) is not age, or length of time married, or even number of children, but wife's employment. That the wife's employment would prove to be so important is not new or startling. Researchers and parents have long known that the number of hours per week that a mother spends at paid work significantly affects both the decision to have children and the character of child care in the home. We soon realized, however, that just knowing whether or not a mother is employed is not sufficient to understand how work, parenthood, and family interaction are related to each other.

Equally important is the couple's definition of the wife's employment situation. For example, a wife who voluntarily quits her job after her baby is born is in a different situation than a wife who involuntary quits her job. And as Flo and Fred graphically demonstrate, the husband's definition of his wife's employment situation is also a factor; housewives who do not have the endorsement of their spouses are in a situation different from that of housewives who do. Finally, definitions can change, or be more or less stable; the working woman who is ambivalent about leaving her child in a day-care center is in a situation different from that of the woman who has no qualms at all.

This first case study illustrates all three of the above situations. Carol voluntarily decided to stay home full-time with her new baby, but she soon became a reluctant homemaker. In contrast to Fred, Chester comes across as sympathetic—both to his wife's decision to quit her job, and to her decision to return to work. And ambivalence, or the general theme of being betwixt and between, is central to the couple's experience with parenthood. All in all, they are a good couple to begin with, one whose story, we suspect, is common among the middle class today.

When Carol and Chester were asked why they decided to have a child, they said that, basically, they were hoping that parenthood would add meaning to their lives.[2] Yes, work and marriage were enjoyable, but they felt that there had to be more; there had to be something else that would make it all seem worthwhile ("I think Carol and I just thought there was a little bit more to life than just what restaurant to go to"). After seeing some of their friends' lives change when they had children, Carol and Chester concluded that the "something else" they needed was a baby. They also seemed to be motivated by the fear that if they did not have a child, they could be very sorry later on. One of the few couples in the sample to have seriously considered remaining childless, Carol and Chester had thus concluded that the risks seemed greater if they opted *not* to become parents.

Since the transition to parenthood was viewed as such a momentous change, they took great pains to insure that everything would be just right for the big event. First, in terms of their mental outlook, they reconstructed their past life, so to speak, by redefining the time before the baby arrived not as time lost, but as a preparatory stage to a successful transition. Having "waited" as long as they did, they maintained that they could now feel comfortable with the idea that they "really wanted to do it." Second, they decided that Carol would quit her job and remain home with the child because, like Flo and Fred (and others), they did not think a day-care center was a suitable place for an infant. Carol's move to full-time motherhood was also part of their search for meaning. Carol wanted very much to be a part of her child's "growing up," and they were both intent on creating a traditional home life, one in which family (marriage and parenthood) would occupy center stage and work would assume a peripheral role.

When they were interviewed during the third month following their daughter's birth, they gave the impression that everything was going according to plan, and seemed to be particularly pleased with their decision to adopt a breadwinner-homemaker family structure.

INTERVIEWER: What's it like going from working full-time to being at home?

CAROL: It is definitely a big change because your whole lifestyle changes. And for the first two or three weeks you rattle around the house, and then you get used to, you know, start finding that you have a lot of it free and you can do the things you always thought you wanted to while you were working.

INTERVIEWER: What do you mean by lifestyle change?

CAROL: Well, you don't get up in the morning and rush in there and gobble down a bowl of cereal and rush in and put on your makeup and run out the front door. Your pace of living changes, and you have a chance to do things together. Like, we never used to have weekends together, ever, when I was working because I also worked on Saturdays, and sometimes I worked on Sundays. And now we have all weekends together, every weekend, and it's just great. We had weekends together when we were dating, but not after we got married. . . .

CHESTER: When she was working, we would both come home and she'd be dead tired and I'd be dead tired and we would go out somewhere and get a few drinks and have supper and go to some friend's house. It was great, but it seemed like we did that every other night. After a while, we just sort of got in a rut. So I like it better now.

INTERVIEWER: What do you like better?

CHESTER: Well, I just like seeing the baby grow. I just feel like we've got something that's ours, and you see her changing every day, and I don't know, I just really like it. It's hard to put it into words.

CAROL: You said to me one day, "It's nice to come home and have somebody there instead of walking into an empty house." It just makes you feel better. . . .

CHESTER: Well, it's a lot more fun. . . . I guess before I would unburden my job on her and she would do the same to me when we came home, and now we just, you know, she asks me how the day was going, that's great and stuff, but you know, we talk about the baby and then we make plans for this weekend and next weekend. It just seems like jobs are just not all that important a topic of conversation. . . .

INTERVIEWER: What's it like being with the child all day?

CAROL: Well, it's different, it's very different, but it's not what I had always thought it would be. I always thought it would be boring, and I always thought I would absolutely go stark raving mad the first three days. But it's really not like that, or at least it hasn't been so far, because she's really exciting and she's always doing something different. And she's, you can see her do something today that she didn't do yesterday, and you can see her, I mean, it's just exciting because you see her look at you when you say her name, and you realize that she recognizes your voice. And it's getting better because she's getting more alert.

From the above account, we can discern two dimensions in Carol and Chester's new world. First, they speak repeatedly, and with great affection, about how their pace of living has slowed down since Carol stopped working. Since they no longer have to contend with the duration and intensity of two jobs, they now say they have the time and energy to enjoy each other's company. The fact that they are not going out "every other night" to "get a few drinks," etc., is probably due mostly to their unwillingness to leave the baby with a sitter. However, they also imply that their heavy night life was their way of letting off steam. Thus, it would appear that since they have eliminated one of the specific sources of their stress, they do not need their extracurricular activities as much as they did before. Then, of course, there is the baby, who now provides them with some previously unavailable home entertainment, which brings us to the second dimension in Carol and Chester's change to a traditional lifestyle—their shift to a child-centered family system. Although Chester is still working, his job does not command the attention it once did ("It just seems like jobs are just not all that important a topic of conversation"). The focus of their lives is now their daughter—what she is doing and where she is going. Her physical and psychological growth is, in their minds, both the stimulus and a metaphor for the new directions their relationship has taken. They have apparently transformed themselves; they are out of their "rut."

It would be incorrect to assume that Carol and Chester had become prisoners in their home. They still enjoyed going out once in a while, both alone and with each other, and they spent considerable time during the first interview talking about how they had achieved what they believed was an ideal balance. The key, they confidently pointed out, was "forethought" and "planning." It should be noted, however, that the couple took basically a permissive or adaptive approach to child raising, which means that, for the most part, they permitted their daughter's needs and developmental changes to dictate what they could and could not do. Thus, when the words "forethought" and "planning" are used, what is meant is that by anticipating the baby's moves they have found that they can often schedule their leisure time around her.

Few, if any, young parents believe that they will not have to make concessions to an infant. As we noted in Chapter 3, new fathers and mothers quickly learn that a baby wields a considerable amount of power; despite the resistance of the parents, the baby's "will" often prevails (cf. Weber, 1947: 152). Parents can, however, be classified according to the degree to which they will allow a child to run their lives. In other words, most parents are relatively permissive, but some are more permissive than others. Carol and Chester appeared to be one of the more permissive couples in the sample. Not once did they mention, as some of the other couples did (e.g., Ted and Thelma in the next chapter), the idea of imposing a schedule on the baby, forcing the baby to eat and sleep when *they* wanted her to.

The sixth-month interview was pretty much like the first. Carol echoed her commitment to being a career mother. She would return to full-time work only if she and Chester were "strapped financially," which she thought unlikely; and she would consider a part-time job only if something really "super" or "fantastic" came along. Ostensibly absent from Carol's list is the possibility that taking care of a baby day in and day out could prove to be "boring" (a word she used during the first interview), and that she might, therefore, decide to return to work. On the contrary, when she and Chester talked about what it was like to be the parents of a six-month-old, they described a world which was far from tedious.

> INTERVIEWER: Do you notice any changes in the meaning of your life now that you have a child?
>
> CAROL: Well, right now, it's very, she's the center pretty much.
>
> INTERVIEWER: And what's that like?
>
> CHESTER: I don't know, it's really hard to describe, you know. We're still just fascinated to think that she came from us, developed the whole time, the whole nine months, and actually came out a baby. So, I don't know, it's fun to see her growing all the time.

INTERVIEWER: What's it like for you with the child as the center of your life?

CAROL: I guess I'm really kind of enjoying her. I don't resent having to spend time with her. I enjoy having her here, and it's just really an exciting thing to see her learn to do different things. Like tonight, she was just playing with her foot. I mean, you know, how simple, playing with her foot. . . . One week she will not be able to do something, and the next week she can pick up something in one hand and then put it in the other hand. It's really amazing. You stop and think, you take everything for granted. I mean, I've always been able to pick up something with one hand and put it in the other, and you see this little baby who, one week she can't do it, and the next week she can. And it's really fascinating. It's an experience that I think we both would have missed something had we not done it. I think we both benefited.

INTERVIEWER: With the child as the center of your life, what does that do to the meaning of your relationship with each other; has that changed?

CHESTER: I don't think it has, do you?

CAROL: No.

CHESTER: I think it's still the same.

CAROL: Well, when I said the center, I didn't mean—

CHESTER: That that was all there was for us.

CAROL: I didn't mean that that's all we live for. It's difficult to explain. Like Chester said, It's just a whole new aspect of living that's opened up to us rather than, and of course, she's totally dependent on us. She can do nothing for herself. She can't change her diapers. She can't feed herself. She can't take the dog out for a walk. I mean, you have to do everything for her. But both of us, I think, are happy to do everything for her, and I guess that's what I meant by the center. She can't do anything, at this point, for herself, so she takes a lot of time. But neither of us resents giving her that time, so we are glad that she, I mean we are glad to have her and we're glad that we can do those things for her. . . . It's just that she's a whole new thing; she's an addition to what we had before.

CHESTER: Sounds good to me.

Asked whether there have been any changes in the meaning of their life, Carol and Chester return to one of the key themes of their third month interview, namely, their shift to a child-centered family system; only now they make a genuine effort to describe in detail the character of that system. In doing so, they mention several important points.

First, when Chester is pressed to define what they mean when they say that the baby is now the center of their lives, he starts with a disclaimer—"I don't know, it's really hard to describe." This is actually not the first time he has made this point. During the first interview (in the segment reproduced earlier), he also said that it was "hard to put into words" the reasons that their life seemed better now. His caveat may help to explain why so few couples in our study spoke at length about the positive aspects of having children. Although there were times every now and then when the fathers and mothers would light up with enthusiasm and try to convey the joy of having their own baby, generally these times were both rare and brief. We think it would be wrong to assume from this that the couples in our sample were not positive or, in more general terms, that early parenthood is not a positive experience. We believe that one of the main reasons that couples did not talk at length about the positive qualities of infant care is that it is extremely difficult to put these qualities into words. It is difficult, for instance, to describe the love that parents have for their own child, the rush that they periodically experience when they look at their newborn, and the fun they get out of playing with a baby that is theirs. Affection, stimulation, and fun are, in fact, the very words that parents use to characterize the advantages of having children (Hoffman and Manis, 1978). However, these labels do not adequately communicate the emotional "high" that often accompanies the transition to parenthood.

The fact that it is Carol who does most of the talking in the above sequence is also significant. She is in the best position to answer the question about how the baby is the center of their lives because their daughter is literally the center of *her* life; no other person, not even Chester, occupies so much of her time. And the events she selects—her daughter's playing with her own foot, and transferring objects from one hand to the other—are things which can easily be missed by a parent. As Carol says, these are things that people "take for granted." Thus, identifying these acts as worthy of note requires an experienced eye.

What about Chester's parental role? You will recall that during the first interview much was made of playing down the importance of work ("It just seems like jobs are just not all that important a topic of conversation"). During the second interview, it seemed that Chester was trying not only to mentally withdraw from his job, but to physically withdraw as well. Whereas before he (and Carol) would work regularly on the weekends, now he was trying to stay home more to be with his family ("I worked a lot more when she was working and wasn't here. I didn't mind being in the office that much. But now . . . I want to be here with them.") Some fathers in the sample responded in just the opposite manner; soon after the baby came they would begin to put in longer hours at work because of what they saw as their increased "financial burden." But not Chester. Although it was felt that Chester's responsibilities as a father included financial matters ("He sees that she has food to eat and clothes to wear and blankets to cover her up"), by no means was this considered sufficient. He was also expected to provide some direct baby care. However, Carol and Chester left little doubt that Chester's contribution in this capacity, like that of most fathers, was basically as a stand-in, and that Carol was grateful for whatever "help" she received ("He's usually pretty good about taking her and changing her diapers sometimes, and if I need him to help me do whatever or bring me things when I have her and I can't get up to get something").

The fact that Chester's direct care responsibilities were relatively circumscribed when he was at home did not seem to pose any problems for Carol. As she says, although the baby is very demanding, she does not "resent having to spend time with her." Indeed, she argues that her daughter's total dependency on them (her need for them) is a cause for celebration, not dismay; parenthood has given meaning to their lives. Carol's remarks stand in sharp contrast to Flo's comments about what it is like to be a full-time mother. Her remarks also seem, at first, to paint a different picture from the one presented in Part Two, when we spoke about how parents negotiate with each other for release time from their infants. Actually, Carol's remarks do not contradict what was said then, but serve to illustrate a point made in Chapter 4.

You will recall that when we discussed the relationship between activity and human energy and time, we noted the importance of not simply taking an economic (quantitative) approach. Essentially, the point made then was that it is fallacious to assume that time availability and energy expenditure can be measured solely by the amount of activity that one "puts in" during the course of a day or week. The fact is, depending on one's commitment to an activity, time and energy can generally be "found" or "lost": the higher the commitment, the more time made available and the more energy produced (Marks, 1977).

Carol gives the impression that she is very committed to parenthood. Thus, being with her daughter day in and day out does not entail a major energy loss, and does not put her in a position where she resents her daughter's demands on her time, or feels cheated, as Flo evidently did, by her husband's "helping" (versus sharing) role in baby care.

Commitment, however, is a variable that is not only different from one parent to the next, but can change from one time to another. Commitments are also organized both horizontally and vertically, which means that one's stance (commitment) to a particular activity can only be understood by knowing one's overall organization of commitments.

The phenomenon of "shifting commitments" is something which many of our couples experienced during their transitions to parenthood. Significantly, we found that first-time parents were likely to experience more dramatic shifts in their commitment structures than second-time parents. This is not surprising, given the fact that the arrival of the first child is one of the major milestones in an adult's life (Hill and Aldous, 1969; Jaffe and Viertel, 1979; Rossi, 1968). Shifting commitments were also more dramatic among the first time parents because they seemed more likely to strongly embrace the parental role early in the transition to parenthood and then, either by choice or circumstance or some combination of the two, withdraw in a relatively short period of time to a more moderate level of parental commitment. Carol and Chester illustrate this second situation.

Although by the sixth-month interview Carol did not resent the minutes, hours, and days she was "giving" to her daughter, by the ninth-month interview her view of things had changed considerably. The beginning of the final interview was basically a replay of the earlier sessions. Even though the baby required "a lot more watching" because she could now crawl on all fours ("If I go to the kitchen and come back, I can be assured that she will not be in the same place she was when I left"), Carol still felt that taking care of her daughter was "great." However, a radical change in the theme of the interview occurs after about thirty minutes. The change is precipitated by Carol being asked what it has been like for her not to be working the past twelve months (Carol had quit her job in the middle of the pregnancy). For the first time, Carol discloses that she intends to return to work not in five or six years when her daughter is in school, as she had said earlier, but in three or four months. When she is asked when that decision was made, both she and Chester embark on a series of explanations (aligning actions) which indicate that the couple's transition to parenthood has taken a definite turn.

The transcript that follows is long, but can be divided into three parts, each of which is unique. The first part emphasizes balancing their daughter's needs with their own needs, especially Carol's. The second part focuses more on Carol's needs versus Chester's needs. Both parts bring to mind some of the conflicts discussed in Chapters 3 and 4. The third part is basically a synthesis of the first two, and constitutes a level of self-analysis which we found rare in our sample. Here, Carol and Chester conclude that the problems they have started to experience are not any one person's fault but are endemic to the transition to parenthood. The series begins with the question about Carol's working.

INTERVIEWER: What has it been like for you? I guess you've been home over a year now without working?

CAROL: What's it like? Well my time is very occupied and very full at the moment, and, you know, almost totally with the baby. And, uh, it's like I have a new job. Uh, it's a job that I like, I enjoy. Uh, at the moment it's occupying my whole time, and I have met other women in the same, who have the same job and it's good. I like that. Uh, that's not to say that at some point I would not want to go back to work. I think at some point I probably will want to go back to work, but it's like at that point then I'll have a third new job. It would be as if, it's just like if you change companies, you know, you have a new job.

INTERVIEWER: When do you see yourself like wanting to, you know, get a paying type of job?

CAROL: I would say probably by the winter [three or four months from now].... But not full-time. Just something a couple days a week, perhaps.

INTERVIEWER: Is that a change or did you plan that, you know, before she was born, that you would stay home about a year or so?

CAROL: Well, we had decided that I would stay home, yes. And that was fine, and I'm glad, you know, I wouldn't have rushed back to work under any circumstances. But you find, which is a surprise to me and that I didn't realize, that when I do go, like to my dancing class or whatever, and she stays in the nursery, that she really enjoys the company of other children. There aren't any babies on the street [that we live on].... She gets all excited and she's really happy to see the other kids.... When you get together with your own contemporaries, it's just an exciting thing. She gets so elated, so excited, that now I feel a couple days a week I could take her someplace where she would be with children her own age, that she doesn't have in the neighborhood, and I could go someplace where I could be with adults my age. And it would be good for me. . . .

INTERVIEWER: Is her going back to work, you know, essentially . . . her decision?

CHESTER: Yeh, yeh, pretty much, because she's really just doing it because she wants to, you know, she just sort of feels a little cooped up at home, I think. And she wants to get back into a position, you know. I mean the money's going to be great, but it's not—

CAROL: Yeh, the money—

CHESTER: You know, [we're not] doing it just for the money; it's something that she wants to do. . . .

INTERVIEWER: Is Chester accurate in his saying that you're beginning to feel a little cooped up here?

CAROL: Well, perhaps a little, yeh. I'm getting to the place that I feel like I would enjoy being out a little more often. I'm not crawling the walls, but you get to a point you feel like you can leave the baby. She's not going to, you know, stop breathing if you're gone from the house for two minutes. You feel like there are other people in the world who can change her diapers and give her a bottle or feed her lunch or whatever. New mothers feel like they have to do every, new mothers always have like a compulsion, nobody can take care of their baby better than themselves. At any time, then, as the baby grows and survives and gets stronger and bigger you realize that they're not going to break and that you can be away for a little while and everything will be fine. So I'm getting to that point now too. . . .

CHESTER: I think she's ready to get back to work. I just don't think she was ever cut out to be a housewife, and I think she's ready to get back and get some kind of a position and just, I don't know. We've got neighbors and friends that are sort of professional housewives, and, you know, we just can't see ourselves in that mold, their whole life is just whether the grass was mowed or whether the shrubs were done right. Maybe if Carol had never worked, you know, maybe she would be happy at home, but since she worked for, what, five years after we got married, four or five years?

CAROL: Yeh, four I think.

CHESTER: I just don't think you can give all that up in just one shot. So I think it would be good, I really do.

INTERVIEWER: Does it surprise you; did you think she would be content being at home taking care of the child and being a housewife type?

CHESTER: Yeh, I kind of thought so right after she had the baby, you know, because your whole world is just covered up with the baby, and that's all you can think about, and that's just everything. But after a while, you just start thinking about yourself again. I guess that's where we are now, you know, we still love the baby, but we're also thinking about our own lives to. . . . I don't think you're doing the baby or child any good if you're not happy. I mean, you can be at home with them and cleaning their nose, but if you're miserable, then you're not doing them any good.

Carol seems intent on conveying that by returning to work she will not be deserting her daughter. On the contrary, she will be facilitating her growth. She claims that she has discovered that leaving her child in a nursery is not harmful but beneficial; day care gives the baby the opportunity to be with children her own age. She also is quick to claim that some of her comments during the first two interviews about wanting to be with her daughter virtually all of the time were basically the normal but naive concerns of the "new mother." Thus, her message is that she is not forsaking the baby, she is just less compulsive about how much her child needs her. And finally, she notes that since she will soon stop breast-feeding, the baby will not starve as a result of her periodic absences. Here and there, almost as afterthoughts, Carol mentions that she too will benefit by not being with her daughter all the time. For example, when she says that day care gives her child the chance to be with children her own age, she slips in the remark, "and I could go some place where I could be with adults my age."

Chester, however, pursues a different line altogether. As he presents it, the principal reason Carol is returning to work is not because the role of full-time mother has become obsolete by the baby's development, but because Carol was not cut out to be a housewife; she needs "some kind of position" for her *own* well being. And the baby? He says the baby will also benefit because Carol will not be "miserable." Thus, what is Carol's main message is Chester's afterthought, and vice versa.

It is interesting that when Carol talks about how one can be overprotective with a new baby, she does not include fathers; rather, "new mothers" feel like they have to do everything. Like many women, Carol has evidently been socialized to believe that the baby is her responsibility and that she will be held accountable, should anything go wrong.

What happens next in the interview is that Chester is asked whether there has ever been any time in the previous nine months when he has felt that *his* needs have not been met. He answers yes, there have been occasions when he has not had the opportunity to do some of the things he likes to do but, for the most part, it is Carol who has made the concessions. The issue of Carol's needs versus Chester's needs would probably have ended right there. However, for some reason—perhaps she was just daydreaming at the time—Carol gives the impression that she had heard Chester say that both of them have equally sacrificed. Disagreeing with what she thought she had heard, she responds to Chester's asking whether she agrees with him by saying, "I gave up a lot more than you did." The vehemence with which Carol responds to Chester's query prompts a question intended to uncover why Carol feels that she gave up so much more than Chester. The result is an argument over who is "slaving" more—full-time parents or full-time breadwinners? The problem of computing equity comes to the fore.

INTERVIEWER: What about your own self? Has there been any time when you've not felt that happy because you weren't attending to your own self and your own needs and your own wants and stuff as much?

CHESTER: Um, no, not really. I don't know. Sometimes, I guess. Before Carol used to work on Saturdays, so I had all day Saturday to pretty much do what I wanted to. You know, I would play tennis all day or something and now we're usually taking turns feeding the baby, and so I just sort of have to squeeze in tennis when I can. But, you know, I don't mind that. I mean, I love tennis, but it's not the whole world, so, but I'm not feeling hemmed in or anything. I think it's Carol that's ready for a change.

INTERVIEWER: So you think that the impact of the child, in terms of your own personal adjustment and happiness, has been more on her and has had more of an effect on her than it has on you?

CHESTER: I think so, yeh. What do you think?

CAROL: No, well, no, not really. I think it's had an effect on both of us too. But you've got to look at it in its true, true relationship. I by giving, you know, by not working and staying at home all the time, if you want to talk about giving up things, I gave up a lot more than you did.

CHESTER: That's what he's saying.

CAROL: So it's bound to reflect on me more.

CHESTER: That's what he's saying.

CAROL: Okay, then I agree.

INTERVIEWER: You say you gave up a lot more?

CAROL: Well, sure . . . if you want to look at it from a strictly selfish point of view, I'm not working anymore. And if I go out and go shopping, uh, I have to be home for her nap. I can't go out and spend all day shopping. I've got to come home at lunch. I have to come home at suppertime. You have a more regulated, regimented life, because you have the total care and responsibility for another human being.

INTERVIEWER: Do you ever feel resentful of Chester, that he did not have to give up as much?

CAROL: No, I don't feel resentful of Chester, that he did not have to give up as much. [However], sometimes I feel that it would be educational for him if we could reverse our roles for like over the period of, oh you know, a few days or a week, so that he could see what it's like. I don't think any father who works forty hours or more a week could ever understand exactly or see exactly what it's like to be in the house forty-plus hours a week with a child or children.

INTERVIEWER: You think it's hard for him to—

CAROL: I think it's hard for him to relate to me and what I do with the baby as being a job, a *position.*

INTERVIEWER: How would you like him to relate to you? Other than the way he is?

CAROL: Well, basically I think we have related to each other pretty well, but just for the sake of clarifying, I think every father, not only just Chester, but every father should assume the role of motherhood at least a week when a child is an infant. . . . I mean, you know, so that they would have an opportunity to see the child do all the little things that they do. . . .

INTERVIEWER: What do you think about what she said?

CHESTER: Oh, I don't know. I think everybody thinks they've got the weight of the world, you know, they don't realize what anybody else does. Everybody else—

CAROL: No, now wait a minute, now I worked at a job for four years, so I know what it's like on the other side. But you don't have the benefit of knowing what it's like being a mother.

CHESTER: Well, yeh, maybe so, but you don't have the benefit of having to be out there being the sole breadwinner. . . . When I was a kid, you know, I used to just get used to my father going to work. He'd go to work same time every morning, and he'd come the same night. And I just thought that's what parents did, you know. I just figured he just sort of went off, and, I don't know, just had a good time. When it was time for the news to come on, he'd be coming home. I didn't really think about him being out there sort of slaving, and—

CAROL: Now, now, Chester, you're not, this is not the right, I'm not talking about, I know you go out there and work hard, I know you do. I worked, and I worked hard. I'm not saying, and this is not really directed at you even, it's just a statement in general for all fathers. I think all fathers should be at home with their children eight hours a day for like a period of time. I'm not picking you out individually.

CHESTER: I realize that, darling. All I'm saying is that the fathers that you want to come home are also out there working and for it to be fair, you need to go out and do what they're doing.

CAROL: I agree.

CHESTER: All right.

CAROL: Okay.

Carol's first long passage makes it clear that she now believes that, as the principal caretaker for her daughter, her life is more curtailed than Chester's ("*I* have to be home for her nap. . . . *I* can't go out and spend all day shopping"). And her emphasis on what she has "given up" by quitting her job is implicitly a claim that her comparison level for alternatives (full-time employment) is higher than her present position (full-time parenthood) and that she is, therefore, worse off than Chester is. Thus, as she sees it, she is the one who deserves the credit, and she is the one who deserves more of the rewards (e.g., time off). But like Flo and Fred, Carol and Chester cannot agree on what full-time parenthood is worth. Although Chester does not go so far as to say that Carol is on vacation (which is what Fred said to Flo), he is not impressed by Carol's claim that she is relatively deprived. Carol, on the other hand, feels that Chester does not appreciate her sacrifice, and says that if he stayed home for a week he would soon understand how much work it takes to care for a baby. Asked what he thinks about Carol's perception of things, Chester replies that being "the sole breadwinner" has meant some pressures on him which he feels Carol is unable to understand. The segment ends in a stalemate, with both agreeing that each of them might learn something if they changed places.

If the discussion had ended here, we would have had but another example of how the problem of equity can prove to be central to the transition to parenthood, and we would have had but another example of how husbands and wives often square off against each other, perceiving their problems in egocentric terms ("It is your fault." "No, it is your fault.") rather than

recognizing the systemic and reciprocal character of social interaction (see Watzlawick et al., 1967: 54). But the discussion does
not end here. Unlike Flo and Fred (and Alex and Amanda in
Chapter 7), Carol and Chester seem to be able to "step outside
of themselves," as it were, and "look down at" their relationship and their transition to parenthood. The shift in their
perception of things to a "higher logical level" (cf. Bernal and
Baker, 1979) is prompted by a question about whether they
believe their inability to fully understand what the other is
going through has now made them more distant from each
other. The couple quickly dispenses with their egocentric communication pattern and begins to talk about their "relationship" and the difficulties of their "situation."

> INTERVIEWER: Do you find that because, you know, he hasn't stood
> in your shoes, you know, and can't fully understand what you're
> [going through], that you've become a little more distanced from
> each other over the past few months?
>
> CAROL: Well, any relationship is going to have its ups and downs. You
> know, it just is. So long as you have an up following a down, then
> you're all right. If you don't have any ups and downs, then you're
> in trouble. . . .
>
> CHESTER: You know, it's just a hard situation, I mean a housewife to
> me is just, pretty much just the biggest ripoff there is, you know.
> It's just, it's the most thankless job there is. It's just really hard,
> you know, there's just no reward for it, there's no real pay for it.
> But, by the same token, you can't take care of the baby all day
> long, and then when your husband comes home and say, "Well,
> it's your turn now that you're home, you take care of him, take
> of her or him." You know, that doesn't work either, because
> while you've been at home taking care of the baby, your husband
> has been at work working. So you both have been sort of doing
> your own roles during the day; then when you come home, you
> need to share. I think we have about come around to that now.
>
> CAROL: We have tried to do it together.
>
> CHESTER: But Carol doesn't meet me at the door with the baby and
> then leave and say, "Here's the baby till 9:00, she's all yours."

INTERVIEWER: Has there been any point over this, these past three months, where things became more difficult, where you were feeling more strain in your relationship?

CHESTER: I guess in the last month or so everything's just sort of surfaced and everything. I think a lot of it's Carol wanting to really go back to work and not, I don't know. . . .

CAROL: Being a housewife is a thankless, just—

CHESTER: *It's the pits.*

CAROL: It's the pits, it's a thankless job, and if you don't stop and realize that she is working all the time too, if you take the attitude that because she's at home all day, she's been doing nothing, then, uh, you don't get paid or anything, and you don't see any other people. You're basically isolated during the day from other adults.

INTERVIEWER: And you felt that Chester was relating to you that way?

CAROL: Well, you go through periods of time, you know, he feels like he's overworked and burdened, and he's working his ass off, and then I go through periods of time where I think I'm working my ass off and, you know, it's just, you got to get together on it. And I can't expect him to come home and take over completely, and he can't expect to come home and sit down and expect me to do everything completely. You have to work together and you have to do it together. You went together to create this child and you have to go together and stay together to raise it. . . .

CHESTER: Yeh, you can really get out of balance. . . .

CAROL: Yeh, I think any relationship, any time any two people have a relationship you go through periods of time where you are out of balance. You just have to stop and regain your balance and go on from there, hopefully as a better relationship.

CHESTER: Plus you were really frustrated because you really wanted to go back to work, but you didn't want to say anything. . . . We finally got that out in the open, then everything was cool.

CAROL: Yeh, well, that's true.

INTERVIEWER: You didn't want to say anything to Chester about your wanting to go back to work?

CAROL: I don't think that I realized that I did want to go back to work. And then . . . when we finally talked about it. I guess it finally came out in the middle of all of that, that, you know, "Yes, I really would like to go back to work." Sooner than I had thought. . . .

CHESTER: Well, I just don't think you ever really ever wanted to be a housewife, you know . . . I think that part about work and wanting to have a position, a title or whatever, I think that's just too deeply ingrained to be taken out. And I think it's great. I didn't marry Carol to be a housewife. . . .

CAROL: The baby's needs [have been] absolutely foremost, before me and Chester, and before us. And then, you . . . come up and you and your husbands are on the short end of the stick and you say, "Wait, wait a minute," you know, "let's reevaluate the situation, and go forward."

INTERVIEWER: Was it a surprise that all of a sudden you just realized that you were on the short end of the stick?

CHESTER: I think once the newness of the baby wears off, you know, the first few months, or maybe even the first six months, it's just so new and so great and everything, and it's still great, but it's just not quite as new as it was, and I think you just have to—

CAROL: Well, you're making her sound like an old toy.

CHESTER: No, I'm not. I just think the first few months is just, especially the first baby, you know.

CAROL: You know, it, there's got to be time for the baby, and there has to be time for Chester, and there has to be time for me, and there has to be time for Chester and I, and there has to be time for me and Chester and the baby, and, you know, it takes living with a child, uh, or husband, or in a relationship to learn that each person is important, an individual in their own right, and I think that what we've experienced is simply just the normal, natural way of getting it all together and working it all out.

There are several things worth noting in this final section. First, there is the striking difference between Chester's perception of the housewife role and Fred's perception of the housewife role. Unlike Fred, Chester does not believe that his wife has an easy life. Just the opposite in fact: being a housewife "is the pits." He is not moving from his earlier position, namely, that Carol is not necessarily worse off by staying home than he is by going to work each day. But he is also not trying to argue that he is relatively deprived compared to his wife, which is what Fred was trying to say. Interestingly enough, later in the conversation, Chester also gives the impression that he was the one who first noticed that Carol was not happy staying at home, that "deep down" she was committed to a career, and that he was the one who helped Carol to verbalize her true feelings. Thus, in contrast to Fred, who seemed to view his wife with distrust, Chester comes across as a sympathetic partner, one who serves as a "watchdog" for signs of personal stress and unhappiness.

Why did Carol find it difficult to admit that she wanted to go back to work? There are several possible explanations, and in all probability, each is partially correct. Most obvious is that because she had so strongly embraced the full-time motherhood role, denying that role placed her in a severe state of cognitive dissonance (cf. Festinger, 1957). Part of the problem, in this regard, is that she may have approached the transition to parenthood with overly romantic notions about what it would be like to stay home with a baby. Of course, such notions do not separate her from the majority of new fathers and mothers. But, because of her social psychological ties to employment, she evidently was less willing to accept anything that was too much unlike the world she had imagined. A recent study comparing new mothers who planned to and did stay home from work in their babies' first year of life with mothers who had also planned to stay home but instead returned to work by the twelfth month suggests that (1) Carol is not alone—there are apparently many women whose commitments shift *back* to their jobs soon after the baby arrives, despite what they had originally planned—and (2) Carol's anxiety over the shift is typical of this group—"inconsistent mothers" (term used in study) were, for example, less positive than "consistent mothers" in their attitudes about the maternal role at three and eight months postpartum, even though they did not differ at birth (Hock et al., 1980).

This study also covers another point which directly bears on an earlier section of the transcript, in which Carol is talking about her changed opinion about day care. Although the researchers did not find significant differences between the "consistent" and "inconsistent" mothers in their anxiety over "nonmaternal child care," they did report that the anxiety levels were significantly higher in the "inconsistent" group than they were in a group of mothers who had not given up their jobs after their babies were born. This third group was part of an earlier study (Hock, 1978). Thus, Carol's emphasis on the needs of her child is perhaps another sign of the difficulties she is having with "cognitively reworking" (aligning) her orientation toward parenthood.

The third noteworthy point raised in the previously mentioned segment is the couple's approach to equity. The problem is initially phrased as a two-person game: when both the husband and wife have had especially "exhausting" workdays or weeks (either on the job or at home), and when both feel that they deserve a rest in the evening or on the weekend, how do they solve the problem that someone must remain in a primary or secondary status vis-à-vis the baby? We know how Fred managed this problem. He discounted his wife's responsibilities at home and unilaterally decided that only he deserved to get "down time." Carol and Chester take a different tack; they care for the baby "together." We believe that what they mean by this is that when both of them are at home, both are responsible for the baby, and that the sharing involves not a system of *conjunction* (e.g., husband holds the diaper while wife pins it) but one of *coordination* (e.g., husband changes the diaper while wife prepares the dinner).

We would be more inclined to take Carol and Chester's definition of the situation at its face value were it not for the fact that earlier in this interview (in a segment not reproduced above), Chester said that in his opinion, Carol was "better equipped" to care for their daughter because of "something inborn with mothers and children . . . like in the animal world." Carol disagreed with Chester's analysis, arguing that whatever expertise she had was solely a function of the fact that by staying home, she had more opportunities to learn how to care for their daughter. But Chester was not moved by her presentation. Thus, although they claim to have worked out an arrangement whereby they care for the baby together, Carol is still the principal caretaker. There is no denying, however, that she gets more "help" from Chester than most of the wives in the sample got from their husbands.

We said before that the equity problem is initially phrased as a two-person game because, at the end of the segment, Carol rephrases the problem in more complex terms. Basically, she notes that in a three-person family consisting of a father, mother, and infant, there are more than two competing interests; there are seven. In addition to the father's and mother's time there is also the baby's time, the father *and* mother's time, the father *and* infant's time, the mother *and* infant's time, and the father *and* mother *and* infant's time. (In a family consisting of a father, mother, and two children, there are fifteen different interests.) Once made, this point seems rather obvious. Yet there were very few couples in our sample who seemed to realize that some of their difficulties derived from this simple fact.

Finally, the way that Carol and Chester interpret the changes they have experienced is significant. Viewing their relationship as a homeostatic or balance-seeking system, Carol plays down the problems that they have been having by saying that "periods of time where you are out of balance" are "just the normal, natural way of getting it all together." This is a justification that permits them to define their conflicts as nonbasic, and within the rules of the marital game (cf. Scanzoni, 1972). And, as with all aligning actions, it allows Carol and Chester to conceptualize their life in stable terms, and, if used repeatedly, it can facilitate a change to a family system in which fluctuations in attitudes and conduct are more the norm (e.g., the "open" or "random" type described by Kantor and Lehr, 1975).

Although it could be said of all the couples who were interviewed, it is particularly true of Carol and Chester: the opportunity to see what happened beyond the ninth month would have been most interesting. We wonder whether Carol returned to work, as she said she would, or whether she continued as a full-time homemaker. We also wonder whether their movement in the opposite direction to what is the standard pattern—their movement toward a nontraditional structure of baby care—persisted beyond our last interview, or whether they reverted to the segregated system that they were using just before they decided to "reevaluate the situation." And last, we wonder whether their being "out of balance" was as temporary as they felt it was, or whether their transition to parenthood sparked a cycle of increasingly sharper and longer imbalances.

NOTES

1. Labor-force participation rates for white women in the months surrounding the first birth are as follows (Shapiro and Mott, 1979):

Months Before Birth				Months After Birth	
18-13	12-6	5-0		1-5	6-12
.84	.75	.43		.33	.39

2. In this case study, as well as the others, some characteristics (e.g., age) are deliberately excluded, while others are disguised to help protect the identity of the couple.

Chapter 6

TED AND THELMA

Whereas the major organizing frame for the case studies is the wife's employment, the minor organizing frame is the number of children in the family. Thus, this case study continues to examine the breadwinner-homemaker family, but it does so within the context of the transition to *second*-time parenthood.

This was a difficult case study to write because, unlike the other three case-study couples, there was no readily observable change over the course of the nine months. Whereas Carol and Chester and Alex and Amanda experienced major changes in the way they thought and behaved, and Sharon and Stuart demonstrated how difficult it is to try to create a relationship which is at odds with the larger society, Ted and Thelma presented a fairly consistent picture. That picture depicted them as a strongly familistic couple. Every other aspect of their life seemed to be subordinated to the needs of the family, and every other aspect of their life appeared to be interpreted by them within a family context. This second element of their familistic orientation proved to be especially important in our attempt to understand them. Through successive readings of the interviews, the extent to which family life constituted an epistemological benchmark–providing both meaning and order to their existence–became increasingly clear (cf. Berger and Kellner, 1964; McLain and Weigert, 1979).

The key to this couple's familistic orientation is their persistent concern with boundary maintenance and interpersonal ties. What seemed to bother them the most were threats to the integrity or identity of their life as a family. Threats were defined as anything which intruded into their home life or blocked the relationships which they had with each other.

The first evidence we have of the couple's strong bounding efforts emerged in the opening minutes of the first interview. Immediately, Ted began to question the interviewer about the nature and projected outcome of the study. It was, of course, not uncommon for the first interview to begin this way; all of the couples were interested in knowing a little bit more about what they were getting themselves into. But no other couple in the sample engaged the interviewer as aggressively as Ted and Thelma did. Actually, it was Ted who took the offensive; Thelma remained quiet. At first, we assumed that Ted may have been simply showing off to the interviewer and to his wife. However, later we came to the conclusion that his show of intellectual force may have been an expression of his role as the family's protector. A stranger had entered their domain and had to be verbally frisked.

Strangers were not the only ones considered to be outsiders. Ted and Thelma also indicated that they felt that it was important for them to erect boundaries between themselves and their own families. Thus, when we say that they were familistic, we mean that they were concerned about the identity of their *household.* This concern was expressed in a variety of ways. When they got married, they stayed in their hometown, which proved to be especially problematic when their first child was born. Because Ted Jr., their first child, was the first grandchild on both sides, the grandparents, aunts, and uncles became almost permanent fixtures in their home ("There were very few nights when somebody didn't come over"). When the opportunity to move away—in response to a job offer for Ted—presented itself, they took advantage of it. As far as Ted was concerned, this move was "the best thing [they] ever did." Isolated from their families, they were forced to rely on each other for support and companionship ("We turned to each other all the time for everything"). Furthermore, since they could not use their families as allies when arguments arose ("I couldn't go running home to Mom saying Ted is being a bully and I want to spend the night here"), they said that they were compelled to "work at their relationship" and that this resulted in their becoming "terribly close."

Having established a strong bond with each other without their "family interfering in their lives," Ted and Thelma were not comfortable with the attention which their families expected of them when they finally returned to the Southeast several years later. Although they did not move back to their hometown, they did live close enough so that weekend trips were possible. Thelma mentioned that she liked the "distance" between them and their relatives because she did not have to be "right in the middle of everything" ("I tend to hear everybody's troubles when I go home, you know, my mother's always talking about my sisters and everything like that"). She was, however, unprepared for the amount of time that Ted would spend with his brother on these weekends because, as Ted said, "she never had to share me with anybody before." After some confrontations on this issue, they now have a standing rule that no matter how tired Ted is after having spent the day with his brother, he must agree to go out with Thelma that evening.

Another threat to the integrity of their family was the increased jealousy which Ted Jr. would exhibit when, on visits home, the relatives would pay more attention to the baby than to him. This was especially bothersome to Thelma, who mentioned more than once how important she felt it was that both boys know that they were equally loved. Thelma's own concern about dividing herself between the two boys was the source of what she termed her "baby blues" after the second child was born. ("I would just find myself in tears thinking, 'How am I going to manage and not make Ted Jr. feel slighted?' ") By the ninth-month interview, however, she said that this was not the dilemma that she had originally thought it would be. For one thing, Ted Jr. seemed to be less demanding of her time (though there were days when he would regress, and want to be babied). Second, she found that more often than not, she could "find" time for Ted Jr. For example, the baby was often asleep when Ted Jr. would come home from school, and she would take this opportunity to sit her older son down and ask him how his day was.

People were not the only potential threats to the family's identity. Work also had to be kept from interfering with their home life. Although Ted took pride in what he did for a living, he also was very conscientious about not letting his job come between him and his family. In the beginning of the third interview, he is in fact asked whether work is the most important thing in his life, to which he responds: "I think my family's the most important and the other thing would be my personal philosophy on life, and the next is work."

We happened to catch Ted at a time when his priorities were being put to the test. When Ted and Thelma agreed to participate in our study, they had been living in their new home for only a short time; in other words, they had just ended their hiatus, and Ted was still getting the feel of his new job. Thus, it came as a surprise to us to learn during the sixth-month interview that Ted had decided to look for another position.

Although he did not go into much detail, he gave the impression that the job had not proved to be as challenging as he had hoped. But this was not the principal reason he had finally decided to look around. The key factor was that the job had become so dissatisfying that it had begun to interfere with his home life.

Families which are in the midst of a crisis will, in their efforts to meet the crisis, or simply in talking about the crisis, often reveal aspects of their lives which might otherwise go unnoticed (Lewis, 1959). This is precisely what Ted's job hunt did. So adept were Ted and Thelma at shielding their family from outsiders that there exists the strong possibility that if Ted had not decided to change his job, the character of their family might have remained beyond our reach. But the job change, coupled with the addition of their second child, provided the opening we needed. In the sequence that follows, Ted and Thelma talk about the job and provide a wealth of information about the substance of their lives.

TED: I am not making the change for the money. I am not making, not making it for pressed needs. I am making it so that I could be content in my work, and thus be content all over. I am not content right now.

INTERVIEWER: And do you find that that flows over into your family life?

TED: Sure, sure. Right now, there's a lot that, you know, I'm not as, how do you say it? I spend a lot of time worrying about things at work, rather than coming home and enjoying the time that I am at home.

THELMA: Well, not even [just] your evenings, but the whole weekend you spend your time at the TV set rather than us getting out and doing things. Or maybe even just doing jobs around the house that you save for the weekend. And I am so preoccupied with his unhappiness at work and what he's going to do about it in looking for something else. And it is a noticeable change, you know, within himself, sure, but as far as, he doesn't take it out on us or anything like that. . . .

TED: I find myself vegetating around the house. I don't go for that. I just, I don't feel happy in my mind, and I don't know if it's extended to the family or what. I have not stepped back and said, "Oh, let's see if it has or not." I don't know if it has. . . .

INTERVIEWER: What do you think? Do you think it's extended over to the family?

THELMA: Uh, it's lacking, because I felt it had this morning [laughing]. That's awful. No, I understand what he's going through, and I'm trying to be patient, and you know, I guess I keep a lot of it inside me, knowing what he's going through. But like this [weekday] morning, I was feeling really crummy, and it would have been nice for him to stay home and take care of the baby, and there was just no way he could stay home today because of what he's doing in his job and job interview after work. And I felt like his job had a lot to blame with, you know, why he couldn't spare the time. . . .

INTERVIEWER: How do you perceive his interaction with the children?

THELMA: Oh, normal there. I think Ted is much better about that [than I am], about not taking his problems out on the kids. As much as I might lose my temper much quicker when I got a lot of things on my mind, when company's coming, or when I clean the house and got to buy groceries, and I want to bake this, and I find myself sending Ted Jr. to his room to play rather than [letting him] mess up the den, and things like that. I probably much more lose my temper and show my impatience to them.

INTERVIEWER: What about playing with the kids and taking responsibilities, that kind of stuff? Do you think that's slacked off now?

THELMA: Oh, no, he comes in the door with a big smile for both of the kids, and you know, a big hug and how was their day, and especially Ted Jr., and playing with the baby. All that kind of stuff doesn't suffer. Usually from the time he walks in the door things go normally, see real well, usually.

INTERVIEWER: Do you think it's affected your interaction with the children?

TED: No.

INTERVIEWER: You spend as much time playing with them, taking them, as you had when you were more jolly?

TED: Oh, sure, absolutely. The only thing that I feel that is a bad effect is I have not felt to be as active around the house or in my going out. I don't feel like we, everything is here that I need.

INTERVIEWER: What do you mean, being active around the house?

TED: I don't do things. . . . Take a look at my stereo set-up there. See all the wires, you know. I could take off one good evening and run the wires back in, tie them all together and things of that nature and get it all nice and clean in there. Uh, there's a table down in the basement that I need to finish for the kitchen. A foot's off the coffee table that I'm stripping now. I started that a long time ago and have not finished it yet. The backyard needs to be [worked on]. I just would rather sit around and think about the job and think about what I've got to do with it rather than be doing things like that. My "get up and go" up and went.

INTERVIEWER: How do you feel your wife feels with you?

TED: I don't think there's any difference.

INTERVIEWER: You don't think she minds that this is to be done and that's to be done?

TED: Oh, absolutely, sure, you know. But she doesn't nag any more than she usually does.

THELMA: I used to have good days and bad. I could really be a nag on some days, and you know, maybe a lot of it is just this house, because we feel there is so much left to be done within the house or that we want to do to improve it, you know. And sometimes that just catches up with me after a while. The things that he talks about aren't major important things, life and death things. But, you know, it's even woodworking, his hobby, he has had no interest for. He has this huge workshop down there that he hasn't been down there except to pick up a tool and bring it back up here.

INTERVIEWER: What's that like for you, seeing him in the state he's in?

THELMA: Well, oh, we've talked about changing jobs a lot, and the different job interviews he's been on, and you know, I've told him how I've felt about it, if I thought one sounded good or one sounded crummy, things like that. But then, after a while, there's just so much talking you can do, and you have to back off and let him really decide what he wants to do. That's where we're at right now. And it's been hard before, but it seems like the longer we've been married, the more patience I've gathered, and learned when to quit nagging and when to quit talking and back off. And sure, I wish he would get out and [work in the backyard] or he would work on that table and stuff. But I just don't mention it, you know.

What is most striking in this sequence is the picture that Thelma paints of herself. It is obvious from her remarks that she feels most directly affected by the unhappiness which Ted is experiencing in his job. The kids are not being shortchanged; Ted still has a smile for them when he comes home. It is she who must suffer through Ted's lethargy, which has manifested itself in his unwillingness to "get out and do things," and, most importantly, in his refusal to get as involved as before in home improvements.

Understanding Thelma's chagrin requires an appreciation for what the absence of finishing touches in her home means to her. First, since she spends virtually all of her time in her home, things like an unstained table leg or an untilled garden are more a part of her everyday life than they are for Ted. If she went out to work each day, she too would not be constantly reminded that "there is so much left to be done within the house." Second, and more important, is the fact that Thelma views her home as an extension of herself. It is her responsibility, her domain. We suspect that Thelma's attitude is quite common among women who are housebound. Even the mother on a short maternity leave may be surprised by her increased interest in the appearance of her home.

It is significant to note that in the final analysis, it is Thelma and not Ted who accepts the blame for the conflict of interests which Ted's job has precipitated. Although it is acceptable for her to express some annoyance with his refusal to work on the house, she has learned that if she presses him too much she runs the risk of being seen as a chronic complainer. The power of words is clearly shown here. Whereas men may be seen as aggressive or forceful if they persist in making a point, women who do the same are seen as nags. The pejorative connotation of this label provides men with a weapon that they can use if a discussion gets too heated. Actually, the real power of the label lies in the degree to which women, like Thelma, have internalized the idea that persistency is unbecoming; these are the women who will stop short of pressing a point, for fear that they will violate their *own* image of themselves.

The same principle apparently applies to Thelma's feelings about the job itself. When she talks about how much she participates in Ted's decision over his search, she communicates that although she has at times tried to influence his perception of things (for example, she mentioned elsewhere that she thought that Ted was not giving the job a chance, since he had been working there only a short time), she has concluded that "there's just so much talking you can do, and you have to back off and let him really decide what he wants to do." In other words, although Thelma may exercise some veto power (and maybe not even that, if Ted feels very strongly about a job), the specifics of Ted's decision about the job are solely his.

Thelma's analysis of how she is more likely than Ted to lose her patience with the children also says something about their traditional division of roles. What Thelma defines in personality terms ("Ted is much better about . . . not taking his problems out on the kids") can also be explained sociologically. First, Ted's day-to-day activities are less likely to be interrupted by the children because his life is more compartmentalized; there is a time and a place for work and a time and place for family (even Ted's workshop is in the basement, away from Thelma and the kids). But Thelma's work and family life are temporally and spatially fused; when she is enacting her role as a home-maker and wife, she must also care for the children. In other words, whereas Ted can move to a tertiary level vis-à-vis his job or his family, Thelma rarely has the chance to isolate herself from one role while she enacts another. Second, since Ted is more likely to play with the children than feed or change them, he is able to interact with them at a lower level of personal attention. As noted in Chapter 3, child play activities require less involvement by the caretaker than child work activities, and they can often be "successfully" enacted on a secondary rather than on a primary level. Thus, the children do not test Ted's patience as much as they do Thelma's. This second point actually suggests that the general pattern of limiting the father's interaction with his children to play activities may serve an important latent function in some families. If Dad has had an especially bad day—and some fathers and mothers may assume that every day in the "rat race" is a bad day—the chances that he will "take it out on the kids" are lessened if he can limit his interaction to play. Thus, specializing in play can allow the father to shield his children (and indirectly his wife) from his troubles on the job. Some families may, in fact, feel that this advantage outweighs the negative aspects of role specialization.

Although child care was not anathema to Ted, generally he would not volunteer his services but would have to be asked to do things. At one point, when he was trying to communicate how involved he was with the children, he boasted that he and his brother did "babysit" once while Thelma and his sister-in-law went shopping. But his use of the word "babysitting" said perhaps more than he intended. Babysitting is, by definition, a stand-in role; it means caring for children "usually during a short absence of the parents" (Webster's New Collegiate Dictionary, 1977: 81). It is, however, noteworthy that Thelma mentions that if Ted were not so consumed with looking for another job, she would have asked him to stay home one day to care for the children because she was ill. We do not know how often Ted did this, or, for that matter, whether he ever stayed home from work to pitch in. Nevertheless, the fact that Thelma would mention it does indicate that it was in the realm of possibility, and suggests that Ted was more committed to child care than many of the other fathers in the sample.

Thelma did say elsewhere that since the second child came along, Ted was taking care of the children more. For example, he was now responsible for making sure Ted Jr. got ready for school each morning while Thelma fed the baby and prepared the breakfast. Several of the second-child couples in our sample chose to adapt to the increased demand for child care in this way. In every case, however, the father would take the older child, while the wife tended to the baby. The significance of this pattern should not be underestimated. In terms of both the number of activities involved and the attention levels needed to perform those activities (the primary/secondary ratio), it takes more "work" to get an infant ready in the morning than it does to get a preschooler ready. Thus, fathers with two children probably get more time for themselves in the early hours than their wives get. Although this may be viewed as fair in families like Ted and Thelma's, where the father must go to his place of employment while the mother stays at home, studies have shown that the inequities do not change substantially when both the husband and wife are employed. In fact, what often occurs in two-paycheck families is that the wife will get up a half hour earlier than the husband so that she can accomplish her disproportionate share of the morning's work (Berk and Berk, 1979).

Ted may not have wanted to have much to do with baby work, but he did insist on sharing, and sometimes controlling, how their children would be raised. For example, during one of the interviews, the couple reported that their older son was having some problems with one of the other children on the block. Ted Jr. would get into fights with a neighbor's boy, and he would always manage to lose because he was smaller than the other child. Ted insisted that Thelma should not go out and scold the neighbor's boy for picking on their son. Drawing on his own childhood experience, he said that to do so could prove disastrous for Ted Jr.'s self-image ("All of a sudden you get tagged a mother's boy"). Without either personal or indirect experience to refute Ted's argument (as a woman, she never had to suffer from being labeled a sissy, and she also had no brothers whose childhood experiences she could offer as evidence), Thelma acceded to Ted's point of view. However, she indicated that it was one thing to believe parents should not become involved in their children's battles and another to put that belief into practice ("It was a hard situation, especially for me, to stand and hear what was going on and not rush out to Ted Jr.'s aid"). Thelma's remark may shed additional light on why, despite the unequal division of baby care in the home, there is only a small minority of mothers who would like to see their husbands help more. If women envision that increased baby-care assistance by men will mean only that fathers will gain more rights over how children should be cared for without also acquiring more duties and responsibilities, then it is perhaps understandable why so many women do not want their husbands helping more. Speaking metaphorically, we could simply say that having someone in the back seat telling you how to drive your car does anything but make the task of driving easier.

By the third interview, Ted had secured another position. And although his new job often required that he work overtime, he was back to his old self: "the family man," as he put it. The beneficial impact which Ted's new job had on the family prompted a question about Thelma's career aspirations. (Thelma had quit her job when their first child was born.)

> INTERVIEWER: What's it like for you [Thelma], not having a career of your own?

> THELMA: Oh, that's, that's an interesting question [laughing]. Uh, gee, I don't know, it's, well it's not that I want to have a career, or at least not right at this moment. I'm quite content with my life. Uh, I don't know. I don't know an awful lot about Ted's work, but I'm interested and am always learning about things, and maybe more interested in the people he works with and in getting to know them.

> INTERVIEWER: I was meaning more in terms of, uh, you know, your own personal kind of career, or something like that. You know, does it make you, you know, like envious that he has one and you don't?

> THELMA: Not necessarily the nine-to-five part of the job, you know, having to get up, having to go. But now Ted does a lot of traveling, and I've often thought, "Gee, it would be nice to pick up and go with him." You know, to pick up and see the places that he's seen, that part of his job, yes, and envious of that because I've seen so little of what he has. But no, I really, I'm really quite content, I'm just, I guess if it were possible to have a job with flexible hours, I might be more interested in a career, but nothing that I'm going to have to be tied down to like that, you know, shuffling the kids off to sitters, and I'm not, not really envious at all. I guess maybe because I share as much of his that I can. He shares as much of his work with me that I can and learn about it.

INTERVIEWER: But you, at this point in your life, you don't feel like it's really important for you to have some sort of job or career or anything like that?

THELMA: Well, I have a job [laughing]. Some people might debate whether it's, they would call it a "career," no, I know what you are talking about, but, but no, and even now, you know, people say, "Oh, why don't you join this and that," not even work, but just different activities around. And I would be beating myself to get, you know, the baby and I ready, and to get the baby off, and I said, "No, I'm just going to sit back the next three years and do what I want around the house, or, or be selective about what I do, so I enjoy it." You know, take care of the baby, and then, once he gets ready for nursery school and we'll be doing things, his few mornings make it a little easier. You know, then I'm just not going to rush things. I'm enjoying what I'm doing right now.

INTERVIEWER: Do you see it, in part, as work?

THELMA: Taking care of the kids? Oh sure, to a certain extent. Uh, you know, you just don't sit and play with a baby all day. There are needs that have to be met that are certainly a great deal of work. But it's enjoyable work.

Thelma epitomizes the traditional wife/mother, which is one reason why she and Ted were chosen for case analysis. There were several women in our sample who defined their relationship to the world of employment in precisely the same way that Thelma defines hers. In contrast to Carol (and others), who was ambivalent about being a full-time homemaker, Thelma is not only unambivalent about what she does, she is genuinely proud of it.

The sequence begins with Thelma telling us how she related to Ted's job. Her primary role seems to be to interact with the people he works with, "getting to know them." Essentially, what she may be saying is that her role is to make a good impression with Ted's coworkers, to be agreeable at the office parties, to prepare a meal which Ted can be proud of when he brings someone home from the office.

When she is asked whether she has any intention of pursuing a career of her own, she says that she has a career—she is a mother. On this point, she is, however, cautious, because she knows that not everyone would agree that motherhood is "a job." But she obviously values the parental role more than anything else that she might do outside the home. Her decision to "sit back the next three years and do what [she wants] around the house" may be seen by some people as simply a rationalization. After all, one might argue, what choice does she really have, given her commitment to a traditional ideology? Yet in some respects, her characterization of how she sees her life is somewhat enviable. As difficult as it may be for some people to believe or understand, there are many people (male as well as female) who would love the opportunity to do what Thelma does, to become a full-time parent.

Thelma subsumed her role as mother under her general responsibilities as homemaker. As the homemaker, she was the manager of the house, which meant that it was her responsibility to see that things (dinner, housework, children) ran smoothly. She was, in effect, the captain of the house—and she ran a tight ship. Everything was on a schedule. Dinner, for example, was always served at five o'clock. The children's awake and asleep periods were also closely monitored ("You could set your watch by the time the baby gets up because Thelma put him on that schedule").

Thelma's fanaticism for scheduling ("I kid her about it sometimes") was perceived positively. Her ability to run things on time was seen as evidence that she was a good mother. Ted, in particular, felt that it was extremely important for children to learn self-discipline. He liked the idea that the boys' lives were regimented, and he and Thelma prided themselves on the fact that their children had to adapt to their schedule, not vice versa. As they saw it, they did not make the mistake of many parents, whom Ted and Thelma felt were too permissive with their kids.

As hard as Ted and Thelma sound, they actually were quite flexible. They did not force schedules on the children which the children were not developmentally equipped to deal with; they did not, for example, try to "schedule" their three-month-old to eat only three times a day. Nor were they so self-centered that they ignored the fact that there might be days when, for illnesses, etc., even the best-planned schedules might have to be altered. One of the reasons that they were able to strike a balance between being both strict and flexible is that they had a relatively open attitude toward time. Despite their infatuation with scheduling, they never seemed to lose sight of the fact that the schedule was their creation. This is an important point. There were several couples in the study who would set up a daily schedule and see that schedule as too sacred to be changed. Thus, when events did not proceed as planned (typical with a baby), they would become very upset over the disorder in their lives. More first-child than second-child couples seemed to fall into this trap. The open attitude toward time that Ted and Thelma exhibited was best illustrated when the couple was talking about how important it was to have moments when just the two of them could talk without being distracted by the children. Usually, because of the children's schedule, these moments would be available at the end of the day, when both boys were in bed. If, however, for one reason or another, the children cut into their time, Ted and Thelma would "make" (up) the time that they needed by either getting up early or staying up late. This may seem to be an obvious solution to a simple problem. Yet, although most of the couples complained about not having enough time for themselves, only a few of these couples would "take away" time from their sleep. Perhaps this just points to another obvious fact, namely, that couples who can get along on little sleep are at a definite advantage during the transition to parenthood.

Ted and Thelma's traditional orientation extended beyond their work roles. They also took a relatively traditional stance toward decision-making and their long-term plans. In the sequence that follows, they talk about how they go about charting and steering their course in life. Few couples come as close as they do to illustrating the classic husband-navigator/wife-helmswoman pattern.

INTERVIEWER: Do you see either one of you as more the boss in the family?

THELMA: That's a good question. No, not really. I think we pretty well sit down and discuss things that need a decision. That's what a boss does, he makes the final decision, and we pretty well, you know, even just buying things for the house, small things like that. Do you feel like you're the boss?

TED: Oh, I don't think there's a boss.

THELMA: Or do you feel like I'm the boss, since I have the check-book?

TED: Oh, I don't know, you know, there's, I think all the topics that have been brought up, or major decisions, I've always brought the topics up. "Okay, we are going to make a decision on this, here we are going to make a decision on that." Okay, but I don't think it's a boss thing. I have, okay, *growl*. There it is.

INTERVIEWER: So you think that you initiate things more and then you come to a joint kind of decision?

TED: Oh, it's for the simple reason that I have, am in a position to do more, okay.

INTERVIEWER: What do you mean?

TED: Because I bring the bread into the house, okay, there are more decisions that, or more topics for decisions that come up, just because of that. Simple nature. I mean, it's the idea of changing jobs and moving down here, things like that. But I don't think there's any large decisions that I made by myself. I may have made a decision prior, okay, and I may start talking about it and see what Thelma thinks about it, not letting her know my prior decision. I would like to see if she comes to the same decision. I don't think anything has been decreed from the burning bush: "We shall do this!"

INTERVIEWER: Do you see it that way, that he initiates topics for decisions?

THELMA: Oh, probably, especially major things, because I've always been accused of, I don't want to use the word "rut," that isn't the right word, but just liking my lifestyle and order and not wanting to make any—

TED: "Complacent. . . ."

THELMA: I was laughing though when he said he might already have his decision made. I wondered if the talk with me ever changed his decision . . . his initial decision. . . .

TED: Thelma would make a perfect computer. Once she gets programmed to do certain things, I mean that's it. She must stay right on the same routine. Anything that upsets the routine is very, very unnerving because she can't multiplex. "Why can't I do that, and why do this, go here, go over there, do that." She gets into a very complacent type of thing. Which in a lot of ways and a lot of times is very good, and I wish I could get into routines like that, but I'm just the opposite. I had rather multiplex than stay in a routine. It's a thing of, I don't know, it is, there's two different ideas on how to do things.

INTERVIEWER: How do you think that affects your relationship?

TED: I think it is good, all right, because Thelma stays in that type of thing, you know, and I can multiplex, all right, and she has the stability that is really needed that I like, and you know, I'm very spontaneous. If somebody presses me for a decision real quick, I'll give it and stand behind it. Okay, Thelma wants to take it a little more slow. Things like that, because it's going to upset the complacent world that she lives in. So I think it's good. I'm glad she is that way, more often than not.

Thelma's remark that perhaps she is the boss in the family because she manages the money is a testimony to how *implementation power*—the power to make unimportant and time-consuming decisions—can give one a false sense of superiority (Safilios-Rothschild, 1976). In the third interview, she almost acknowledges that her handling of the money is hardly a measure of her power when she says that she is grateful that Ted is "more than generous" about her "spending [his] money" ("I pay all the bills and buy all the groceries, and he doesn't want to know where each and every dime goes"). Significantly, it is only after Thelma tries to claim that she is the boss that Ted makes it clear that he sees himself as the leader in the family. He says that he is the one who is responsible for determining the direction the family will take, while Thelma is responsible for maintaining the course which he has chosen.

Ted's comment that sometimes he will have already made his decision before he sits down to talk with Thelma is very much like the relationship which autocratic executives have with their staffs. Via meetings and conferences, these executives give the staff members the false belief that they are really having an impact on the direction of the department (company, country, etc.) when in fact the staff operates only in an advisory capacity, if that. Thelma is not oblivious to the full meaning of Ted's remark and wonders just how many decisions Ted had already made before he consulted with her.

Ted's role as initiator gives him more power than Thelma may realize. Her comment that the one who makes the final decision is the boss is only correct if both parties start out with the same opportunities to influence the other. But if Ted is the one who initiates the discussions, then he has the power to frame the decision that is to be made. Even if Thelma does make the final decision, Ted is likely to have constructed the options of that decision. Ted's power here is an example of *orchestration power* (Safilios-Rothschild, 1976). And what resources does Thelma have? While we suspect that there are many which were not discussed at length during the interviews—Thelma did not come across as powerless—she mentioned one which is perhaps an indication of just how little power she has: She said, "I cry easily."

Ted's explanation for why he is the one who initiates major decisions is a familiar one—he is the breadwinner. He does not, however, lord his breadwinner status over his wife, as Fred did to Flo, and as many husbands do to their wives (LaRossa, 1977). He does not, in other words, use his status, at least overtly, as a resource to base a claim for overall power in the marriage. In fact, Ted is unlike several of the husbands that were interviewed (and like others) in that he gives the impression that he very much values his wife's "traits." He does cast himself in the role of leader, but he is at least a benign leader who sees his marriage as a team effort. Thelma is important to the functioning of their family, in his opinion. She is more than simply someone who carries out his ideas; she is the one in the family who provides the ballast. Without her "stability" to counteract his "spontaneity," they would really have no direction because they would be continuously changing course. We suspect that one of the reasons that Thelma is so committed to the homemaking role is that she is married to someone who makes her feel good about performing that role.

Perhaps the clearest indicator of Ted and Thelma's familism is their pattern of recreation. No other aspect of their lives so graphically illustrates the bounding and bonding process that was central to their identity as a family. In a word, *they* were family.

TED: A lot of things that we do as a family, we enjoy.

THELMA: I think that started a lot after Ted started traveling, you know. He would come home, and he would want to take me out because he knew I had been home the whole time. But then we would feel bad about leaving Ted Jr., after Ted Jr. and Ted had been separated. So I think especially then we started looking for things to do as a family.

TED: You start realizing there's more to do as a family.

THELMA: We can all do the things together like that. And we didn't have to take him [Ted Jr.] out to even fairly nice restaurants.

TED: Well, there was one time, a company that I was thinking about going with a few years back flew me and Thelma to Florida for an interview trip for me. And we spent the weekend there looking at houses and things of that nature and went to Disneyworld, and then, going through Disneyworld, we really felt guilty that we went when we knew Ted Jr. would be enjoying it as much and a lot more than we were.

THELMA: You know, getting excited and—

TED: You know, you start thinking about things like that.

THELMA: You know, getting excited and saying, "Oh boy, Ted Jr. will like this." And, you know, we really catch ourselves. So next summer we had our vacation and we took him to Disneyworld just because we knew after seeing it ourselves how much he would enjoy it. I don't think we necessarily took him out of guilt, but we enjoyed it ourselves so much that we looked forward to going back and taking him and and seeing his reactions. And he talks about it now, wanting to go back, but he knows the baby has to get bigger, and he has it all planned. "When the baby is four and I'm eight, we can go to Disneyworld," you know, because he knows the baby will be big enough to enjoy it.

TED: You see, that's the thing. That's the kind of environment I like to maintain in a family here. And Ted Jr. knows that when we go on something like that, the baby won't enjoy it. Therefore, the family won't enjoy it as much. If we can keep it in that kind of context, then I think things will always go right.

Ted and Thelma's togetherness philosophy was not limited to vacations but applied to virtually all recreational activities (e.g., "The baby does not enjoy doing things that me and Thelma and Ted Jr. could do right now, okay? So we have to opt for the total family's needs like that, okay. You have to do things that the baby would enjoy doing. Uh, the baby wouldn't enjoy going to a baseball game or a hockey game or something like that. . . . We want to do [things] as a family unit."). Thus, the couple took it for granted that the only way to handle the leisure time problem that families with infants are confronted with was to limit recreation to activities that everyone could participate in. The possible advantages of encouraging individual pursuits—to include even giving the baby the opportunity to interact with nonfamily people (e.g., day care)—were never explored (or at least discussed during the interviews).

Ted and Thelma's closed-ranks stance on leisure time places an important qualification on a point made in the last chapter when we were discussing Carol's complex approach to the problem of equity. We noted then that in a three-person family there can be seven competing interests, if you count relationships as well as people (e.g., the husband *and* wife's interests as well as the husband's *or* wife's interests), and that in a four-person family, like Ted and Thelma's, there can be fifteen competing interests. But Ted and Thelma demonstrate that these interests are only potential interests. Families may choose to discount some interests altogether, or at least define some interests as less important than others. Thus, although Ted and Thelma can, if they want to, try to juggle fifteen competing interests, they seem to be especially concerned with satisfying the interests of the whole group. The relative weight that various families give to their potential interests is an empirical question, and is another way of operationalizing the separateness-connectedness variable. The way in which families determine the weights for their potential interests is also an empirical question, one that is within the "social construction of reality" tradition (cf. Berger and Luckmann, 1966).

When Ted and Thelma were asked whether they intended to have more children, they said that they had adopted a wait-and-see attitude. That such a we-oriented family would be so cautious about having children may, at first, seem contradictory to their familistic ideology. But just the opposite is true. Although they loved their two sons ("the union of our love") and, in the abstract, loved the idea of having a large family ("If Thelma and I could afford it, we would have a thousand of them"), they seemed to recognize that, given their family system, each additional child was a potential intruder to their lives; each additional child would mean that they would have to rearrange their lives to find yet another series of activities which everyone in the family could enjoy. Contrary to what is generally believed to be the case (see, for example, Rossi, 1968), families which are individualistic or husband-wife oriented are not the only kind that can be "threatened" (in a sociological sense) by the addition of a child to the fold; families which are superfamilistic can also have a difficult time adjusting to the birth of a baby. It would seem that what is true in general would be true for the transition to parenthood: families which strike a balance between separateness and connectedness would be best able to absorb a newborn child (cf. Olson et al., 1979; Russell, 1979).

PART FOUR: CLOSE-UPS OF TWO-PAYCHECK FAMILIES

Chapter 7

ALEX AND AMANDA

In this part of the book, we shift our focus away from bread-winner-homemaker families to two-paycheck families. The two couples analyzed, like the two previous couples, represent first- and second-time parenthood respectively.

When Alex and Amanda were asked why they decided to become parents, they said that they knew they would have children at some point in their lives—they loved children too much not to have their own—but that it took them a while to be in a position where they felt they could afford the additional expense a child would impose upon them. Since Amanda seemed to be getting somewhat bored with her job, the time seemed ripe. Though she planned on returning to work once her maternity leave expired, she would at least have the opportunity "not to have to work for a while."

Amanda would have preferred that her leave be permanent, but because of heavy loans she and Alex had incurred over the years, they could not afford to be without her income. Amanda's working was a controversial topic, one which came up over and over again during the interviews. She felt that by leaving her daughter every day to go to work, she was not being a good mother ("I feel like I'm forsaking her for money"). Alex also would have liked Amanda to stay home ("When the baby is growing up, the first few years, it's important for one of the parents, preferably the mother, to be at home with the child"). But he said that they had gone over their monthly expenses innumerable times and that each time the results had been the same—they could not make it financially if Amanda did not have a job.

During the first-visit with them, three months after the birth, they were still up in the air about what they would do with their daughter when Amanda's maternity leave expired in four weeks. They were very much against leaving her in a day-care center, arguing that day care was expensive, unhealthy (too many kids with colds and flu), and, most importantly, not a suitable learning environment for a child (too much "dirty language" and not enough "attention"). What they were hoping was that Amanda's mother would agree to take care of the baby. There was, however, a snag in that plan; Amanda's father was objecting to the arrangement. Though earlier he had said it was a splendid idea ("Why not? She [your mother] is not doing anything"), when the baby came his feelings changed.[1] First, he felt that no one could substitute for a mother's care (not even a grandmother) and that his son-in-law and daughter should try to do something in order that Amanda would not have to return to work. As mentioned, both Alex and Amanda would have themselves preferred this arrangement, but there was "no way" they could afford it. A second reason Amanda's father wanted Amanda to stay home with his granddaughter was that he felt that babysitting on a daily basis would be too much of a strain on his wife. Finally, he said that they had been looking forward to his retirement and the freedom to travel it would bring, and that he had no desire to be stuck at home because his wife was a "parent" again.

Although Alex and Amanda said that they did not want her parents to feel "obligated" to take the child, since they were the only relatives available, only Amanda's parents could, in their minds, save their daughter from what they perceived as the cruel world of nursery life ("It would just be better for the child's growing experience and all. It will mean a lot later to the child . . . we want somebody in our family . . . to take care of the baby."). Much to their relief, Amanda's father did eventually yield to their request. When it came time for Amanda to return to work, her mother took the baby.

The couple talked a little during the first interview about what the pregnancy and birth were like for them. Amanda said that pregnancy was an extra-special time during which she felt very "womanly." She also said that she had assumed that she would receive a lot of "extra-special treatment" but that this was not always forthcoming from either her coworkers or her husband. She seemed particularly surprised and annoyed with Alex's unwillingness to help her more around the house or to come to bed earlier when she grew tired in the evening. Alex's response was that he only helped her if he thought she needed help. Also, he contended that Amanda did not "really" need his help. He said that if he had helped her, she would have insisted that he not help, to which Amanda replied that she was reluctant to press Alex to do things for her because she did not want to be labelled a "nag" (cf. Ted and Thelma). Unknown to us at the time, Alex and Amanda's differences over who should do what, discussed here within the context of the pregnancy, would prove to be especially significant during the sixth- and ninth-month interviews.

The birth was described as a joyous experience. Alex, who witnessed his daughter's arrival, made a point of telling us how important he felt it was for husbands to be at the delivery. He said that he could not imagine not being there, that it would not be "fair" to Amanda if he had waited outside, and that he could not believe that husbands throughout history had been missing it all.

While Amanda had wanted a girl, Alex had been hoping for a boy, and he talked during the first interview about having another child to try to fulfill that dream. Amanda confessed that when she brought her daughter home she was very concerned about whether Alex would be disappointed ("I remember three or four weeks after she was born starting to cry, because I said, 'I want you to want a girl and I think you wanted a boy' "). Alex had told her that she had no reason to believe that he would not want the baby, so Amanda eventually dismissed her concern as "postpartum blues." As far as having another child, she said it was too early to even think about it. She said that people should never ask a woman so soon after she has given birth whether she would like to go through it again; the experience is still much too clear in her mind.

A good portion of the first visit was devoted to a discussion of two interrelated issues which would be central themes throughout all three interviews. These issues were the loss of free time and the division of child care responsibilities. The principal message of the first interview was that the largest impact on their lives was that they were forced to stay home much more than before and that, because of the incessant demands of their baby, their lives had become more hectic. But they felt that, on the whole, they were doing well.

Being forced to stay home was a tremendous restriction on this couple, considering just how much they went out before the baby came. Without a doubt, Alex and Amanda were the most active of the twenty couples. Sometimes out every night of the week, their recreational pursuits had included, among other things: singing in a choir, acting in a theater group, participating in community and religious affairs, and playing and attending several sporting activities. Though they were somewhat disappointed over being homebodies now, they were optimistic it would all work out. All they had to do, they said, was to "plan better." What they meant was that they needed a list of reliable babysitters whom they could call. Once they had that, they said that they were confident they could return to their former pastimes.

One thing which Alex and Amanda were particularly proud of was that, whatever limitations parenthood had imposed on them, they were in it *together.* As far as child-care responsibilities, they definitely gave the impression during the initial visit that they had every intention of sharing the load. Alex was especially vocal about how important it was that fathers take an active role. He knew that some of his friends would be disappointed that he was not as involved with them as before, and he could see that there might be some conflict at work when he insisted that he had to take time off to escort his child to the pediatrician, but he claimed that he was not going to be the absentee father; he would be different.

> ALEX: I've got a good friend of mine, he's the ultimate male chauvinist pig. He will not change a diaper, he doesn't wash a dish, and he doesn't do any of those things. The baby is the mother's responsibility. He goes and earns a living and his wife takes care of the baby; and he wouldn't stay up at night for anything. But we don't look at it that way. . . . I mean, she's nursing . . . [so] right now I don't have anything to do with that, but I share in changing the diapers, and in rocking her, and in doing those kinds of things. . . . I love babies. I have always loved little babies. And I love to play with her, and I play with her a lot when I come home.

Amanda was appreciative of the fact that Alex was so willing to pitch in, and said that she "felt a whole lot of love for him" as a result. Alex too believed that their marriage was now stronger because of his responsible attitude.

> AMANDA: I remember the first two weeks that she was, right after I got home from the hospital. I felt like I loved him more than I ever had in my life. And I think it was because he, I just remember that one, two [o'clock] in the morning and he, like I would feed her, and then maybe she would scream for two hours . . . and he would come in here and rock her and let me lie in bed for an hour, and then I would get up and feed her again, and all that kind of stuff, and just things like that. I mean, he helped me a lot, and I really felt a whole lot of love for him then.

> ALEX: Yeh, I can really see how if a child was unwanted or if the father really didn't feel any responsibility, it could become a split in the marriage. I think that we have some friends where sometimes he doesn't want to do anything, have anything to do with

the child, and there's got to be some resentment there on her part. But in a situation where both people feel there's a responsibility on both their parts, I think it could be a strengthening kind of relationship. I think our daughter has been a strength in our marriage.... Like Amanda said, I think that one of the things that helps to strengthen our marriage is my helping Amanda more around the house and doing things like that when she knows she has to work. And I've been doing more of that, and largely because of the baby coming along, and that helps, I think, to strengthen our relationship.

AMANDA: I think you respect each other a little more. Like you think about, before you just think about whether you are a good husband or a good wife, you know, even if I don't think he's the best husband, I mean I do think he's a real good husband, but I mean, if [hypothetically speaking] I didn't think he was the best husband, *right now* I think he's just the best daddy in the whole world!

In sum, the overall impression that Alex and Amanda tried to convey during the first interview was that of a couple who were very much in love with each other and with the idea of being parents and who, although their situation was not ideal (with Amanda working), were quite capable of dealing with whatever problems should come along. There were other impressions given, but at the time these did not seem to change the picture presented above. If the interviews with Alex and Amanda had ended at this point, the above summary would have been their story. But the interviews did not end here. During the sixth- and ninth-month visits, we discovered that there were several statements made during the third month which were highly significant, statements which during that interview seemed to be only minor comments and asides but which, in conjunction with subsequent comments, would prove to be critical in dramatically altering our characterization of their transition to parenthood. The statements dealt with the fact that Alex and Amanda were not equally committed to their former recreational activities, and with the fact that the couple had, throughout their marriage, disagreed over how housework should be divided. With respect to the first point, Alex was, by far, more committed to getting out of the house on a regular basis. While Amanda liked for them to spend quiet evenings at home ("She's an incurable romantic"), Alex felt that staying home was not only not relaxing, it was downright boring ("It really just kills him to have to sit home on Friday or Saturday night"). Their ongoing battle over housework generally came down to their not being able to agree on how much of it was being done by Alex. Consistently, Alex felt that he was doing a lot more than Amanda was willing to give him credit for. For example:

ALEX: Washing clothes and all that; I'll do it, but I don't like to do it.

INTERVIEWER: Have you been doing more of that since the baby's been born?

ALEX: Yeh, yeh, washing my own clothes most of the time.

AMANDA: No, you haven't been doing that since I've been home [on maternity leave], washing your clothes.

ALEX: Yes I have.

AMANDA: No. He doesn't realize how much I wash.

ALEX: Yes I have. She doesn't realize how much I do.

The couple's sixth-month interview begins innocently enough with a question which is intended to do no more than bring the interviewer up to date: what has been happening in the three months since he has last seen them? The baby is awake, and the interview starts with her sitting on Amanda's lap. We first are given a description of what their day is like, now that Amanda has returned to work. Initially, one gets the impression that there has been no substantial change in their relationship. Life has just gotten more "crazy," because they say they are trying to do too many things at the same time. The tone of the conversation is light. Then there is a shift. In their account of who is doing what with their days, it is revealed that Alex has returned to some of the extracurricular activities which he had been so involved with before the baby came, and which he had said, during the first interview, that he was going to sacrifice for fatherhood. Amanda, on the other hand, is involved in no outside activities whatsoever, but is left at home to care for the child. The conversation gets increasingly heated until it reaches a point where Amanda, misty eyed, picks up the baby and leaves the room, ostensibly to put her to bed. Because the sequence is so long, we will divide it into five parts and comment after each.

INTERVIEWER: Okay, what's been happening in the past three months, since I haven't seen you?

ALEX: Had she gone back to work?

AMANDA: No.

ALEX: Well she has now [laughter].

AMANDA: I went back to work when she was four months old, and that's the worst part. I'm enjoying my job a whole lot, but I just go crazy because I don't have a third enough time to do the things I need to do. Don't have time to get the house cleaned and things like that.

ALEX: We have to get up about an hour earlier now than we did before, get up at 5:30. It means we have to get to bed about 10:30, hopefully. A lot of times we end up going to bed at the regular time [a later time], so we cut down on our sleep, now we get tired.

INTERVIEWER: So you're getting up at 5:30?

AMANDA: Uh-huh.

INTERVIEWER: Then what happens?

AMANDA: Okay, we get ready and we leave the house about 6:30.

INTERVIEWER: She [the baby] is still sleeping at 5:30?

AMANDA: I don't get her up until 6:30. All I do is change her diapers and wrap her up in a blanket, and I take Alex to the bus stop, and then I take the baby to my mother's. And I get there about 6:50 and then I feed her, breast-feed her over there, and then leave about 7:35 to go to work. And then I get back over to my mother's at 4:30 in the afternoon, and I breast-feed her again, breast-feed her over there, and then leaving and coming to pick

Alex up. But just this past week she started on solid food. Alex started getting a ride home with someone, and I'm coming straight home so I can feed here. So I've been getting home at 5:00. We've only done that about two days.

The sequence starts with Amanda describing a relatively common problem for working mothers. Not only must she meet the demands of her job, but she is also expected to be the principal caretaker for her child as well as be the one who is responsible for whatever household chores need to be done. The working mother thus has *three* jobs. Particularly significant is Amanda's use of the personal pronoun "I" in her description of what her morning is like. She says that she, not Alex, gets the baby up in the morning, and she, not Alex, changes the baby's diapers. And since she is the one who takes the baby to her mother's, there is a very good chance that she puts the baby's things (extra diapers, clothing, etc.) in a carryall bag before they leave the house. Remember that she is doing all of this on top of getting dressed. Is she also in charge of breakfast? They do not say. Time-use surveys do, however, indicate that employed wives are usually responsible for breakfast in addition to child care in the early morning hours (Berk and Berk, 1979). The interview continues:

INTERVIEWER: So what's it like for you being back at work; are you enjoying it?

AMANDA: I'm enjoying work, but I'm going crazy. I don't recommend it to anybody.

ALEX: She hasn't got time to go to the bathroom. That's what I feel like sometimes.

INTERVIEWER: Since she started back to work?

ALEX: Uh-huh. It's bad.

INTERVIEWER: What's the bad part about it for you?

ALEX: Too much pressure on her. When she doesn't have time to do anything at home, that puts more pressure on me to do more things; so that puts pressure on anything that I would do.

INTERVIEWER: What kinds of things?

ALEX: Right now, for instance, we got, this has just started the last couple of weeks. The first three months was bad too, but I've been involved with some plays, player's group over the past several years. And I didn't participate last year because of the baby, the pregnancy and all. But this year I decided I was going to go ahead and do it, and so I'm gone quite a bit at night and—

AMANDA: Not to be specific [laughing], he's off every night of the week till about 11:30.

ALEX: Yeh, from about 7:30 to about 11:30.

AMANDA: 11:15 [laughing]. I'm already asleep when he gets home.

ALEX: That's been going, that'll last for about six weeks, but it's bad enough even without that. The thing about it is, see, what the pressure is, is not to be able to do *anything* like that. See, those are the kinds of things I like to do with my life, you know, outside the home, and all that kind of thing. I feel like after seeing this, you know, that if she stays at work, I'm not going to be doing too many things in the future because it's just too much of a hassle.

It is interesting that Amanda says she is enjoying her work. In the first interview, she had said that she would have preferred to stop working, not only because she felt it would be better for her child, but also because she was getting bored with her job. The different attitude she now has toward her job may reflect the effects of having been away from it for a while (absence makes the heart grow fonder), or it could indicate that she has found the tertiary time (vis-à-vis the baby) resulting from the job to be rewarding. Interestingly enough, there was one working couple in the sample who said that they found the weekends to be the most difficult because they were not used to spending so much uninterrupted time with their baby. In other words, they appreciated the "down time" that their jobs afforded them.

Anyone who has experienced the transition to parenthood can empathize with Alex's remark about not having enough time to go to the bathroom, now that there is a baby in the house. Humorous as such a predicament may sound to the childfree or to the parent who can afford a live-in nanny, his comment is a significant statement about what happens to one's private time when an infant is yours to keep, and is a reminder of some of the points made in Chapter 3.

When Alex says that Amanda does not have time to go to the bathroom, he also includes himself; he too feels "sometimes" that he cannot go when he would like to. Note, however, that Alex located the cause of his time loss not with the presence of the baby per se, but with the fact that Amanda is working. Given that it was Alex who during the first interview was so adamant about Amanda's having to work, it is puzzling that he now sees her employment as his personal burden. If she stays on the job, he may not be able to continue to do the kinds of things he likes to do because it would be too much of a hassle (for him, not Amanda). The conversation is starting to get heated:

AMANDA: Well, he still does everything, and I've given up everything.

ALEX: That's not true.

AMANDA: And that makes me mad.

INTERVIEWER: What have you [Amanda] given up?

ALEX: What have you [Amanda] given up?

AMANDA: Well, I mean, I'm not in anything anymore like that at all. And I have been some, but not as much as he is. But I've just had, like two or three times people have called me up and asked me to do something, and I just can't do anything, *period*, during the week anymore.

INTERVIEWER: How did it work out that you get to do things and you wouldn't.

AMANDA: Probably the best, the number one excuse is that I'm breast-feeding, probably. But I don't think it will change when that stops.

Several critical remarks are made in this short section. First of all, Amanda's opening comment ("Well, he still does everything, and I've given up everything") shifts the topic of conversation to the problems she is having with Alex. Implicit in her comment is the assertion that the current arrangement is tipped in Alex's favor, that it is, in other words, inequitable. When asked how this unjust situation came to be, she says that the number one excuse is that she is breast-feeding, *but* that she does not believe anything will change when that stops. Her prediction does eventually come true; by the third interview, Amanda has stopped breast-feeding but the perceived inequities in Alex and Amanda's relationship remain. Why?

Before answering this question, we must first ask what is it about breast-feeding that can make it an "excuse" for an inequitable child-care arrangement. There are at least two ways that it can serve this purpose, one of which is alluded to by Amanda, and one of which is not. Let us first cover Amanda's definition of the situation.

All other things being equal, mothers who breast-feed are generally more tied down than mothers who do not. Breast-feeding mothers must be available to their babies more often and more regularly. Even if a mother chooses to pump her breasts and store her milk so that someone else can "breast-feed" her child, it is rare that a mother will use this substitute procedure more than twice a day. For one thing, breast milk given in a bottle defeats what for some parents is the most important reason to breast-feed, namely, the personal contact which a baby and mother receive. And many mothers find the pumping procedure difficult or just inconvenient. Thus, when one considers the fact that infants expect to be fed every three or four hours, and that even under the best circumstances only a few of those feedings can be handed off by the breast-feeding mother, one can begin to appreciate what the decision to breast-feed can entail, in spite of its psychological and nutritional benefits.

But it is not breast-feeding itself that is solely responsible for tying a mother down. Yes, the mother who insists on strictly breast-feeding may, in the middle of the night, temporarily regret her decision because she and not her husband must be the one to respond to their hungry son or daughter. But there are many breast-feeding mothers who contend that they are not restricted by breast-feeding. If they want to go somewhere, they just take the baby with them and feed him or her "on the run"—in the car, in the shopping mall, in the restaurant, etc. The interviews suggest, however, that Amanda was not one of these women. For her, breast-feeding was something that you did not do in public.

Amanda's attitude toward public breast-feeding was suggested in her discussion of what took place in the morning, after she brought the baby to her mother's house. She noted, during the third interview, that since she had stopped breast-feeding she could now sit at the table with her parents while they were having their breakfast, whereas before she had to retire to their bedroom to breast-feed the baby. It is not clear whose idea it was that Amanda not breast-feed at the table. It is noteworthy, however, that Amanda did not once mention the possibility of going out at night with the baby in tow. Thus, her attitude toward breast-feeding may have partially contributed to her "imprisonment."

There is another way that breast-feeding can be used to account for an inequitable child-care arrangement. Amanda does not use this excuse during the interviews, but it could have been a relevant factor; we cannot say for sure. As noted, many parents opt for breast-feeding because they feel that it creates a very special emotional bond between a mother and child. Some parents (and some researchers [e.g., Rossi, 1977]) believe that the bond that develops from this experience makes the relationship between the mother and the child more special than the relationship between the father and the child, and that since fathers cannot breast-feed, the father should reconcile himself to the fact that the baby will prefer his wife to him, and that his wife will have certain "insights" into the child's behavior which he can never have. Under these conditions, it is only "natural" for mothers to be the principal caretakers while fathers assume a lesser role. What makes this account more potent than the first is that the bond between the mother and child is presumed to be permanent. Thus, even after the wife has discontinued breast-feeding, the special relationship lingers and supposedly serves to explain why the baby prefers the mother and why Dad just does not have the "know-how" or "patience" to comfort the child.

We have yet to come up with an answer for what Amanda meant when she said that breast-feeding was probably the number one excuse but that it was by no means the only reason that there existed what was, in her opinion, an unfair arrangement. As soon as Amanda made this statement, she was asked to explain what she meant, so let us begin to answer the question posed by returning to the transcript.

INTERVIEWER: How come [breast-feeding will not change things]?

AMANDA: [Laughing] You tell him "how come."

ALEX: What do you mean, me "tell him 'how come' "?

AMANDA: Well, this is going to be an interesting tape! He just gets his way more, I mean.

ALEX: That's not true. Well, I don't know. That's not true.

AMANDA: What's the answer?

ALEX: We're going to have a fight here in a minute?

AMANDA: What's the answer?

ALEX: See what you [the baby] are causing; see?

AMANDA: Well, I want to stay with her more. I think he should want to stay a little more than he does. But, I mean, I want him to be in the play because he enjoys it so much. . . . But I still resent a whole lot that he's gone.

INTERVIEWER: What do you resent about his being gone?

AMANDA: Because I could barely, I don't even sit down. Come home, like we're putting stuff in the, heating stuff in the oven for supper. We're not even eating decent; we're not cooking decently.

ALEX: It wouldn't matter whether I was here or not.

AMANDA: But then like, quick as he leaves, by the time we finish eating, it's still on the table, I have to—

ALEX: No, because *I* clean up the dishes after we get through eating.

AMANDA: Anyway—

ALEX: Let's get all the story straight.

AMANDA: Sometimes it's still on the table, sometimes it's not. He leaves at 7:00, 7:15, around there. And then she has to have her bath, and then she has to eat, and all these things *I* have to do, like any clothes that are washed, *I* have to wash them, and all these things, and it's almost impossible. She's not at the stage I can just leave her, and, you know, you can't even, it's like you need four arms to do things because like you are having to hold her and she's not always going to be content to be in her bed or in her playpen or something like that. And the last week or so, I've been getting her to bed as early as 8:45 or 9:00, but sometimes it's been later than that.

INTERVIEWER: And then what do you usually do when you're by yourself?

AMANDA: Well, usually by that time, it's just about time to go to bed by the time I get her done. Like I'll have some clothes that are in the wash or something like that, or I'll wash my hair or take a bath or something.

After they bicker over who is going to explain why things will not change when the baby is no longer breast-feeding, Amanda discloses that the real issue for her is not that she can no longer go out as much as before or that she cannot go out as much as Alex does, but that Alex does not "want" to stay home with her and the baby. In other words, as she sees it, Alex seems to place more value on his outside activities than he does on his family activities. Her complaint about not eating "decent" is more a comment about wanting a relaxed *family* dinner than it is a statement about the quality of their food. The point she is trying to make is, however, missed by Alex, who replies that his presence at dinner would not "matter."

It is obvious from the above transcript that Amanda has more of a stake in Alex's staying home than she had before the baby arrived. If she chose to stay home before, the only thing she lost was Alex's company (something she valued very much). Now, if she chooses to stay home, she not only loses Alex's company, but she also is saddled with all the baby work. Describing what her evenings are like, she again uses the pronoun "I" (only here more emphatically) to denote the fact that, for all intensive purposes, she is a single parent. When she says that she needs "four arms" sometimes, she does not seem to be aware of the irony of her statement; if Alex stayed home, she would have the second set of arms she wants. Her description of what it is like to be with someone who refuses to take no for an answer ("She's not always going to be content to be in her bed or in her playpen or something like that") is a familiar comment, one that was echoed by the other parents in the study. The demands of an infant are, to some extent, nonnegotiable. In short, Amanda's comments graphically illustrate the adult-alone-with-an-infant-at-home picture that was sketched initially in Chapter 3.

At this point in the interview, Alex is asked how he feels about leaving Amanda alone with the baby. The question precipitates an argument which ends with Amanda picking up the baby and leaving the room.

INTERVIEWER: How do you feel about leaving the house? I mean, you know she's got things to do?

ALEX: Well, I feel guilty about it, but it's, I take exception to the fact that it stays like that because before I mean she, for five months I've been home, haven't been doing much at all, that's true, what I have done. . . . I want you to explain that.

INTERVIEWER: You [Amanda] see it differently.

AMANDA: Yeh, I do.

ALEX: You haven't thought about what I was doing before, during the first five months.

AMANDA: Okay, he still, he has choir practice every Thursday night
until 9:00. . . . He did not play football this year for the first
year, first time ever, but he did play softball during the summer—

ALEX: Wait a minute. Tell him about when she was born. Softball was
over.

AMANDA: Yeh, that's true, and then now he's started basketball, and
he has basketball every Tuesday night.

ALEX: Wait a minute. When did that start? Two weeks ago. I said the
first five months. Tell him about the first five months.

AMANDA: I'm not going to do this anymore [long pause] if you are
going to argue on the tape [said in an emotional whisper, after
which there is silence].

INTERVIEWER: So you think you were around a lot during the first
five months?

ALEX: Well, I *know* I was.

AMANDA: It just doesn't *feel* like he was [said in a very weak whisper,
followed by her getting up with the baby and leaving the room].

The argument that erupts is actually the same argument that
Alex and Amanda have been having ever since they got married.
They cannot agree on how much Alex works around the house,
only now they are focusing on baby care instead of doing the
laundry and the like. True to form, Alex insists that he is doing
a lot more than Amanda is willing to give him credit for, while
Amanda implies that Alex's standards must be worlds apart
from hers because she does not "feel" that he has done what he
claims to have done. During the third interview, Amanda said
that she and Alex must have different concepts of time because
somehow Alex always sees himself doing more work than she
sees him doing ("He must have a crazy concept of time").
Alex's focusing on the first five months may seem strange at
first, even manipulative (is he skirting the issue?). But what
Alex may be trying to assert is that because he "gave up" his
most valued activities during the first five months (his theater
group, his sports, etc.), he should be credited with having made,

qualitatively speaking, a greater sacrifice. Since Amanda does not value outside activities as much as Alex does (though she suggests that there were some that she liked a lot), she finds it difficult to understand Alex's point. All she knows is that Alex is not there when she needs him. Thus, Amanda is correct when she says that they have different conceptions of time, but it is not clock time that they disagree on, but quality time.

The fact that Alex and Amanda's conflict over baby care is basically the same conflict that they have been having all along is significant. Many of our couples found themselves confronting problems from the past. In some cases, problems which were only minor before were now major, while in other cases, problems which were presumed to be dead and buried were reawakened with the arrival of the child.

The most important comment in the above segment is Alex's initial response to the interviewer's question. He says, "I feel guilty about it [leaving the house], *but*." Alex sees the question for what it is—an attack on him ("You know she's got things to do")—and tries to defend himself by offering an account of his activities. Introduced in Chapter 4, an *account* is a "statement made by a social actor to explain unanticipated or untoward behavior" (Scott and Lyman, 1968: 46). Such a statement may be phrased as either an excuse or a justification. An *excuse* is an account "in which one admits that the act in question is bad, wrong, or inappropriate but denies full responsibility." A *justification* is an account "in which one accepts responsibility for the act in question, but denies the pejorative quality associated with it" (1968: 47). Alex's reference to the first five months and the opportunities lost as a result of his staying home is his way of justifying his apparent "untoward behavior." He accepts responsibility for his actions, but denies that his absence in the evening is all that bad in light of his contribution during the first five months. His response to the question is important because it marks the beginning of a series of aligning actions used by him during this interview and the next to try to mend both the breaks between him and Amanda (interpersonal misalignments) and the breaks between his semiegalitarian ideals, offered during the first interview, and his current conduct (culture-conduct misalignments).

In the course of the interviews, Alex offered no fewer than twenty different accounts to explain why his baby-care activity (or lack of baby-care activity) should not result in his being cast as a villain. ("Every account is a manifestation of the underlying negotiation of identities" [Scott and Lyman, 1968: 59].) Including the one just discussed, the twenty (paraphrased) are: (1) "I did a lot the first five months." (2) "It's her job that's making it so bad." (3) "She'd rather stay home more than I would." (4) "I help out more than most husbands do." (5) "She's expecting more from me now than she did before." (6) "As the mother, she's more naturally suited to care for the baby." (7) "I do a lot now that I don't get credit for." (8) "Disagreements about responsibilities are normal in a marriage." (9) "She always complains about how little I do" (she is a nag). (10) "I've changed more than she has to make our marriage work." (11) "We're just two strong-willed personalities [with some honest disagreements]." (12) "I'm not good at taking care of the baby; I don't feel comfortable making bottles or bathing her, for example; I am good at playing with her, however." (13) "I worry about the baby's welfare and well-being; she feels more of an obligation for her day-to-day care." (14) "There are more outside demands on my time than there are on hers." (15) "First, she says I could become involved again in the play, and now she's complaining" (she does not know what she wants, she is fickle). (16) "I couldn't stop now if I wanted to; I made a commitment to my friends." (17) "Her staying home alone with the baby is her problem; she refuses to get a babysitter." (18) "She thinks I like to go out every night; well, even a lot of the youth work that I do is not always fun and games." (19) "The baby does not give her as many problems (crying, etc.) as she does me." (20) "It's a lot easier for her to change than it is for me to change the way I like to live."

Why does Alex use so many accounts? For one thing, Amanda did not honor or accept many of the excuses and justifications Alex offered to explain his conduct. Only if an account is accepted is the misalignment repaired. Thus, some of the accounts were proposed only *after* others were disqualified. For example, account 18 was offered immediately after account 7 because as soon as 7 was proposed, Amanda glared at Alex, indicating that she did not accept that explanation ("See the look she just gave me"). Surprisingly, Amanda did not challenge, at least during the interview, account 18, despite the paradox implied; Alex has time for "youth work" with other people's kids, but not his own. Other accounts which Amanda found somewhat acceptable were 12 and 19. Although they were not sufficient to completely legitimate Alex's behavior, they did have, in her mind, some merit, and could explain why, when they were both together with the baby, she ended up carrying the bulk of the responsibility. Accounts which place the blame on Amanda (3, 5, 9, 15, and 17) were difficult for her to parry. Account 17 was especially problematic because it centered on something that Amanda held dear. She believed that since she was working all day, she would "not be a good mother" if she "went off" and left her baby with a sitter several nights a week. Alex felt no similar compulsion and accused Amanda of being overprotective. If she insisted on personally keeping track of the baby, then in his mind she could be the one to care for her. He was not going to be tied down by her preoccupation with responsibility.

Sometimes Alex would offer an explanation for his behavior without being overtly accused of wrongdoing by Amanda. He could have been responding in anticipation of Amanda's position on a line of questioning, or the general context of the interview situation may have made him defensive. Another possibility, one that is suggested by the overall structure of the conversations, is that Alex felt compelled to offer explanations to himself, and that he was not always willing to honor his own aligning actions. He was quite aware that during the first interview, he had made statements which said he would do one thing, while he now did another. He was aware that, despite his claim that he did more than most husbands (account 4), he could be grouped with the "male chauvinist pigs" that he had alluded to then. Thus, the excuses and justifications were as much for his own self-image as they were for Amanda's image of him. He too needed to come up with a set of explanations that would leave his identity untarnished. The fact is that Alex was probably a little surprised by his own behavior. We suspect that he genuinely believed much of what he had said during the first interview. But his commitment to his recreational pursuits was much stronger than he had realized. More importantly, the commitment he thought he would have to his daughter did not develop to the level that he expected. Certainly, he felt committed to her in an obligatory way and assumed responsibility for her welfare and well-being (account 13), but he did not develop the intrinsic commitment that he thought would; he did not, in other words, find his daughter as much fun as his recreational activities. Thus, his daughter could not compete for his attention; she was not a big enough attraction.

No other couple in the sample employed as many aligning actions as Alex and Amanda did. No other couple experienced as many misalignments. Every other couple, however, did use one or more of the accounts listed above to explain their traditionalization. Hence, the twenty accounts are a fairly comprehensive list of the kinds of aligning actions couples use during the transition to parenthood. If fathers and mothers do indeed talk themselves into traditional roles, these are the kinds of words they will use.

The third interview was pretty much like the second, with one important exception. Although Alex had not stopped his gallivanting and the accounts flowed freely throughout, Amanda was not as angry as before but seemed resigned to what was happening. One segment of the interview seemed to sum up her feelings fairly well:

AMANDA: I think what he's doing is wrong, but, you know, but I mean she's going to have a mother at least. So it's as simple as that.

INTERVIEWER: So you feel like in some ways she doesn't really have a father?

AMANDA: Yes, I sure do. Now, in a lot of ways she does, but I think the last three months, I think it's been, you know, he's been gone most of the time and so that's hard. Now, I don't know that it makes a whole lot of difference to the baby or not, you know, at this point in her life.

INTERVIEWER: Does it make a difference to you? Do you feel like you don't have a husband?

AMANDA: It makes a lot of difference to me. Because it probably only makes about an hour's difference in her time because she goes to bed at 8:00, 8:15, you know. It doesn't, it probably doesn't make as much difference to her as it does to me.

INTERVIEWER: What's the big difference that it makes to you? What is it that you're missing?

AMANDA: I'm lonesome, you know. And I'm envious because I would like to be doing a lot of things [that he does] too. And I'd rather that he be home with me, you know, doing things together rather than, you know, doing them separately. . . .

INTERVIEWER: Do you feel that you've been changing over these nine months?

AMANDA: I don't know. I don't think I'm as nice a person as I used to be. I think it's more of a result of I've been nagging more, I guess just because he's gone so much, but I don't otherwise, I don't think I have. . . . I think what's changed the most has been our relationship, my husband's and my relationship.

INTERVIEWER: And what, what do you mean by your "relationship"?

AMANDA: I mean, I just think it's, I haven't, it's just not as pleasant as it was, you know. It's more conflict oriented than it used to be.

INTERVIEWER: And you think that's directly related to the birth of the child?

AMANDA: No, not really. Well, maybe, I guess so, in that I feel · responsible, maybe so, not directly, kind of indirectly.

INTERVIEWER: Does the increased conflict in your relationship ever get you to feel regretful for having a child?

AMANDA: No.

The above segment is one of the most poignant in all the interviews. Lonely, and seemingly depressed, Amanda reflects on the past nine months and concludes that her family is a shambles: she has become a single mother, her husband has deserted her, and her marriage does not seem as enjoyable as it once was. The most gripping comment is her remark about how she feels about herself. Because she tried to stand up for what she believes in, she now sees herself as a "nagging wife," which means that, to her, she is not as "nice a person" as she used to be. Damned if she complains, and damned if she does not, Amanda is trapped in a classic double bind.

The portrait of Alex that she paints stands in sharp contrast to the pictures of Chester and Ted that emerged in the interviews. Both Chester and Ted appeared to be relatively sensitive to the expressed and implied needs of their wives. Chester, you will recall, played an important role in helping Carol to recognize that she was not happy as a full-time homemaker. And Ted bragged about what a great wife and mother Thelma was, which made Thelma very proud because these were central roles in her identity. Alex, on the other hand, seems to be oblivious, at some points, to how much he is hurting Amanda and, at others, gives the impression that he just does not care how she feels. During the third interview, Amanda said, "He told me he was going to do these things [his extracurricular activities] whether I wanted him to or not." Amanda's disapproval is evidently not a strong controlling factor in Alex's life, at least with respect to his evening activities.

Amanda says that the changes in her relationship with Alex, indirectly prompted by the birth of her daughter ("indirect" perhaps because, as noted before, their transition to parenthood did not cause new problems but accentuated old ones), does not make her regret having a child. One might conclude that she is lying, or at least deceiving herself. Yet when she is asked later in the interview whether she would like to have a second child, she unhesitatingly answers yes. (Alex gives a qualified yes: "We have to straighten out the conflicts we have now before we have another one.") Again, one could say that she is lying or that she is confused about what she really wants. Perhaps. We think that it is significant, however, that when Alex and Amanda were asked at the end of the study whether there were any topics that should have been covered but were not, *both* of them immediately started to talk about the positive ("We have spent all of our time talking about negative things instead of good things"):

> ALEX: When you go off some place with her to church or some place like that, uh, it gives you a sense of pride and all that, because everybody comes up and says how pretty she is. . . . She gives you a lot of enjoyment and pleasure and you're proud of her and that kind of thing, you know, and that's worth a lot. . . . I think she's a real pretty baby, and that makes me feel good about myself; and she's healthy, and all the doctors say she's real intelligent. . . . She is the best baby in there, and she's their favorite and all that kind of stuff, and, uh, you know, that makes you feel good about yourself, about the way you're, you know, what you've produced, I guess. . . . *Despite all of our conflicts,* she seems to be pretty happy most of the time, which is, she has a real pleasant personality and all that kind of thing, and that makes you feel good about what you're doing with them.

> INTERVIEWER: What about yourself [Amanda], can you add anything to that?

> AMANDA: Well part of, well, she's probably, having a baby was probably one thing that I feel I had to do to be fulfilled as a woman, or something like that, you know, I really felt that. And now that, you know, I'm real glad I have her. . . . It's nice having someone that's so perfect, that loves you so much, and that depends on you so much. You know, things like that. . . . Just having another little person that's part of me, part of me and it's part of Alex, and, I don't know. Having her, it makes you feel proud to be successful at something, even if it's little things, like nursing her was real fulfilling to me. . . . It feels like that's the way human beings were made, and if you're able to do it, it makes you feel good, that you are able to produce a child.

The juxtaposition of the above comments with what has come before may seem inconsistent. Who are the real Alex and

Amanda? The answer is that both the negative and the positive expressions are genuine. Parenthood is, in many ways, a paradox (Hoffman and Manis, 1978). On the one hand, there are the problems of having to contend with a demanding infant. But on the other, there are the joys of knowing you are very important to someone. The paradoxical character of the transition to parenthood is not simply a function of the fact that both of these experiences are part of it all, but that the "lows" and "highs" are so extreme and so intense that they make you want to cry at one moment and laugh at the next.

NOTE

1. Alex and Amanda thought it amusing that Amanda's father would see his wife as not doing anything. What she was doing, they pointed out, was trying to be a super homemaker. Her house was always spotless, and she cooked wonderful meals—feats which took a tremendous amount of her time but which her father assumed were effortless.

Chapter 8

SHARON AND STUART

This case study is about a couple who is like Alex and Amanda in that they, too, both work. However, unlike Alex and Amanda, this husband and wife voluntarily chose a two-paycheck family system. Highly committed to their jobs, they are what is called a *dual career couple* (Rapoport and Rapoport, 1976). More than anyone else in the sample, they represent the future.

Sharon and Stuart were one of the first to stand out as a potential case study. What impressed us initially was the positive way they seemed to approach parenthood. Here was a couple who wanted to have children when they did (He: "Both our children were planned, planned down to the day; it was a very, very deliberate decision"), who seemed to relish the parental experience (He: "I'm tremendously inspired by the lifestyle of children, and that's a moving force for me." She: "I really feel like people who don't have children miss a lot."), and who believed that they had been blessed with two wonderful kids (She: "We see a lot of people with children these days, and ours seem to be amazingly free of hassle for us. No bedtime hassles, no eating hassles, no jealously hassles, no, none of that kind of thing, no particular disciplinary problems. You know, they seem to be really just contented kids."). So positive were they about the whole thing that during the final interview, Sharon felt compelled to apologize, saying that as luck would have it, we just happened to interview them at a high point in their lives ("It all sounds so Pollyannaish. We do have horrible days when we want to cook both the kids. [But] I mean, it's, I think in all three interviews we have been so, we have been caught at such a good time."). The thing that really made their inclusion as a case study certain was that Sharon and Stuart were a couple who seemed to be trying their darnedest to create a nonsexist atmosphere in their home. After reading so many stories of couples whose marriages had undergone severe traditionalization, it was refreshing to find a couple whose role structure appeared to be unaffected by the transition (He: "Having children hasn't changed our relationship one iota"), and who seemed to be immune to a traditional division of labor (He: "We could trade roles in a night, it wouldn't affect us; I could stay at home and take care of the kids and she could bring home the salary check"). In short, Sharon and Stuart were chosen because they were a significant contrast to the other couples.

When the time came to begin the serious chore of writing, some of our first impressions were found to be false. The most important of these was our impression that Sharon and Stuart were nontraditional. While there is no denying that they were far less traditional than all the other couples, they were a lot more traditional than they had initially appeared; they were also a lot more traditional than they believed they were. Had the couple been given a standardized sex-role questionnaire, they would have scored very well; that is, they would have scored toward the nontraditional or feminist end of the scale. This is because they were very conscious of sexist attitudes, sexist language, etc. But in open-ended interviews, ambivalances and self deceptions are more likely to surface. Confronted with questions that place them "on guard," couples will reply with fairly stock answers. But during "the interim"—those time periods when they believe that they are between questions— they will often slip into a level of conversation that represents a more taken-for-granted or natural attitude. It is during these "off guard" moments that Sharon and Stuart would generally make their traditional feelings known.

A good portion of the first interview is devoted to a description of the couple's philosophy of life. This was as a result of their trying to set the stage for discussing some of the changes they were going through. The philosophy which they presented is interesting in that it is just the opposite of Ted and Thelma's. Whereas Ted and Thelma's goal was to protect and defend the integrity of the family, to create boundaries around their family life, Sharon and Stuart's goal was to protect and defend the integrity of the individual, to create boundaries around themselves. This does not mean that Sharon and Stuart did not consider family life important, only that they were less dependent on their family, and that instead of planning things for the family to do together, they tried to come up with things for each of them to do apart.

STUART: Contrast is one of the essential ingredients of life, and anything you get too much of, that just runs you down hour by hour, day after day, week after week, month after month, is just alienating and debilitating. And so while it may not be working at a job, it may be raking leaves every day or something, but something where a few hours you've got to yourself in doing your own thing is really crucial. And as a result, we don't, because of the trade-off of times [spent with the children] and everything, we seldom get, we don't find ourselves getting as uptight and possibly upset with our kids as might be possible, you know. You sometimes see on TV where we [parents in general] sort of feel like they [children in general] are taking something from us. Now, we feel less that way because we are still pretty much doing our own thing, even while they are around. And we help each other make that possible. And then the time we spend with them, we don't feel cheated.

Stuart's remarks are in line with points made in Chapter 3 in the discussion of primary, secondary, and tertiary time. We noted then that because of the repetitiveness and pace of baby care, even the most dedicated parents can feel the need to get away for a while, to get tertiary or "down time." Stuart says that they are aware of the predicament that some parents find themselves in, the situation in which, for one reason or another, the father and mother do not get the time they feel they need, and end up blaming their kids for "taking something from" them. This is precisely the kind of zero-sum situation they are trying to avoid, and they feel they have been successful because of their "trade-off" system. Rather than adopt a system of *coordination* (each does part), as Carol and Chester did, or *specialization* (one does it all), as Alex and Amanda did, Sharon and Stuart use a system of *alternation* (each does it all in turn). For example, one "sort of simplified therapy," as Stuart called it, was for one of them to take a few hours and go out alone, perhaps take a drive or see a movie, while the other stayed home with the children. The longer the "therapy" the better: "One of the greatest things in the world that I could give, do right now for Sharon, would be to take the kids and disappear, not for half a day [but] a whole day, all day, everybody be gone and you have the whole house to yourself."

There is an important difference between coordination and alternation that should be noted. Coordination is a system that relies more on secondary ("ready" but not "up") activities vis-à-vis the children to get the release that is needed. Alternation, on the other hand, is a system that relies more on tertiary activities. Because of this difference, it is logical to hypothesize that a couple's decision to adopt a system of coordination or alternation (or some combination of the two) will partly be a function of the couple's location on the connectedness-separateness continuum. We-oriented couples would be likely to employ coordination to minimize the demands of parenthood because it still allows them to be together, though perhaps more often than they would like on only a secondary level. I-oriented couples, on the other hand, would be likely to employ alternation because it allows them to get the time alone they want.

Sharon and Stuart, an I-oriented couple, could not always get out of the house and away from their children. Thus, they developed spatial and temporal strategies that could be used in the house to control the amount of primary time that they spent with their kids. These strategies are not unique to them, but are, in fact, used by most couples who want to break up the repetitiveness and pace of child care (see Rosenblatt and Titus, 1976). Spatial distance was achieved by having a closed-door policy. For instance, even though their older child no longer required an afternoon nap, they still maintained that the period after lunch was "rest time," during which she would be required to go to her room. And sometimes, certain rooms would be declared off limits to the kids. Temporal distance was achieved by scheduling the children's bedtime (cf. Ted and Thelma). Although they said that they tried not to be autocratic about it, working on compromise rather than proclamation, they did have one hard and fast rule: the children were to be in bed by 8:00 p.m. Achieving this meant that their older child would not be given the opportunity to take an afternoon nap even though she might be tired ("She gets pretty cranky between 4:00 and 7:30, but we just let her get cranky, and by 7:30 to 8:00 she's ready to drop"). Their bedtime policy insured that they would at least have the last few hours of the evening to themselves.

The most important strategy used by Sharon and Stuart to achieve separation from their children was their careers. In fact, no other couple in the sample used their jobs as an "out" to family life as much as Sharon and Stuart did. They were both professors at the same university, Sharon in the department of English, Stuart in the department of History. However, Sharon held a temporary position, which meant that she was hired primarily to teach, while Stuart's position was permanent, which meant that he was expected to do research as well as teach. The fact that Stuart's job demanded more of an intellectual or mental investment proved to be significant, and we will comment on it shortly.

One of the things that sets Sharon apart from all the other women who continued to work after their babies were born is that Sharon did not take a maternity leave after giving birth.

For the first child, she arranged with her colleagues to have them cover her classes, and she was able to return to teaching in three weeks. The second child was born during a recess, so she needed no formal maternity leave. When classes resumed, seven weeks after the birth, she was back on the job. Why did she not take advantage of a maternity leave? She said that she was "just very anxious to . . . get back on the routine" ("Nobody ever asked or was interested in your professional life; everything else took a second place to the pregnancy all of a sudden, and you're so tired of being asked how you feel"). In keeping with the couple's philosophy of life, Sharon believed that returning to work as soon as possible made her "a much better mother" ("When I come home, I have had something interesting to do, been out of the house, and I am just overflowing with motherhood and just want to be with them and do things"). In sum, Sharon felt that getting "down time" from her children (and primary time in something she liked to do, her job) insured that when she was at home she would be willing to be actively involved (primarily rather than secondarily involved) with the kids. Having been recharged outside the house, she would have less need to recharge when in the house; her family would have her full attention.

It was not made particularly clear during the interviews how they handled the child-care arrangements for their first child. The arrangements for their second child were, however, discussed in detail. Taking advantage of the fact that academic life is a flex-time system in which faculty can request certain teaching schedules, they asked for and received a schedule which would permit them to alternate taking care of the baby. It was not that they were opposed to day care; their older child was, in fact, enrolled in a preschool program. They just believed that for "psychological" reasons, it would be better if the baby spent his first six months in his parents' care ("He'll just be better able to face the world and whatever might walk in the door").

The schedule they worked out was fairly straightforward. Stuart arranged his classes so that he could stay home with the baby four mornings a week while Sharon taught. Sharon would then come home by about 1:30 in the afternoon and Stuart would go in to teach his classes. Their daughter would be dropped off at the preschool center on Sharon's way to work and picked up again on the way home. Thus, Stuart was responsible for the baby in the morning, whereas Sharon had both children in the afternoon. When he was asked during the third month interview how the arrangement was working, Stuart said everything was fine.

> STUART: I have the baby to be in charge of, [which has] really been no problem for me at all. But that's because we worked out a schedule where he sleeps a pretty good amount of that time. He gets up and nurses and stays awake for about an hour and goes back to sleep about 9:00 and sleeps for about anywhere from two to three hours. He generally is up thirty minutes before she gets home, and he gets fussy, and I will use that time. I generally sort of have to be with him in the sense of paying attention to his crying or dirty diapers or something like that for anywhere between thirty to forty-five minutes, sometimes an hour, depending. But usually I can have two hours of my own to count on each morning to do my own work, so it's no big problem. That's just the breaks that go with it. I mean, some people, some kids don't like to sleep, they are crying all the time, fussy, this, that, and the other thing, and it could have been the other way around. I'd be on pins and needles around here from 8:00 in the morning straight through. Not have a chance to do anything. But we were lucky in being able to get him through on this schedule.

In the preceding passage, Stuart implicitly acknowledges how crucial the distinction is between primary and secondary attention when one is alone with an infant. If the baby is crying or in need of a diaper change, Stuart must "pay attention" to the baby, meaning that he is forced by the baby into a primary level of activity. But, he says, fortunately the baby sleeps for two hours, and that allows him to do some of his own work, meaning that he can "count on" two hours of time during which he need only be at a secondary level of attention vis-à-vis his son. He notes that if the baby did not sleep at all, he, Stuart, would be "on pins and needles" the whole morning, an apt metaphor to describe what it is like to be "up" or "ready" for concentrated periods of time.

Interestingly enough, nowhere in the above passage does Stuart say that staying home with his child has given him the opportunity to get to know his son better. Rather, his son is his "charge," a person committed to his care. Stuart apparently views staying home as an obligation; he believes he owes his son six months of personal care. So far, however, this debt has proven to be relatively easy to "pay" because the baby sleeps a good deal of the time. Thus, his son is a good child in the same sense that people who sleep a lot are perceived as good patients by a hospital staff. And a good morning is not one in which Stuart and the baby have had an interesting time together, but one in which Stuart is able to squeeze in a fair amount of work.

In all fairness to Stuart, we should point out that, first, he is doing something which no other father in the sample even tried to do; he is repeatedly taking full responsibility for the baby for whole blocks of time. And second, the fact that he is preoccupied with his job while he is home with the baby is partly a function of the pressures of that job. Although he has reduced the number of hours per week that he devotes to his work, as far as the university is concerned, he is still on a full-time schedule; he is still expected, as Stuart put it, to "produce" the same number of "scholarly things" (books, journal articles, etc.) as before. Consider this: If on each of the four days that he stays home, he is able to get in two solid hours of academic work, he would still be putting in approximately three fewer hours of work per day, which would mean twelve fewer hours per week. By the third interview, Stuart had been on his unsanctioned semipaternity leave for six weeks; thus, by this time, he had put in seventy-two (12×6) fewer hours at work. Of course, there exists the possibility that he may be making up for some or all of this lost time by working after dinner, late at night, etc.—periods which he formerly had free. Or he may just work more efficiently than he did before, perhaps spending less time around the coffee pot at work. Whatever the case may be,

Stuart gives the impression in the above sequence that, at this stage of the game, staying home is not a "problem." However, by the sixth-month interview, the situation has changed substantially.

The interview begins with the standard question ("I would like to know what's been happening and changing since last time?"). Stuart says that he is still "babysitting" four mornings a week with his son ("an incredible amount of exposure for the average American male-father"), but that he has begun to "see" that he has his "limits in that sort of thing." Asked what he means, he replies:

STUART: Well, I get pretty frustrated and pretty angry sometimes, sometimes at the baby, sometimes at myself, sometimes at Sharon, but for no particular reason other than just the fact that I want to be doing something else.

SHARON: The housewife syndrome.

STUART: Housewife syndrome or househusband syndrome or whatever, but I—

SHARON: Houseperson syndrome.

STUART: Houseperson syndrome. I can, I suppose that's a small benefit that before at an intellectual level, I suppose every man can empathize with the problems of a working mother and so forth, but before, [but now] I have felt [what it is like] . . . changing the diapers and doing all that sort of stuff on a very full-time basis for four or five hours a day. So it's been something of an exercise in growth in that respect. I've seen exactly what my limits are, and I think they are considerably more than what the average man might be able to contend with.

Stuart says that he is getting more frustrated and angry at both himself and his family because when he is home with the baby he wants to be doing something else. The "something else" that Stuart wants to do is primarily academic work; the time that he is spending with his son is apparently beginning to take its toll on his research productivity. At this point—six months after the birth—Stuart has stayed home twenty-one weeks which means that, at twelve hours per week, he has put in two hundred fifty-two (12 × 21) fewer hours at work. That amounts to six forty-hour weeks.

Many, if not all, of the women in the sample would have loved to have had Stuart say to their husbands what he says to the interviewer in the above sequence. Certainly, Flo and Amanda could have used Stuart as their spokesman. He has concluded from his experience as the morning parent that there is a world of difference between the "intellectual" understanding that most husbands have of their wives' baby-care responsibilities (especially working wives) and the understanding that emerges when a husband has to do "all that sort of stuff" himself. He does, however, qualify his remarks in a significant way when he says that he has seen what his "limits" are. He suggests that he has gone beyond the limits of most men when it comes to baby care and he has also pushed himself beyond his own limits. The implication is that he and all men have dispositional limits which can be tested but which should not be tested too much or too often. As we will soon see, the idea of *fixed* limits (stemming from biological or psychological or sociocultural forces) will be an important account used by Stuart to explain his pullback from child care.

Worthy of note is the semantic game which Sharon and Stuart get into when they are trying to label Stuart's frustration and anger. Moving from "housewife syndrome" to "househusband syndrome," and finally to "houseperson syndrome," they seem to be trying to communicate to the interviewer—and to each other—that they are very much the nonsexist couple. Parenthetical statements such as these, however, are somewhat inconsistent with the traditional attitudes which emerge in the above and subsequent sequences, and provide examples of the different levels of reality which we discussed earlier. Ideologically, Sharon and Stuart are model feminists. But day in and day out, they are traditionalists—less traditional than the other couples in the sample, but traditionalists just the same. Related to this point is a comment made by Sharon during one of the interviews. She said that sometimes she wished they they were not so committed to being the androgynous couple, that there were moments when she wished that Stuart would treat her more as a woman and less as a person. "I'm not knocking what he does; I think it's great. [But] I think it could be supplemented. I think it definitely needs more of the equilibrium. . . . I mean, sometimes I would rather him not be so helpful in clearing off the table and putting the dishes away, and do something more spontaneous, like, I don't know, whatever, bringing flowers or whatever."

The daily alternation of baby care was about to change. Stuart was not able to schedule his classes for the next semester so that he could have his mornings free because it was the policy of the History department to rotate the faculty's schedule, and some of his colleagues were demanding the time periods which Stuart had been monopolizing for a while now. Disbanding their personal system of child care did not, however, pose a problem, as far as they were concerned. When the next semester started, the baby would be old enough in their opinion to be left with someone else. They had, in fact, by the sixth-month interview, already lined up someone to come to their home the mornings that Sharon (and also Stuart) would be at work.

While discussing the change, they said that they had seriously considered the possibility that Sharon could take a leave of absence from her job, but that the idea was quickly dropped because of the importance of Sharon's work to her. In their ·explanation, however, of just how committed Sharon is to her job, they make a critical point: although Sharon's job is indeed important to her, it is not as important as Stuart's job is to him.

INTERVIEWER: You both had discussed your [Sharon] not working and taking care of him?

SHARON: Yeh.

INTERVIEWER: And how did you reach the decision that you [Sharon] would continue to work?

SHARON: Every time I spend the summer at home, I go perfectly bananas all day. I'm not a very good mother on a twenty-four-hour basis, and I enjoy it [teaching] when I'm doing it; it's a fantastic opportunity. And I would really hate to give it up, because there's no going back once I give it up.

INTERVIEWER: Yet if there was someone who was going to give something up, it was going to be you.

SHARON: I think so, yes. But for many reasons other than just the fact that I'm a woman. I like my position. I like what I'm doing. I think it's a fantastic thing. I think it's the only thing I would take while my children were younger, because, you know, it's a full-time job, but I work only in the morning four days a week and it keeps me alive intellectually and everything, and I just enjoy what I'm doing. But anyway, I would give it up because I could be doing an awful lot of other things that I would enjoy also. Whereas I think Stuart in a way is more limited, career-wise, in what he can do. Since my income is a supplementary income, I can either have a lot or a little, and it comes in handy. But I also think I have many more choices to make, careerwise, than he does.

STUART: I read that question a little differently.

SHARON: Oh.

STUART: I think you probably have more choices than I do, but I read that question as applying, suppose you had to give up anything and everything, or one of us did, then it would be you, supposedly. And why would it by you? The question was not could you do something else, but could you *just* be home? On what basis would the decision be made that you would stay at home and I would be at the university?

SHARON: Oh, well, it would be me, because you certainly make more money than I do and in a sense are more committed to what you are doing.

STUART: Okay, well that's, those are two reasons.

SHARON: And the old idea is true, for you work is more [important] than [it is] for me, you know. I think probably the family life plays much more of an important role for me than it does for you. I mean, I could certainly exist without working, without having a professional identity, not very well, I wouldn't like it

very much, but I don't think you could survive psychologically
without any professional identity.

The different commitments that Sharon and Stuart have
toward their work and parental roles explains in part the different ways they interact with their children. The linkage between
commitment and action is, in fact, especially clear in the next
few minutes of the interview. But before we get into this
sequence, we should mention one thing: when the interview
began, the baby was in a playpen next to the tape recorder.
Periodically, his babbling would make it difficult to hear what
was being said. Soon after Sharon remarks that Stuart could not
survive psychologically without a professional identity, Sharon
decides that the baby is making too much "noise" and picks
him up to put him to bed. The tape recorder is shut off until
she returns. When she comes back, the baby can be heard crying
in his room. We have no way of knowing for sure, but it seems
logical to suggest that the baby's crying was responsible for the
direction that the interview then took.

While the baby is sobbing in the background, Stuart, on his
own initiative, begins to talk about his and Sharon's abilities to
calm their son when he is upset. He mentions that he finds
himself "thinking a lot" about whether women are programmed, either instinctually or environmentally, to be better
parents, and says that he has not "come to any great conclusions," but has deduced that he is "less tolerant" and "less
patient" than Sharon is when it comes to dealing with a crying
child. He just does not have as many "little tricks" in his
"repertoire." At the very moment he makes this point, Sharon
excuses herself from the interview to go to her son. While
Sharon is gone, Stuart is asked why he is not as good as Sharon
is at calming the baby. He suggests that it might be due to their
different personalities ("I'm an uptight person. . . . Sharon
is . . . a more peaceful and tranquil person"). He says also that
he does not feel badly about his lack of expertise in that area
because he makes up for it with the housework ("Hell, I do
more than my share"). Moreover, the situation is not going to
last forever ("Kids grow up"). Finally, in the most important

part of the sequence, Stuart talks a little about his one-on-one behavior with his son, and provides some insights into how parents can subconsciously disconfirm their children. When Sharon returns from putting the baby to sleep, the conversation remains focused on how Stuart relates to his son on a day-to-day basis, only now Stuart talks about some of the reasons behind his behavior and mentions again the pressures of his work. In the conclusion to the sequence, the different attitudes that Sharon and Stuart have with respect to their son's capabilities or competencies come to the fore, giving us another clue as to why Stuart finds it difficult to concentrate on his son when he is with him.

STUART: One of the things that I find myself thinking a lot about is the question of who really is made better by nature, if there is such a situation, to take care of a child? I thought about such things as mothering instincts, whether there's a similar thing in the father, what seems to be environmentally programmed into the different sexes, and what part is just biologically determined. But I haven't come to any great conclusions about any of it except that I am thinking about it more. I know that I simply have less tolerance and less patience for the, you know, well, not helping out, but the kinds of things, you know, with a crying child, who cries and cries and cries, and there's something wrong, and the mother's going to feel sympathy, or at least Sharon will very often feel sympathy, although she has her limits too, but her limits extend beyond mine. I can only take it for a short period of time.

INTERVIEWER: So she'll feel sympathy in situations where you'll feel—

STUART: Anger.

SHARON: Desperation.

STUART: Yeh, desperation is a good word. Desperation. Like, "What the hell's wrong?" you know, "I've tried everything and nothing is working; you do it." And, of course, I have a very limited repertoire of little tricks in the bag: the bottle, hold him up and see if there's anything wrong with him, or change him, or something like that. But I mean apart from that, it's—

INTERVIEWER: Do you think she has more of a repertoire?

STUART: Uh, slightly more in terms of amusing him with something, seeing what the problem is.

SHARON: I think my services are called upon now, and I'll be back. [Sharon leaves the room to tend the baby.]

INTERVIEWER: What do you attribute that to?

STUART: Well, it may just be the fact that I'm an uptight person with limited tolerance for situations [in] which I am not the controlling factor. But Sharon is not like that. She is generally a more peaceful and tranquil person with or without children. But what I am saying is that as far as she and I are concerned, she is certainly better suited for a broad range of the kinds of necessary functions, where I just sort of go off the deep end. And that's not a sexist sort of thing. I mean, hell, I do more than my share. I mean, it's not, I'm not talking about just changing diapers and so forth. I'm talking about washing clothes, shopping every weekend; I do that all. And part of the housecleaning sometimes and dinner about half the nights of the week, so she really does less than I do in many cases. So that's my way of effecting a trade-off. I mean, I would rather do the garbage, the dishes, x, y, and z, and all these extra things, and spend less time with the actual necessities of even changing diapers and stuff like that. It's kind of a sense of fairness, you know. "Well, I can't do that very well, but I can do something else. I can whip dinner together in ten minutes, but I'm not very original when it comes to seeing why my son or daughter is crying, what the problem is." Where she could figure that out a lot better, or has the patience to do it. So—

INTERVIEWER: What's that like for you, feeling limited or—

STUART: It's perfectly okay apart from, you know, there's the present buildup in the sense of frustrations. Sometimes I go pound my fist in the wall or something like that. But the thing that makes it all tolerable is the fact that I see the light at the end of the tunnel. This is strictly a temporary thing. Kids grow up. Time passes on. Schedules change, you know. It'll all be over and we're off and running. Awful big difference. I mean, I, my older child now is verbal, you know, she dresses herself, takes care of herself, goes to the bathroom by herself, everything, more or less an autonomous being in a physical sense. And I just enjoy that tremendously.

INTERVIEWER: When you say you see the light at the end of the tunnel, are you saying that you would like for him to hurry up and get bigger?

STUART: No, I wouldn't speed it up one day because, I mean, I'm enjoying him for what he is, you know, at the stage he's at. But it's just that that stage has a lot of other things that are more or less undesirable. You know, I mean, I'm a great believer in letting nature take its course in such matters too. It's a learning experience for me, going through it the way we are going through it. I really wouldn't trade it for anything. I would simply spend a little less time. You know, if you asked me how I would change matters, I would spend less time with him each day. It's not the time, per se, that is a problem. It's just when he, I mean, if he's entertaining himself and I'm in the room, I mean, I'll be happy to sit there all day and occasionally give him a bottle or may change him. That's fine. It's just the thing about the crying or fussing or something like that, that if that comes along, I just don't find myself able to deal with that very well.

INTERVIEWER: How do you spend your morning?

STUART: Well, I try to get something done, which means class preparation, reading, but usually something that I can turn on again and off again. And I've usually been pretty fortunate. I've had between an hour and two-hour block of time where he's taking a morning nap, and then about 11:00 he'll wake up, and between then and 1:30 it's in and out; I may have five minutes to myself.

INTERVIEWER: Then what do you do usually for those two and a half hours when he's awake?

STUART: I will try to do something constructive still, maybe a little reading or some project around the house, but I've generally got an ear out for him and an eye out too, and sometimes I'll be in here in the same room with him, other times I'll just let him play by himself.

INTERVIEWER: But you are not interacting with him that much?

STUART: Uh, not on a continuous basis. But, I mean, I give him a bottle, he's just learning to hold it up for himself now. I continu-

ally will teach him things or try to: how to hold his bottle, how
to get it if it's fallen over to one side or the other, or right now I
am trying to teach him how to roll over. I mean, he should know
by now, but he's got this funny way. He tries to roll over with his
arms stuck straight out like that. And also I will interact with him
to a limited extent by trying out new toys and sort of keeping
some kind of scale on these things, you know. Like I know
certain things he likes first, and then later, and work it up in some
organized fashion, and not overwhelm him with too many things
all at one time. And I talk to him, hold him, and walk around
every so often, but not very much on a sustained basis, you
know, like now is the hour to learn the alphabet or something
like that.

INTERVIEWER: Do you hold him much?

STUART: A fair amount, probably during that two-and-a-half-hour
period up to a half an hour. That seems to be a fair amount, you
know, perhaps with some people it might not seem like much,
and that will be broken up of course, two- to three-minute
segments, or a two-minute segment here, if he seems particularly
disconsolate about something. [Sharon returns from putting the
baby to sleep.]

SHARON: Where are we?

STUART: Talking away. The question was just how much actual time
that I spend with the baby, how much did I interact with him and
how much did I hold him. I was trying to give some kind of
answer to that. There may be something of a sense of guilt, not
guilt but perceived external pressure, feeling like I ought to be
doing something, quote, "constructive" with my time, like
writing or reading or whatever. Uh, and I think that probably
grates on me to an extent, when I'm at home as much as six or
seven hours at a time with the baby, when Sharon had to stay late
at school or something like that. And I find a certain degeneracy
in myself. I found, for example, that I've taken to eating. By high
noon, it seems like I've gotten all I'm going to get done [work-
wise], and there's still another two hours with the baby; he's
beginning to get cranky, and I start inventing little things to do to
sort of occupy my time and eating is one of them. And so I've
put on a lot of weight since he was born, probably fifteen or
twenty pounds. And I'm assuming that part of that is going to

disappear when I get back in somewhat of a more normal schedule, leaving the house at 8:30 in the morning, coming back at 5:00 in the afternoon. Because I'm just not, me in the same room with a refrigerator just don't work, and I don't have any alternative. I mean, I don't work it off, like you [Sharon] do, like some people might. I'm not into that consistent an exercise program.

INTERVIEWER: You say that you feel guilty about not using your time constructively with writing or reading or etc. How do you frame the time that you spend with the baby? If that's not constructive, what is it?

STUART: I feel that that is constructive time, but, you see, let's say there's a total of three hours that he's awake and I have to be on top of him, and an hour and a half or two hours that he's asleep. Well, it's not that I don't feel like that time I spend with him is not constructive. It's just that I continue to feel the pressure from outside concerns, school concerns is one thing. There is a committee report coming up that I feel like I ought to be working on. Even though I'm in one sense perfectly happy to be interacting with him and using that time in the way that I do, and I think it will pay off, and have long range benefits. But I'm a firm believer in both parents spending as much time as they can with their children, and I really have a unique opportunity here, one which a lot of fathers don't have, but—

SHARON: I think it really shows in your relationship with our daughter.

STUART: In what way?

SHARON: Well, there's a lot more intimacy between you and her than there is with other parents and their children.

STUART: Well, as I pointed out a little while ago [while you were out of the room], it's because our daughter has reached a stage where she and I can interact more. I don't think it has a thing to do with the baby. I would be exactly the same with her.

SHARON: No, I don't think it has anything to do with the baby. I think the time you spent with her is paying off with her now, that's what I meant.

STUART: Oh, okay.

SHARON: It's been maybe not as, time with her, but you spent a lot of time with her too. Far and beyond what most other parents do, I mean actively changing diapers and that type of thing, that sort of thing, you know, whoever changes them and whatever.

STUART: Well, I don't know what kind of correlation there is with that kind of time and when they're getting older. Maybe there is, but—

SHARON: The relationship is *active*.

STUART: It's active because she's capable of inter-*act*-ing too.

SHARON: No, because she's capable of interacting now, but so is he. *They're capable of interacting at different levels.* But it's carrying through though.

STUART: Right, but [he is] at a level that's more frustrating to deal with.

SHARON: Sure.

We think it is significant that Sharon took responsibility both for putting the baby to bed in the first place and for going in and quieting him when he refused to go to sleep. We believe that her actions (and Stuart's inaction) were behavioral confirmations of the points that they were making during the interview. Stuart *says* that he is not as good as Sharon is at dealing with the baby when the baby is crying, while Sharon is *showing us* that, indeed, she is the one responsible for quieting the baby ("I think *my* services are called upon now").

Stuart indicates that as a result of his experiences with his son, he finds himself thinking more about the differences between the sexes. Several fathers in the sample said exactly the same thing, namely, that after watching how they and their wives interacted with their babies, they too began to wonder whether there was anything to the theory that men and women are "programmed" differently when it comes to parenthood. As sincere as Stuart is in trying to come up with an explanation for why he finds it more difficult than his wife does to calm his son (and as sincere as some of the other fathers are), we think that physiological or personality explanations for differences in parental expertise can be seen as attempts to account for sexism in the same sense that physiological and personality explanations for racial differences in expertise (e.g., intelligence) can be seen as attempts to account for racism. In both situations, the theories can become ideologies to excuse and justify institutionalized discrimination.

This applies to "liberals" as well as to staunch sexists and racists. In fact, it is a particularly important point for people who do not think of themselves as sexist or racist to remember. As one study of racism found, liberals can avoid defining themselves as prejudiced (and hence exclude themselves from the problem of racism or sexism) by developing "ways of explaining their opposition to change *that do not explicitly contradict egalitarian ideals*" (Wellman, 1977: 33; his italics). Thus, for example, Stuart's insistence that his unwillingness to deal with the baby when he is crying is "not a sexist sort of thing" allows him to oppose any change in their situation while at the same time letting him hold on to his egalitarian beliefs; by accounting for his behavior, he excludes himself from the problem.

Stuart's description of a typical morning with the baby is unique and highly significant. Stuart is one of the few fathers in the sample to speak about his baby in specific rather than general terms. Because he has a vast amount of parental experience, he is able to come up with concrete examples of how he interacts with his child. More importantly, the examples that he uses go beyond play activities; he *works with his son,* teaching him how to hold his bottle, how to roll over, how to play with his toys, etc. Through his experience, he has also *learned from his son.* He is aware that the baby does not like to be overwhelmed with too many toys, but prefers to play with them one at a time. Hence, Stuart is less likely to dump a pile of toys in front of the baby and then be annoyed when his son is not amused.

As sophisticated as Stuart's understanding is, it is still less sophisticated than Sharon's, and less sophisticated than the understanding that most mothers have of their infants. Part of the problem may very well be that Stuart's forced preoccupation with his job has claimed some of his attention and prevented him from concentrating enough on his son to develop a higher parental understanding. (Stuart's income was not "supplementary," as Sharon's was; like it or not, he had to work.) Whatever the reason, some of Stuart's remarks do give the impression that, to a certain degree, he views his son as something akin to a wind-up doll. In other words, implicit in the above sequence is the following metaphor. Before Sharon leaves for work in the morning, she winds her toy son up. Stuart's responsibility then becomes one of maintaining the toy's equilibrium; if it should fall or bump into something (impeding its progress), Stuart picks it up or redirects it ("occasionally give him a bottle or change him"). Toward the end of the morning, the toy is losing some of its spring tension and is beginning to act sluggishly ("By high noon . . . he's beginning to get cranky"). But Stuart cannot wind the toy himself, and hopes that Sharon, who can, will get home in time. If she is late, he begins to get uptight, and he has found that the best thing to do is to take his mind off the fact that the toy is running down ("When Sharon [has] to stay late at school or something like that . . . I find a certain degeneracy in myself . . . and I start inventing little things to do to sort of occupy my time").

The reason behind Stuart's somewhat reified conception of his son can perhaps be traced to the point he makes at the end of the sequence. Stuart sees the baby as less interpersonally competent than Sharon does. In his mind, the baby is not capable of interacting; in her mind, he is. The differences in their points of view may hinge on the importance that each attaches to verbal skills. Stuart may define interaction as *symbolic* communication; Sharon may define interaction as *signal* communication. Thus, as far as Stuart is concerned, since the baby cannot talk, he cannot interact. Sharon prefers to believe that the baby can interact, but on a "different level"; the level she is referring to is the level of indexical signs. Babies can, in other words, "tell you" when they are hungry, dirty, tired, etc., if you are willing to listen, if you are willing to come down to their level. If you are not willing to learn the baby's language (or if you do not "have" the time to learn it on your own or from others), then the probability is increased that your efforts to deal with the baby when he or she is crying will be unsuccessful, which will, in turn, increase your frustration and anger. Most mothers find themselves in this situation on a regular basis, partly because the child's "vocabulary" changes so often and so quickly. What they end up doing then, through a series of trial and error experiments, or through reading what others have to say (e.g., Dr. Spock), is *learning* how to cope with the problem. However, when fathers find themselves in this situation, they often turn to their wives to "translate," or, as in Stuart's case, they give up entirely, letting their wives specialize in dealing with the kids when they are cranky. The key point is that the differences in the responses of mothers and fathers are not a function of inborn traits, but a consequence of the fact that mothers have no one to hand off the job to and fathers do. Stuart himself supports this explanation; because he could not relinquish his child-care responsibilities when he was home alone with the baby, he learned, on his own, some of the things that do and do not satisfy his son. We would hypothesize that if he had continued to care for the baby, and if he had not accounted for some of his failures, but had tried to figure out for himself how to deal with his child, then he would have been as skilled as Sharon is. It was the ready availability of socially approved accounts, coupled with the pressures of his job, that created their different conceptions of their son.

The third interview opens with Stuart announcing that the period of the past three months has been "a particularly favorite time" for him. The baby has begun to develop a "primitive personality" and can now crawl and stand unassisted. Best of all, his son is being cared for in the morning by someone else, which means that Stuart is "able to enjoy the good things about [the baby] without the responsibilities" ("It's the typical explanation that grandparents always give"). No change has occurred in Sharon and Stuart's levels of expertise in dealing with their son when he cries. If anything, Sharon's position as the specialist in this department has become more firmly entrenched (She: "I can read him very well, what he wants and what he doesn't want." He: "Yeh, I think that's right, you've been very good at interpreting just the slightest crying instantly."). In short, the basic pattern discussed during the first two interviews has remained essentially the same.

Looking back over the previous nine months, Stuart ventures a comparison between their parental experience and the experience of others, and concludes that he and Sharon are very "untypical" and very "fortunate" ("We're living in a sort of quasi-heaven"). He says that their "stories about children don't overlap very much" with the stories of a lot of the people that they know. Many of their friends, he surmises, are "probably a little bit more negative" and "a little more trapped" or "blocked in" with respect to "what they can or cannot do." The most important reason, as he sees it, that he and Sharon are doing so well is that both of them are in academia and, therefore, have "flexible schedules" which afford them "a lot of options to play around with."

Stuart's hypothesis is worth examining. First of all, Sharon and Stuart did come closer than any other couple in the sample to establishing an egalitarian relationship. Both were employed, and both took responsibility for child care and housework. Though the balance within these spheres was not perfect, it was an impressive effort. Could their system have worked if they did not have jobs with relatively flexible schedules? The answer is yes, but it would have been more difficult. If both of them held nine-to-five jobs, and both wanted to continue to work, they would have had to do what they did when Stuart could no longer get his mornings off; they would have had to hire someone to care for the baby (or convince a relative or friend to care for the child, as Alex and Amanda did). This still would have allowed them to strive for an egalitarian child-care and housework system in the early morning and in the evening, as Carol and Chester were trying to do. But it would not have given each of them the opportunity to be *alone* with the baby, which means, in our opinion, that they would run the risk of drifting even more rapidly than they did into a traditional child-care arrangement. Comparing Stuart with the other fathers in the sample, we believe that there is something to be said for giving fathers the chance to interact one-on-one with their infants. The learning experience that results is very much like what happens to tourists when they are plopped down in a foreign country without an interpreter; they quickly learn the language and customs of that country. Thus, Stuart is probably correct; his and Sharon's special relationship to the world of work did facilitate their setting up a semiegalitarian child-care arrangement which made them feel as if they were in a "quasi-heaven."

One conclusion that can be drawn from this is that until we restructure our economy to allow for more flex-time and part-time work, we can expect that the traditional division of labor in the home will continue to be the norm (cf. Bernard, 1975, among others). But before we jump to the conclusion that flexible hours are the cure-all for sex-stereotyped family systems, we should remember that it was not the inflexibility of their hours that kept Sharon and Stuart from achieving a true egalitarian arrangement, but their different attitudes toward their jobs. Stuart's faculty position may not have "blocked" him in the sense that he had to be at the office eight hours a day, forty hours a week. But it did "trap" him in the sense that it followed him wherever he went; he was unable to separate his work life from his personal life. The character of his work certainly contributed to the "frustration" that he often felt when he was home with the baby but wanted to be at his desk writing. The chief reason, however, that his job continued to force itself into his consciousness was his *supercommitment* to his work.

In a complex society like the United States, there is a tendency for people to become super or overcommitted to certain things; these things (essentially activities) become so important that they "begin to encroach on the time and energy being produced for one's under (or less) committed interests"

(Marks, 1977: 931). This is a fairly accurate assessment of what was happening to Stuart. Though both he and Sharon were committed to their work roles, Stuart, as we have mentioned repeatedly, was far more committed than Sharon was ("I don't think [Stuart] could survive psychologically without any professional identity"). Sharon said that she too once believed that she could work at home while she was caring for the children, but she soon came to the conclusion that such efforts were futile, and decided that the best thing to do was to give her job her full attention when she was at school and to give her children her full attention when she was at home. Stuart was unable to do this not because he disliked his children (he loved them dearly), but because of his supercommitment to his job; so important was it that it began to encroach on the time and energy "set aside" for other important (but not as important) activities (i.e., child care).

To blame Stuart for his intense commitment to his work would be, in our opinion, misdirected. Stuart is not alone. There are many men and women who are committed to their jobs the way that Stuart is committed to his. For the most part, these men and women are middle- and upper-class executives and professionals, people "on the way up." Some sociologists have suggested that these are the kinds of people who are likely to view their children as intruders (Rossi, 1968). The significance of this assertion should not be underestimated. Since our society is rapidly becoming more career oriented, there exists the possibility that there will be more and more children born to couples who find it difficult to "squeeze in" the time and energy for their kids.

Thus, to return to Stuart's hypothesis, Stuart is correct when he says that flex-time jobs facilitate an effective integration of work and family life, but he is incorrect when he assumes that being a young professional in today's society makes the transition to parenthood easier. Given existing social structural conditions, we would hypothesize that career-oriented individuals and couples will generally find having children more difficult to deal with than family-oriented individuals and couples (all other things being equal). If we continue on our present path—encouraging increased commitments to jobs but not setting up institutionalized supports to enable people to balance their work and family lives—the consequences for children and for parents could be extremely serious.

PART FIVE: THE GENERAL PICTURE

Chapter 9

THE TRANSITION TO PARENTHOOD
IN A COMPARATIVE PERSPECTIVE

Confronted with the reality of having to care for a helpless infant, how do parents interact, and what kinds of social organizations do they build? This is the basic question that we have been raising throughout the book, and we would like to deal with it explicitly one more time in this, the final chapter, to recapitulate some important themes and to tie up some loose ends.

The major points to be made are diagrammed in Figure 1. Beginning with the helplessness of the human infant (which varies as the infant matures), the figure pictures four causal propositions and four contingency propositions. Following diagramming conventions proposed by Burr et al. (1979b) and Reiss and Miller (1974), the causal propositions are represented by the chain of variables linked together by plus signs, while the contingency propositions are represented by the bisecting lines with circled notations. By "causal proposition" we mean that

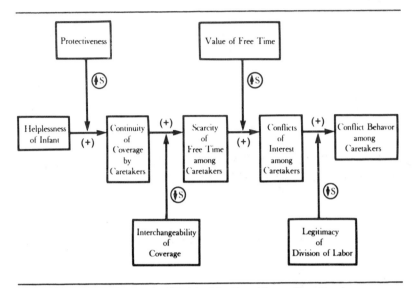

Figure 1. A Conflict Sociological Model of the Transition to Parenthood.

there exists a relationship between two variables such that one variable influences the other. Plus signs denote positive causal relationships; negative signs denote negative causal relationships. All causal relationships in Figure 1 are positive: an increase in one variable in the chain contributes to an increase in the next variable in the chain. By "contingency proposition" we mean that there exists a variable that specifies conditions under which a causal relationship is altered. The use of small arrows, facing either up or down, followed by the letter S, denotes the qualifying effect of the contingency variable: up arrow/S means that as the contingency variable increases, the causal relationship that it bisects becomes stronger; down arrow/S means that as the contingency variable decreases, the causal relationship that it bisects becomes stronger. For the sake of clarity, the two kinds of contingency variables are also denoted by whether they are above or below the causal chain.

The figure is titled "A Conflict Sociological Model of the Transition to Parenthood" because the conflict orientation serves as the overarching sociological framework in our analysis. As we review the relationships depicted in the diagram, it will become clear that the other two orientations used in the book—the choice and exchange orientation, and the symbolic interactionist orientation—are also important, but in this model they are secondary. We want to emphasize that this is *a* conflict sociological model, not *the* conflict sociological model. Other researchers focusing on other conflict-relevant variables could present other conflict models; and other researchers focusing on other conceptual orientations (e.g., using the symbolic interactionist orientation as an overarching framework) could present other sociological analyses. We also want to emphasize that Figure 1 is based on a theory generated by our data and is still in need of testing. Thus, while we depict each relationship in the model as linear and as equally important, if someone were to take the model and test it (via a survey, a simulation, etc.), that person would probably find that some of the relationships are curvilinear, and that some are more important than others. Finally, there are relationships that are not depicted in the model but do exist. For example, the linkage between conflict behavior and legitimacy is absent, despite the fact that the legitimacy of any division of labor is likely to have resulted from the negotiations among the participants in the system. Indeed, our data offer some graphic illustrations of this very fact. Because we wanted to limit our summary statement to a few important points, we have selected certain relationships in preference to others. The reader should assume that reciprocal associations and feedback loops are implied.

The basic pattern emerging from the interviews is represented by the causal propositions in the model. What we would like to do now is shift our attention to the variations in this pattern represented by the contingency propositions. Focusing, therefore, on the four contingency variables, we will now examine Figure 1.

PROTECTIVENESS

In Part Two, we discussed the difficulties of getting "down time" when one is the parent of a newborn. We noted that if an adult is left alone in the house with a baby, the adult cannot move to a tertiary level of activity (a down status) toward the baby, but must remain at either a primary level (up status) or secondary level (ready status). The case studies, however, show that the amount of time that parents devote to primary or secondary levels of activity when left alone with an infant varies. Some parents, for example, believe that the baby should almost always decide if and when a shift from secondary to primary status is to occur, while other parents choose to retain more personal control over these shifts and will often deny their children's requests for primary attention (e.g., "Not now, I'm busy"). Carol and Chester and Ted and Thelma, respectively, illustrate these two parental styles.

The point being made is this: not all parents act toward their dependent infants in the same way; some are, as they say, more "protective" than others. Protectiveness is a continuous variable that theoretically extends from complete protectiveness (total subordination of self to the perceived needs of the child) to complete disregard (total lack of interest in the child). The fact that protectiveness qualifies the impact that a dependent infant will have on an adult forces us to recognize that the statement, "An adult left alone in the house with a baby cannot move to a tertiary status," is a value judgment. Implicit in the statement is the assumption that moving to a tertiary status without transferring custody of the child to someone else (e.g., leaving the house without arranging for a babysitter) is morally wrong. While it is true that in contemporary society, such an act might not only be morally wrong but, under some circumstances, illegal (e.g., if while the adult is gone, the house should catch fire, the adult could be charged with criminal negligence), there have been periods in history when less regard for infants was more acceptable. For example, infanticide, a common practice in earlier times, is the most extreme form of disregard for infants. Less extreme, but still reflecting a relatively low regard, is the custom, also popular at one time, of swaddling babies (wrapping them in bands of clothes to restrain them) and hanging them on tree limbs, often for the whole day, while the parents work nearby.

The issue of protectiveness brings to the fore a point made in the beginning of Chapter 3. We noted then that the helplessness of the human infant places a family that is in the midst of a transition to parenthood within the class of social arrangements that have "coverage" as their primary function. A medical hospital in the United States, for example, is a continuous-coverage system (Zerubavel, 1979b). As with parenthood, there must always be someone (and usually a team of people) who is at a secondary status vis-à-vis the patients. Even when the patients are sleeping, it is required that someone remain available, or ready, to give primary attention, should a request for help be made. But as with parenthood, the continuous-coverage rule in a hospital implies a value judgment. Contrary to American customs, there are hospitals in some parts of the world where medical coverage is not continuous, where coverage is simply not provided "during a long, middle-of-the-day break when doctors are out for lunch" (Zerubavel, 1979b: 41). Similarly, other so-called continuous-coverage social systems, upon examination, prove to operate at various levels of protectiveness which qualify the amount of coverage given to "clients," "cases," etc. Strikes by police and fire departments often have meant increased threats to life and limb, and they are examples of less protective attitudes toward the incessant demands of a city for protection. So also is the policy of most beaches to provide lifeguards only during daylight hours. In sum, the unrelenting demands of anyone, be it infant or victim, do not necessarily result in an immediate response by others, do not necessarily mean that coverage will be continuous. If and when a response will be forthcoming is a function of the variable stance of the community toward the request, a function of the level of protectiveness and, implicitly, the level of commitment that is normatively prescribed.

INTERCHANGEABILITY

No less important than the issue of protectiveness in continuous-coverage systems is the structure of the division of labor. Assuming a decision has been made to provide continuous coverage for an infant (or a patient, a precinct, a beach), the critical question then is, *Who* will provide that coverage? In hospitals (and, in fact, in most coverage systems), "A major solution to the problem of maintaining continuous coverage is the impersonalization of coverage through the institutionalization of functionally equivalent—and, thus, interchangeable—categories of social actors" (Zerubavel, 1979b: 43). For example, when patients are assured by a nurse that should they call, the nurse will be "right outside," it is assumed that the person who offered the assurance is not necessarily the one who will respond to the call. Rather, what is meant is that someone who legitimately occupies the position of nurse will respond. In contrast to the medical hospital, which essentially "runs" like a machine with interchangeable "parts," most parental systems rely on particular people, and sometimes on one particular person, to provide continuous coverage. For example, Alex and Amanda's parental system relied almost exclusively on two people: Amanda and Amanda's mother. And Sharon and Stuart's parental system for their infant consisted only of Sharon and Stuart. Thus, both couples, for various reasons, refused to institute or use an impersonal coverage arrangement; both shied away from day-care for their newborns (though in Sharon and Stuart's case, they were willing to use more impersonal arrangements, once the children were more than six months old, and after intensive personal care made their children "better able to face the world").

As with protectiveness, the interchangeability or impersonalization of coverage for infants is a variable, the extremes of which are total interchangeability and total personalization, with reality for any given couple somewhere in between. Also, as with protectiveness, the estimation of what is the "best" position on the continuum for the infant and/or the parent is a value judgment. Although in the United States we tend to advocate personal coverage, there have been and are societies that stress interchangeability. In the militant societies of Sparta and early Rome, childrearing was exclusively in the hands of officials of the state and not the biological parents. In the Israeli kibbutz, communal childrearing is the rule (Blustein, 1979). Note that when we say the parental arrangement in these societies is relatively interchangeable, we do not mean that the children are not loved. Rather, we are simply referring to the interchangeability of the care. The kibbutz childrearing system, though more interchangeable than the American childrearing system, is hardly devoid of love; indeed, it is one of the most loving and caring systems in the world today. Some readers may still object, and contend that any childrearing system that divorces infants from their biological parents is a nonloving system; their assumption is that infants can only thrive or reach their full potential when cared for by their biological parents, and especially their biological mothers. There is, however, no conclusive evidence to suggest that an infant's biological parents are necessarily the best caretakers for that infant, or that ex officio parents cannot provide the love and nurturance that a baby needs to develop.

It is interesting that when the relative merits of various child-care arrangements on the interchangeability continuum are debated, almost always the question is, What kind of an effect does the arrangement have on the children? Few people seem concerned with the consequences for the parents. Yet the structure of the division of labor in a continuous-coverage child-care system has important, and sometimes devastating, consequences for the parents. All other things being equal, the less interchangeable the child-care coverage, the less free time for the caretakers, and the more likely they are to find themselves in a zero-sum gamelike situation whereby one person's "winning" (being free to pursue his or her own goals) means that the other must "lose" (forego his or her own goals for the sake of the infant). Indeed, if a couple insists that they alone can provide care for their child, then the only way that each of them can get "down time" is to "take it" from the other. They cannot move together to a tertiary status vis-à-vis their child, unless they disregard the needs of the child altogether and simply leave the baby alone, which would, of course, be in direct contradiction to the whole idea of giving the personal contact that they believe the baby needs.

Like protectiveness, interchangeability is instrumental to a sociology of the transition to parenthood, and may help to explain such things as why there is often a "honeymoon period" during the first few months after birth (Entwisle and Doering, 1980; Miller and Sollie, 1980). We would hypothesize that during the first year of the baby's life, interchangeability fluctuates; it starts relatively "high," then dips to "low," then moves toward "high" again. In the maternity ward, interchangeability is the norm. Though there are some hospitals that permit rooming in (letting the newborn stay with the mother), generally speaking, babies are handed off from parent to nurse to doctor, etc. When the baby comes home, interchangeability is still the norm. Because of the mother's "condition," she is likely to be catered to by her own mother or by a live-in nurse, or both. The father is also likely to take an active role at this point, not only to "help" his wife, but because the "novelty" of the baby (as Chester put it) makes caretaking fun. Within a few months, and perhaps weeks, however, "the honeymoon is over." Both Grandma and the nurse will probably have left. And as for Dad, even if he wants to take an active role, his boss is not likely to look too kindly on periodic absences or tardiness (which, of course, were permitted just after the birth). The mother, home alone either permanently (having quit her job) or temporarily (on maternity leave), is thus *the* caretaker for the baby during the day and probably during the night (Dad cannot get up for the 2 a.m. feeding because *he* has to work the next day). It is at this point that some full-time mothers begin to feel overwhelmed with the amount of work involved in caring for an infant. Carol gave the impression that this is what happened to her. Unlike some mothers who are trapped in this position, however, she was able to remedy the problem to some degree, though not completely, by encouraging Chester to take a more active role in baby care. We suspect that mothers who reach this point and want "out," but who do not have husbands who will share the load, if only periodically and under a "helping" context, begin to step up their efforts to locate reliable babysitters, and may, in fact, experience "burnout," taking their frustrations out on the baby (cf. Maslach and Pines, 1977; Maslach, 1976).

THE VALUE OF FREE TIME

A basic axiom in the conflict orientation is that "wherever valued resources are scarce (i.e., not sufficient to meet demand), conflict over the use of such resources is inevitable" (Duke, 1976: 84). The key word in the above axiom is *valued.* Scarcity of a phenomenon, in and of itself, does not lead to a conflict of interests. Rather, the phenomenon must be valued by the participants if they are to perceive themselves in competition for it (1976: 85). Following our discussion of interchangeability and the scarcity of time, we would then conclude that fathers and mothers who valued free time and who, as a result of their specific child-care arrangements, experienced a scarcity of free time would be more likely to perceive themselves in conflict with each other over that time.

Throughout the book, we have treated free time as a valued resource simply because the fathers and mothers in our sample valued free time. Some parents, of course, seemed to value free time more than others (e.g., Alex came across as a free time "addict"), but no parent in our sample indicated that he or she would not be bothered if his or her free time were cut drastically. In other words, on the value continuum from "no value" to "high value," all of our subjects were bunched at the "high" end.[1] This is not surprising. The United States is quickly becoming both a career-oriented and a leisure-oriented society, and the upper middle class (which our sample represents) is at the forefront of this movement. Free time—or, more accurately, "down time"—from children, means time to pursue a career and time to participate in the variety of leisure activities manu-factured in a postindustrial economy. We suspect that if our study had included lower-class couples, or if it had been con-ducted thirty years ago, we would have found less perceived conflict between husbands and wives over baby care.[2] We also suspect that if our study had been conducted in a culture in which time is conceptualized differently from the way we in the United States conceptualize time, we would have found differ-ent levels of husband-wife conflict. For example, whereas we tend to think of time as a "thing" that we can "spend," "lose," "give up," "gain," or "make," the St. Lawrence Island Eskimos think of time in more fluid terms. In their culture,

> neither the concept of "spending" as a process of transaction with an external agent nor the concept of "time" as a dissectible entity which can be used as the object of such a transaction has any validity. The cultural focus of daily activity is not on "time" as a hollow shell which is to be filled with completed tasks or accom-plished relaxation. Rather, the focus is on the *tasks* themselves which must be done [Hughes, 1961: 92; his italics].[3]

Actually, the existence of a culture like that of the St. Lawrence Island Eskimos raises an even more important point than simply noting that the value of free time varies from one place to another. Given the fact that the distinction which people make between work and leisure time is arbitrary, a function solely of the way they choose to cognitively organize the world, why is baby care so often viewed today as an activity that "cuts into" free time? Free time is actually nothing more than optional-use time, time when we are doing what we per-sonally want to do rather than what we are obliged to do (DeGrazia, 1964). Thus, to say that baby care infringes on free time is to suggest that baby care is sometimes seen as a chore rather than a joy. Of course, this is not news to any parent, nor is this the first time that we have raised the point. However, by explicitly recognizing that our definitions of work and leisure are culture bound, we are highlighting the sociological fact that the attitudes and actions of specific husbands and wives cannot be divorced from the sociohistorical conditions under which they live (Mills, 1959). To reiterate one of the principal messages of this book, one which is a truism in sociology but which is too often overlooked by the general public and by some people in the helping professions, the problems which many families experience during the transition to parenthood cannot be solved on a solely personal (one-to-one, or small-group) level, but must be understood as part and parcel of the larger institutional structures that constitute "our society." The answer to the question of why baby care is so often seen as an infringement on people's lives will, therefore, be found not in the experiences of any one parent or couple, but in the experiences of parents in general.

LEGITIMACY OF THE DIVISION OF LABOR

The mere existence of a conflict of interests between a husband and wife does not necessarily mean that the couple will engage in conflict behavior. A conflict of interest simply denotes a conflict in goals. Conflict behavior, on the other hand, refers to specific tactics or strategies (combinations of tactics) used to manage a conflict of interest (Straus, 1979), and includes such things as bargaining, debating, and influencing (powering).

It was apparent from the transcripts that couples could be virtually the same in the degree to which they perceived a conflict of interest, yet be different in their uses of conflict behavior. The variable that generally explained the difference was the legitimacy of the division of labor in the two families. By "legitimacy" we mean the extent to which a husband and wife believe that their system of baby-care coverage is valid, desirable, good, moral, etc. (cf. Weber, 1947). Legitimacy is a subjective variable extending from complete legitimacy (a totally valid arrangement) to complete illegitimacy (a totally invalid arrangement), and its importance in qualifying the effects of conflicting goals on conflict behavior is another basic axiom in the conflict orientation (see Duke, 1976). Thus, for example, families in which the wife had less free time than the husband, but in which her relatively deprived position was deemed *legitimate,* would be less likely to exhibit conflict behavior than families in which the wife had less free time, but in which her relatively deprived position was deemed *illegitimate.* Ted and Thelma and Carol and Chester, respectively, are examples of these two situations. Although both Thelma and Carol were full-time mothers, placed in positions where they were getting less free time than their spouses, only Carol seemed to object, and only Carol attempted to negotiate for a change in the child-care arrangement. Of course, the couple that exhibited the most conflict behavior was Alex and Amanda. As far as Amanda was concerned, Alex's refusal to take a more active part in child care was illegitimate, despite his protests to the contrary. Alex and Amanda also demonstrate another way that the legitimacy of an existing social order qualifies the effect of conflicting goals on conflict behavior. Generally speaking, the less legitimate a social arrangement, the more intense the conflict behavior; if you remember, during Alex and Amanda's second interview Amanda left the room in tears. Illegitimate social orders, if they persist, often escalate to violence or breakdown. In the case of marriage, this can mean anything from verbal abuse to murder, from pseudoconnectedness to divorce.

The more we read the interview transcripts, the more impressed we were with both the conflicting goals of husbands and wives and the amount of conflict behavior in marriage. Couples had set up child-care arrangements which created a scarcity of valued free time. More often than not, it was the wife who "came out on the short end of the stick"; more often than not, if someone had to sacrifice it was she, regardless of whether she was employed. But wives did not sit idly by and let themselves be exploited. On the contrary, they were sensitive to the division of baby care, and, though they did not push for equality of responsibility for the children, they did view marked imbalances as illegitimate and worthy of note.

The picture would have been different if we had conducted our study thirty years ago. Undoubtedly, one of the most dramatic changes that has occurred in this century, and especially in the past thirty years, has to do with the attitudes of women toward what are and what are not legitimate ways of life for them. Although these changes in attitudes have not had as strong an effect on gender roles as some people would like, men can no longer assume that traditional social orders will go unchallenged, and they have learned that they must be ready to defend their unwillingness to participate in child care. Unfortunately for those people who would like to see some genuine changes in the division of labor in this country, our data suggest that women as well as men are quite skilled at wittingly and unwittingly negotiating themselves into sex-stereotyped divisions of labor. For many, the head seems willing but the heart is weak.

CONCLUSION

Our objective in this book has been to present a sociological view of the transition to parenthood. We believe that the transition to parenthood offers the student of social life a unique opportunity to see in action what Mills (1959) meant by "the sociological imagination." Few family experiences provide so vivid a picture of how biography and history are dialectically related. Few family experiences are so close to the cornerstone of a society. We hope that this exploratory study will whet the appetites of other researchers enough to encourage them to embark on studies of their own. There is still much work to be done.

Some readers may feel that we have dehumanized "a blessed event" by subjecting the experience of having a baby to so much scrutiny. Sociology does indeed have a way of demystifying social life (Berger, 1963). But it is not alone in this respect; science in general tends to show that life is not always what it seems. Our bodies, as viewed through an X-ray machine, for example, hardly conform to conventional notions of beauty. But the reality of science is accepted because it is assumed that scientific knowledge is ultimately beneficial. We think that the same is true for sociological knowledge. The picture of parenthood that we have presented may not be as "beautiful" as some people would like. Nonetheless, we think that it will be ultimately beneficial. By laying bare some of the social patterns, social processes, and sociohistorical linkages underlying conflict and sexism during the transition to parenthood, we have at least provided a clue into how we might go about improving the social world of fathers and mothers.

NOTES

1. The value of free time should not be assumed. Some retirees, for example, feel that free time is burdensome. And in some offices, having free time is a sign of low status; what is often negotiated is the opportunity to work.

2. Thus, the value of free time is a function of what can be done with that time.

3. We are indebted to Marks (1977) for introducing us to Hughes (1961).

APPENDIX A
ANNOTATED BIBLIOGRAPHY

Since one purpose of this book is to encourage research on the transition to parenthood, we have provided the reader with an annotated bibliography of the major studies on the topic. The bibliography is, for the most part, an edited verbatim record of relevant books, articles, and chapters, presented in chronological order. The following criteria for inclusion in the bibliography were used: (1) A study had to focus explicitly on the transition to parenthood; studies of pregnancy (e.g., LaRossa, 1977) and studies which simply compared couples with and without children (e.g., Hoffman and Manis, 1978) did not qualify. (2) A study had to be empirical, not theoretical; literature reviews (e.g., Rossi, 1968) were also not included. (3) A study had to focus on the family or husband-wife relationship; studies of the psychology of women or men were not summarized (which explains why Senn and Hartford, 1968, is not here). (4) A study had to have been published or accepted for publication (an arbitrary cutting point used to keep the bibliography within manageable size).

AUTHORS' NOTE: Portions of the following works have been reprinted in this Appendix by permission of their publishers and authors: COWAN, C. P., P. A. COWAN, L. COIE, and J. D. COIE (1978) "Becoming a family: the impact of a first child's birth on the couple's relationship." Pp. 296-324 in W. B. Miller and L. F. Newman (eds.) The First Child and Family Formation. Chapel Hill: Carolina Population Center, University of North Carolina; ENTWISLE, D. R. and S. G. DOERING (1980) The First Birth. Baltimore, MD: The Johns Hopkins University Press; RUSSELL, C. S. (1974) "Transition to parenthood: problems and gratifications." Journal of Marriage and the Family 36 (May): 294-302. Copyrighted 1974 by the National Council on Family Relations. Reprinted by permission.

LeMASTERS (1957)

Research Design

Unstructured joint interviews with a nonprobability sample of 46 urban, middle-class white couples whose first child had been born within the previous 5 years. Crisis scores arrived at by agreement between interviewer and couple. A five-point scale was used: (1) no crisis, (2) slight crisis, (3) moderate crisis, (4) extensive crisis, (5) severe crisis.

Major Findings

Eight-three percent of the couples experienced "extensive" or "severe" crisis in adjusting to the first child. Mothers in these categories cited the following feelings: loss of sleep, chronic tiredness, confinement to home, curtailment of social contact, loss of job, additional housework, guilt over parenting abilities, long hours, decline in housekeeping standards, worry over appearance. Fathers cited the above things, plus: decline in sexual response of wife, economic pressure, worry about second pregnancy, general disenchantment with parental role.

DYER (1963)

Research Design

Likert-type crisis scale administered to a nonprobability sample of 32 urban, middle-class white couples whose first child had been born within the previous 2 years. Crisis score for each couple was the average of the summed items scored for both fathers and mothers. A five-point scale was used (see LeMasters, 1957).

Major Findings

Fifty-three percent of the couples experienced "extensive" or "severe" crisis in adjusting to the first child. Eighty-seven percent of the mothers admitted to one or more "severe problems," including: adjusting to being tied down, getting accustomed to being up at all hours, inability to keep up with the housework, the feeling of anticlimax or letdown. Eighty percent of the fathers admitted to one or more "severe problems," including: adjusting to one income after wife quit job, adjusting to new demands of parenthood, getting used to the new routines, sharing with grandparents and other relatives.

HOBBS (1965)

Research Design

Twenty-three-item checklist was administered to a random sample of urban, lower- and middle-class white couples whose first child had been born within the previous 3-18 weeks. Crisis scores of fathers and mothers were separately analyzed. A five-point scale was used (see LeMasters, 1957).

Major Findings

None of the couples experienced "extensive" or "severe" crisis. The majority (86.8%) experienced "slight" crisis. Mothers' mean crisis score was significantly higher than fathers' mean crisis score. Mothers cited the following as "most bothersome": interruption of routine habits, tiredness and fatigue, increased money problems, feeling emotionally upset. Fathers cited the following as "most bothersome": interruption of routine habits, increased money problems. Correlates of crisis (Fathers): family income (-), baby's age (+). 70% of the mothers and 91% of the fathers indicated that their marriages were more happy and satisfying than before the birth of the baby. Only 2% of the mothers and none of the fathers indicated that their marriages were less satisfying than before the baby was born.

MEYEROWITZ AND FELDMAN (1966)

Research Design

Four hundred primiparous couples from several different geographic areas in the United States were interviewed at three time periods: during the fifth month of their first pregnancy, five weeks after delivery, and five months after delivery. One hundred matching control couples, half nulliparous and half multiparous, were interviewed in a similar manner.

Major Findings

Respondents agreed strongly that having a baby improved the marital relationship, but in response to specific questioning they agreed at a lower qualitative level with statements such as "Our baby's needs conflict with our own desires." Stress between the second and third interview suggested by the mean percentage of times that "things are going well" (85% to 65%). With the arrival of the child, frequency of disagreement over child rearing decreases. However, sexual incompatability, inability to express feelings to spouse, unshared liesure time, inability to discuss husband's work all increased as sources of complaint. The area of sexual adjustment was the leading specific cause of complaint between spouses. Wives reported significantly more dissatisfaction with the physical relationship and saw the husband as being decisive in determining the frequency of intercourse. At the third interview, a decline was reported in the amount of time that husband and wife spent talking to each other on the average day. By this time, there was also a shift toward a more patriarchal power structure with all decision-making, with the exception of the choice of food, being reportedly held by the husband.

HOBBS (1968)

Research Design

Twenty-three-item checklist and focused interview administered to a random sample of 27 urban lower- and middle-class white couples whose first child had been born within the previous 6-52 weeks. Crisis scores of fathers and mothers were separately analyzed. Interviews were tape recorded and coded by a panel of judges. A five-point scale was used (see LeMasters, 1957).

Major Findings

None of the couples reported "extensive" or "severe" crisis on the checklist. The majority of mothers and fathers experienced a "slight" crisis (74.1% and 85.2% respectively). Although the interview method yielded higher crisis scores, few mothers and fathers were coded as having experienced "severe" crisis (18.5% and 3.7% respectively; "extensive" was not a category in the interviewers' code). Mothers' mean crisis score was significantly higher than fathers' mean crisis score. Correlates of crisis (checklist): marital adjustment (−).

RAUSH ET AL. (1970)

Research Design

Individual and joint semistructured interviews with 21 suburban, middle-class white couples at three time periods: four months after marriage, the seventh month of the first pregnancy, and the fourth month after childbirth. Coders tallied frequencies of "I" and "We" type pronouns from typewritten transcripts for each couple for seven areas of discussion: housekeeping, food, budget, parental functioning, sex, relatives, and friends. The couple was the unit of analysis.

Major Findings

There was an increased use of "I" words as marriages progressed from newlywed stage to parenthood stage. The major change occurred primarily after the child was born. Topics which became more "I" oriented: sex, parental functioning, budget, relatives. Topics which became more "We" oriented: friends. The I-We dimension can be conceptualized in terms of a range from task to relationship orientation. Thus, it can be said that across the three stages the relationship/intrinsic aspects of marriage become less salient while the task/utilitarian aspects become more salient. Causal relationship unknown; does orientation predispose couples toward parenthood, or does parenthood initiate a shift in orientation?

RYDER (1973)

Research Design

One hundred twelve urban, predominantly middle-class white couples were interviewed at two time periods: in approximately the third or fourth month of marriage, and then one or two years later (inspection of data indicated little difference between the one- and the two-year follow-up cases). Three groups were defined: (1) childless couples who did not yet at posttest have a first child; (2) child couples who (a) had had their first child as of posttest and (b) were not yet knowingly pregnant at pretest; and (3) pregnant cases, in which the wife was pregnant as of pretest (and which of course had had a child when retested). Two dependent variables were measured for each spouse, one being a general score based on traditional "marital dissatisfaction" questionnaire items, the other a scale which reflected whether or not the respondent felt his or her spouse paid enough attention or was adequately loving; the latter scale was referred to as "lovesickness."

Major Findings

Wives who have a child are more likely to report that their husbands are not paying enough attention to them. The same kind of generalization is not supported in such a solid way for the less specific variable, marital dissatisfaction. There is no evidence that spouses who start off with high scores have a different baby-related change than spouses who start off with low scores. The author cautions that the differences found do not demonstrate that having a child causes some particular result. It is logically possible that only correlates, and not consequences, of having a child have been demonstrated.

FELDMAN (1974)

Research Design

See Meyerowitz and Feldman (1966) for research design.

Major Findings

There was a significant decline in marital satisfaction after birth. Some couples did, however, increase in satisfaction, and it was decided to explore the reasons for improvement. Couples with a more differentiated rather than a more companionate marriage were significantly more likely to experience increased marital satisfaction after birth. The transition to second-time parenthood resulted in greater negative effects than the initial transition to parenthood. The child effects found for both primipara and multipara were: lowered satisfaction in marriage, perceived negative personality changes in both partners, less satisfaction with home, more instrumental conversation, more child-centered concern and more warmth toward the child, and a lowering of sexual satisfaction after birth. Some of the findings reported in Meyerowitz and Feldman (1966) were reiterated. However, in the earlier paper the claim is made that Hobbs's (1965) findings have been confirmed, whereas in this paper the findings by LeMasters (1957) are said to be substantiated.

RAUSH ET AL. (1974)

Research Design

Thirteen suburban, middle-class white couples were observed during a quasi-role playing "conflict of interest" procedure (called Improvisations) conducted in a "laboratory" setting at three time periods: four months after marriage, the seventh month of the first pregnancy, and the fourth month after birth. Verbal transcripts of interactions during the procedure were analyzed using a 36-item coding scheme developed specifically for the project.

Major Findings

The major shift between the pregnancy and postnatal sessions was that husbands became far less conciliatory to their wives during those Improvisations in which the wives were playing the "distancing" (noninvolved) role. Both mothers and fathers increased the proportion of cognitive acts (neutral acts, suggestions, and rational arguments) over the previous stage. Fewer rejecting responses (acts showing a "cold" or "nasty" rejection of the other's argument or person) were also used by the couples. These changes between pregnancy and postnatal periods continued the trends noted between newlywed and pregnancy stages. Smaller and less systematic changes included an increase in coercive tactics (power plays, guilt induction, disparagement), with the mothers increasing more, and a decrease in the use of appeals (acts appealing to the others to grant one's wish), with the mothers decreasing more, during those Improvisations which generated efforts to negotiate "closeness." Thus, with time there was a tendency to use stronger methods to bring a partner into line. There is no evidence to confirm suggestions that the transition to parenthood is experienced as a crisis. If anything, the authors assert, parenthood for this sample of couples was a growth-producing experience.

RUSSELL (1974)

Research Design

Hobbs's (1965) 23 item checklist was administered to a random sample of 271 urban lower and middle class white couples whose first child had been born within the previous 6-56 weeks. Crisis scores of fathers and mothers were separately analyzed. A five point scale was used (see LeMasters, 1957). A 12 item gratification checklist "fashioned after" the crisis checklist was also administered. A follow-up of nonrespondents showed that couples who did not return a questionnaire tended to be both younger and less educated than respondents and were more likely to be premaritally pregnant.

Major Findings

3.1% of the mothers and 4.8% of the fathers experienced "extensive" or "severe" crisis. The majority of the mothers and fathers experienced a "slight" crisis (57.5% and 75.1% respectively). Mothers' mean crisis score was significantly higher than fathers' mean crisis score. Mothers most frequently checked the following as "bothering them": worry about personal appearance, physical tiredness and fatigue, baby interrupted sleeping and rest, worry about loss of figure, feeling edgy or emotionally upset. Fathers most frequently checked the following as "bothering them": baby interrupted sleeping and rest, suggestions from in-laws, increased money problems, changes of plans, additional amount of work. Correlates of crisis (Mothers): months married (−), marital adjustment (−), health (−), ease of pregnancy (−), ease of delivery (−), "quiet" baby (−). Correlates of crisis (Fathers): marital adjustment (−), wanting more children (−), wife's ease of delivery (−), age (−), occupational prestige (−), saliency of father role (−), "quiet" baby (−). While the respondents checked a far higher proportion of "gratification" items than "crisis" items, the gratifications they checked were more likely to be personal ones rather than benefits to the husband-wife relationship or to relationships outside the marriage. Most report that their marriage relationship has either improved since birth (about 42%) or has stayed about the same (about 43.5%). Only 7.5% of the women and 5.5% of the men felt their marital relationship had deteriorated since the baby's birth.

HOBBS AND COLE (1976)

Research Design

Twenty-three-item checklist was administered to a random sample of lower and middle-class white couples whose first child had been born within the previous 3-6 months. Crisis scores for fathers and mothers were separately analyzed. A five-point scale was used (see LeMasters, 1957).

Major Findings

Of the couples, 2.3 percent experienced "extensive" or "severe" crisis. The majority of the couples experienced a "slight" crisis (68.4%). Mothers' mean crisis score was significantly higher than fathers' mean score. Correlates of crisis (Fathers): age (+), parents' income (−). Thirty-nine percent of the mothers and 45% of the fathers indicated that their marriages were more happy and satisfying than before the birth of the baby. Only 2% of the mothers and none of the fathers indicated that their marriages were less satisfying than before the baby was born.

HOBBS AND WIMBISH (1977)

Research Design

Twenty-three-item checklist was administered to a nonprobability sample of 38 urban, lower- and middle-class black couples whose first child had been born within the previous 5-52 weeks. Crisis scores of fathers and mothers were separately analyzed. A five-point scale was used (see LeMasters, 1957).

Major Findings

None of the couples experienced "extensive" or "severe" crisis. The majority of the couples experienced a "slight" crisis (78.9%). Mothers' mean crisis score was significantly higher than fathers' mean crisis score. Mothers cited the following as the five "most bothersome" items: interruption of routine habits of sleeping, going places, etc., worry about loss of figure, worry about personal appearance in general, physical tiredness and fatigue. Fathers cited the following as the five "most bothersome" items: interruption of routine habits of sleeping, going places, etc., having to change plans we had before baby's birth, decreased sexual responsiveness of spouse, increased money problems. Correlates of crisis (Fathers): education (−), age (−). Eighty-two percent of the mothers and 74% of the fathers indicated that their marriages were more happy and satisfying than before the birth of the baby. Only 5% of the mothers and 2% of the fathers indicated that their marriages were less satisfying than before the baby was born.

COWAN ET AL. (1978)

Research Design

A quota sample of 8 urban predominantly middle class couples (2 black, 6 white) participated in ongoing groups of 4 expectant couples and one leader/facilitator couple. Groups began in the third trimester of pregnancy (6-8 months), continued on a weekly basis until the babies were approximately 4 months old, and focused on the couple relationship. Periodically throughout the data collection, a battery of social psychological instruments (e.g., self image scales, arrangement of roles questionnaires) were filled out and discussed by the group participants. To assess the effect of the group sessions on the transition, comparison couples also completed the battery of instruments and were interviewed twice—during late pregnancy and 6 months postpartum.

Major Findings

Group experience provided couples with support, information, and examples/models/alternatives for being parents and partners. Group couples appeared to describe more change in each dimension of couple relationships assessed. In the first 6 months after birth, all couples indicated a shift toward a more traditional division of roles which was most marked in the household tasks, next in family decision-making, and least in baby care activities. Role overload was acute for some couples: the couple spending the highest number of weekly hours on home and baby care seemed to be experiencing the most distress at the 6 month follow-up. Women perceived more changes in time allocation than men did. Discrepancy between partners' perceptions of role arrangements increased; both mothers and fathers perceived that their respective share of baby care tasks was greater than their partner perceived it to be. Conflict over the use of time alone and as a couple, and the division of labor were the most salient areas of conflict or disagreement for the most couples at the 6 month follow-up. The majority of the couples stated that their sexual relationships often felt precarious during late pregnancy and the early months after birth; in most cases couples experienced this change as discouraging but understandable. All couples reported some new feelings of closeness which they attributed to being partners who were now parents and to their baby's growing responsiveness. Some felt that discussing the project materials together led to new closeness as a couple.

JAFFE AND VIERTEL (1979)

Research Design

An unspecified number of urban lower- and middle-class couples, each of whom had taken some part of a LaMaze prepared childbirth course, were interviewed slightly before their first baby's due date and then again at one month, three months, six months, nine months, and one year after birth. All of the interviews were open-ended, free-flowing conversations in which the parents were encouraged to talk about anything that interested them. Six couples were chosen for case-study presentation.

Major Findings

The transition to parenthood is not a homogenous experience. The only general theme, according to the authors, is this: the struggle to become parents is a struggle to become grown. Although growing is a lifelong process, the particular growth spurt associated with the first year of parenting is probably the most intense, compact, and pressurized period of growth in a young adult life. Case studies raised a variety of questions (hypotheses) which could and should be tested by other researchers.

ENTWISLE AND DOERING (1980)

Research Design

Structured interviews with a nonprobability sample of 120 lower and middle-class white women and a subsample of their husbands (60) representing different levels of childbirth preparation. The women were interviewed face-to-face when they were 6-7 months pregnant, again in their 9th month, and then about 3 weeks after birth of their first child. There was also a telephone interview conducted with the mothers when babies were about 6 months old. The men were interviewed twice, at approximately the times of the second and third women's interviews. Variety of standardized measures employed.

Major Findings

Transition to parenthood constitutes a critical period in the evolution of a family. Period immediately preceding birth and the first few weeks postpartum are particularly stressful. Sobering lack of anticipatory socialization for the parent role; it took time for most new parents to relate to their baby in positive terms. The "postpartum honeymoon" may signify stress so intense that most couples do not face it, and thus the honeymoon may actually prolong the crisis. Women's birth preparation (e.g., LaMaze or other formal instruction) and husband's presence at birth favorably impacted on reaction to birth experience. Average behavior of parents was approximately the same by social class. (Some of this equivalence, the authors note, is probably forced by selecting people of similar preparation levels in each class.) Lower-class fathers were present as often in delivery as middle-class fathers. Just as many lower-class women undertook breast-feeding as middle-class women. On all indications of parental responsiveness, the two classes were equivalent. Lower class fathers were as active in caretaking and as emotionally involved with their infants as middle-class fathers. On the other hand, in every instance where models were estimated separately for parents of the two classes (feeding models, mothering models, fathering models), the differences in structure by class were impressive. For middle-class families, preparation and previous experience has positive effects on parenting, and the baby does not appear to be viewed as the "mother's property." For the lower-class families, the influence of mothering on fathering, together with the negative effects of fathers' previous baby care experience on fathering, strongly suggest that baby care is controlled by the mother. Irrespective of class the young men expressed opinions consistent with an active father role. The lion's share of infant care was, however, assumed by all mothers. Couples moved toward a traditional role structure in spite of their egalitarian attitudes, and in fact acted in ways to decrease the pressure of egalitarian beliefs on themselves (e.g., women's work roles were devalued by both husbands and wives). By the sixth month phone interview, 7% of the mothers were back at work full time, 19% were back part time, and 8% had tried to work and had quit; 66% of the mothers thus had remained at home full-time. Mothers had more difficulty than fathers with role integration. This was especially true for employed mothers who still were predominantly responsible for child care. Marital sex was interrupted by the transition; most of the couples (92%) did, however, resume intercourse by the 9th week post-partum (intercourse rate not reported).

MILLER AND SOLLIE (1980)

Research Design

A volunteer sample of 109 predominately middle-class couples recruited from one of three different hospital-based parenthood preparation classes completed questionnaires at three different points in time: First, when the wife was in midpregnancy; second, when the baby was about five to six weeks old; and finally, when the baby was between six and eight months old. Structured measures of personal well-being, personal stress, and marital stress (along with other measures not included in this article) were repeatedly administered.

Major Findings

Personal well-being scores of new mothers were significantly lower at time 3 than at time 2, and personal well-being scores for fathers were significantly lower at time 3 than during time 1 or time 2. Both new mothers and fathers reported significantly higher scores on personal stress items after they had become parents. Wives' personal scores at time 1 were lower than husbands' scores, but new mothers ended up with higher personal stress scores than their husbands. The most interesting sex difference in the changes was evident in the marital stress scale. New mothers reported higher stress in their marriages after the baby had been born than before, and even higher marital stress by the time the baby was eight months old. New fathers' marital stress scores, by contrast, remained essentially the same across the year of the study. Authors contend that their data coincide with Ryder's (1973) finding that new mothers were more likely than fathers to report that their spouses were not paying enough attention to them. The fact that the majority (seven of nine) of the significant differences were between one month and eight months postpartum provides some support for the notion of a "baby honeymoon" in the early postpartum period.

SOLLIE AND MILLER (1980)

Research Design

See Miller and Sollie (1980) for research design. The difference is that in this paper the couples' qualitative responses to open-ended questions were tabulated. Parents were asked to write both positive and negative comments about what their babies had meant to their lives.

Major Findings

The four most apparent positive themes expressed by the couples were emotional benefits, self-enrichment and development, family cohesiveness, and identification with the child. The four most common negative experiences were physical demands, strains on the husband-wife relationship, emotional costs, and opportunity costs and restrictions.

APPENDIX B
DESCRIPTION OF SAMPLE

TABLE B-1   Intentions Toward Conception

Categories	First-Child Couples	Second-Child Couples First	Second
"Planned" pregnancy	7	7	6
Advised off preferred contraceptive, couple "chooses" to conceive	1	0	0
Advised off preferred contraceptive, or birth control failure, couple "unintentionally" conceives	0	0	2
"Unplanned" pregnancy	2	2	2
No information		1	

TABLE B-2   Length of Time Married at Birth

First Child Couples	Second-Child Couples First	Second
1	½	2
3	1	6
5	1	3
6	3	4
7	4	5
7	4	7
7	5	6
7	5	9
7	5	14
8	6	10
MEANS = 6	3	7

TABLE B-3　　Age at Birth

| First-Child Couples | | Second-Child Couples | | | |
| Husband | Wife | Husband | Wife | Husband | Wife |
		First		Second	
23	27	24	24	26	25
28	27	25	25	27	26
29	30	26	19	32	25
29	27	27	26	37	36
30	30	29	26	31	28
30	29	29	26	33	30
31	28	29	24	33	28
31	30	30	27	33	30
32	26	36	31	38	33
37	32	39	28	41	31
MEANS = 30	29	30	26	33	29

NOTE: Tables B-3, B-4, B-5, and B-6 are arranged in ascending order according to the husbands' ages, educations, incomes, and occupations, respectively.

TABLE B-4　　Education at Birth

| First-Child Couples | | Second-Child Couples | |
Husband	Wife	Husband	Wife
HS	PC	PC	HS
PC	PC	PC	PC
PC	GM	PC	PC
PG	PC	CG	PC
PG	CG	CG	PC
GM	CG	CG	PC
GM	GM	CG	CG
GD	CG	GD	PC
GD	CG	GD	GM
GD	GM	GD	GM

HS　　High School Graduate
PC　　Partial College
CG　　College Graduate
PG　　Partial Graduate School
GM　　Graduate Degree (Master's)
GD　　Graduate Degree (Ph.D., Ed.D., J.D.)

TABLE B-5   Income for Year Preceding Birth

| First-Child Couples | | Second-Child Couples | |
Husband	Wife	Husband	Wife
3,000	9,000	9,000	3,000
9,000	7,000	15,000	7,000
9,000	11,000	18,000	0
13,000	9,000	18,000	11,000
15,000	15,000	22,500	0
18,000	11,000	22,500	0
18,000	11,000	22,500	0
18,000	13,000	32,500	0
32,500	15,000	32,500	0
32,500	32,500	40,000	0
MEANS = 16,800	13,350	23,250	2,100

TABLE B-6   Occupation at Birth

| First-Child Couples | | Second-Child Couples | |
Husband	Wife	Husband	Wife
CRFT	HOME	SERV	SERV*
CRFT	HOME	CLSA	HOME
MNGR	HOME	CLSA	HOME
MNGR	PROF**	CLSA	HOME
PROF	MNGR*	MNGR	MNGR*
PROF	HOME	MNGR	HOME
PROF	PROF**	PROF	PROF**
PROF	PROF*	PROF	HOME
PROF	PROF*	PROF	HOME
PROF	HOME	PROF	HOME

CLSA	Clerical and Sales Workers
CRFT	Craftpersons
HOME	Homemakers
MNGR	Managers
PROF	Professionals
SERV	Service Workers
*	Returned to work part-time after birth
**	Returned to work full-time after birth

TABLE B-7   Sex of Children

| First-Child Couples | Second-Child Couples | |
	First Child	Second Child
Boy	Boy	Boy
Boy	Boy	Boy
Boy	Boy	Boy
Boy	Boy	Boy
Boy	Boy	Boy
Girl	Boy	Girl
Girl	Girl	Boy
Girl	Girl	Boy
Girl	Girl	Boy
Girl	Girl	Girl

APPENDIX C
INSTRUCTIONS TO INTERVIEWER

Reproduced below are portions of the "methodological memos" given to the interviewer before the third-, sixth-, and ninth-month interviews. They do not represent all staff communications during the data-collection phase, because most communications were verbal and were not taped. However, they do give a fairly accurate picture of our research agenda.

THE FIRST INTERVIEW

The purpose of the first interview is to: (a) establish rapport with the couples; (b) introduce the study (go over again how many interviews there will be, etc.); (c) get a sense of how the couple came to have a first child (in other words, what was their decision-making process); (d) talk a little about the pregnancy, what were their experiences, what kind of birth did they have (e.g., LaMaze); (e) ask them to compare their expectations during the pregnancy with the "reality" of parenthood; (f) changes—in self, in relationship with each other, in relationship with first child (if second-child couple), in relationships with parents, in relationships with friends.

None of these issues which you will attempt to bring up during the first interview will be "solved" after an hour and a half or so with the couple. Rapport will have to be renegotiated at each interview (and when you bring up sensitive questions, during the interview itself). No matter how well you introduce the study the first time, there will always be something left unsaid—partly because they will not "hear" you the first time, partly because the character of the study will change as it progresses. Their decision to have a child may take on new meaning to them as the parental role develops. For example, during the first interview they may say simply "it was planned"; in a subsequent interview they may say something else: "He made me do it." Their experiences during the pregnancy will also take on different meanings—biography reconstruction is a tricky phenomenon. Before and after comparisons (before birth, after birth) are, of course, retrospective and not a "true" experimental design. What's important, however, is how they perceive their situation. The change question (f above) is one that you should ask in each interview session. They may not understand the question, or prefer to state it in different terms ("Do you want to know if I love him/her more?"). That's fine. Let them lead you. . . .

The key to this type of study is to listen. At first, you will feel that you are getting data on anything and everything. Few things may seem relevant. It will be difficult for you to decide when to let the couples ramble and when to change the subject. However, by letting the couples lead you through their lives, we'll be able to get *their* story, not some story we've dreamed up. It is a precarious thing—the deductive/inductive process. For the most part, and as much as we can, we shall proceed in a quasi-inductive mode. Our value judgments will be minimal. We shall try not to give the impression to the couples that they are being judged. If they ask for your opinion, attempt to parry their request. Do not tell them what you would have done in their situation. This is not therapy, it is research. Look upon their family system as you would look at any social system—a complex of interrelated parts that is difficult to comprehend. Comprehension is our goal, and it will take all of our energies (as you know, depth interviews demand a great deal of concentration) to get just that. . . .

The key in depth interviewing is to phrase the questions and the whole study in a frame that "works" for the couple. In the end, although you may not have asked each couple the same question in the same way (in other words, your measurement is not phenomenally equivalent), you will still have gotten essentially the same information from each (in other words, your measurement is conceptually equivalent). . . .

Finally, remember this: the initial questions that you pose to introduce an issue will not be as important as the probes that you follow with. Your comments are merely stimuli for the couples to get going on what they think. A well-placed "What makes you say that?" or "How do you feel about what your wife just said?" can be priceless. Another point: do not assume that one spouse speaks for both. If necessary, ask each how he or she feels; give each a chance to speak. Be sensitive to nonverbal cues.

In your post-interview comments after the first interview, draw a diagram of the room in which the interview was held. (I, by the way, found it comfortable to have the couple sit on a couch, put the tape recorder on a coffee table, and sit on a chair facing the couple. Make sure you and the couple are not more than three or four feet away from the machine.

THE SECOND INTERVIEW

Listening to a number of the tapes, and reading the two that have been transcribed as of now (couples 4 and 5), I am struck by the importance of the variable *time*. A few of the couples express this variable in terms of their having less time to do what they want to do now that the baby has arrived. Other couples center on the issue of scheduling. At least one woman has said that she feels that she now has more time for herself. I am tempted to focus the study in this direction. Already I have begun to think about how a paper on time and family life would be organized. Already I am imagining how the temporal dimension fits into the problem of social order.

As tempting as it is to narrow the framework to something so specific, I feel that it is much too premature to begin imposing a structure so rigid on the interviews. Still, I must convey to you what it is that I would like you to get during the second phase.

First of all, let me reiterate a basic tenet of this type of research: the idea is to let the subjects lead you rather than vice versa. The questions that you ask are supposed to serve essentially as probes which prompt the couples to talk about themselves. While you are asking questions you must be particularly sensitive to what is important to them, what are the questions that they seem to be interested in, what are they troubled about, and (very important, but often forgotten) what do they take for granted. Given this approach, the paradox of depth interviewing becomes clear: how do you lead them to talk without "leading" them? Wiseman and Aron (1970: 28-29) provide some guidelines.

⌐ Throughout the interview, the social investigator must take pains to be as neutral as possible. He must resist the temptation to moralize, to give advice, or to otherwise indicate how he feels about the information given. Above all, he must encourage his respondents to keep talking. A nod of the head once in a while, to indicate understanding, is sufficient after a relationship has been established and answers are forthcoming. More reaction might interrupt the respondent's train of thought and elaboration of various points.

And Lofland (1971: 81, 85, 89, 90):

> In [depth interviewing], the emphasis is on obtaining narratives or accounts in the person's own terms. One wants the character and contours of such accounts to be set by the interviewee. The researcher might have a general idea of the kinds of things that will compose the account but still be interested in what the interviewee provides on his own and the terms in which he or she does it. As the interviewee gives his account, one is attentive to what is mentioned and also to what is not mentioned but is felt by the interviewer to be possibly important. . . . One caution about wording questions needs to be given. Avoid posing questions in such a way as to communicate what you believe to be a preferable answer. Questions so posed are known as leading questions. Instead of beginning by saying "Don't you think that . . . ?" begin with something like "What do you think about . . . ?". . . . For most interviewing situations, it is most productive of information for the interviewer to assume a non-argumentative, supportive, and sympathetically understanding attitude. . . . I would say that successful interviewing is not unlike carrying on unthreatening, self-controlled, supportive, polite, and cordial interaction in everyday life.

Given the above, we shall continue to ask the most general questions: "What's happened since I last saw you?" "What's happened since the baby arrived?" Start off the second interviews with these deliberately ambiguous questions. First of all, they are the most obvious questions to the subjects. Even though you will have visited them once before, you still must expect that you will have to renegotiate an entree into their lives. Start with the most nonthreatening types of queries. Also, due to your asking in most general terms what they are all about, they may provide leads for you to follow. If the couple asks what do you mean by "What's happened since I last saw you?" (highly likely), meaning that they want you to structure the question more, I've decided that the best "general idea" (see Lofland; he uses the phrase in the preceding quote) is one derived from Kantor and Lehr (1975: 37). They argue that affect, power, and meaning categorize all or nearly all the interactional behaviors manifested by family members. Using their definitions, the kinds of questions you would ask are outlined below.

Affect is intimacy and nurturance—that sense of loving and being loved by someone. Sample questions: "Has the love that you have for each other changed in any way? Do you feel more or less intimate with each other?"

This area is, of course, the most sensitive. If the couple chooses, they can get into their sexual relations. Save this area for points in the interview when you feel you have gained rapport (typically, toward the end). Also try to pose the questions in relatively nonthreatening ways. For example, "Some couples have mentioned that they feel less intimate now that the baby has come. Have you had this experience?"

Power is the freedom to decide what we want, and the ability to get it. Here we are talking not only about decision-making between the couple, but also the idea of constraint. To what degree is the child now running their lives? Do they feel that they have more or less freedom now that the child has arrived? This, of course, gets into that notion of time that I mentioned earlier. So ask, "Who is the principal decision maker?" Or better, "How are decisions reached; any change?"

Meaning is a kind of philosophical framework that provides us with explanations of reality and helps us define our identity. What we are talking about here is also our conceptions of self and other. Relevant questions: "How do you think about yourself? How do you see your husband (wife)? How do you see your child? Your marriage?"

The purpose of the threefold distinction is to give you a framework without giving you a framework. In other words, we want to focus on issues that one would deduce are salient in any family. During the course of the interviews the couples will "flesh out" this framework. Your job is to provide the most general guide and let them fill in the rest.

Also, with respect to the threefold distinction, I think the best way to proceed is to talk first about meaning, then power, then affect. This would seem to be the most nonthreatening. Of course, if a couple wants to jump right into affect, fine. Don't cut them off.

Okay, so you start by asking very generally what's happened. Then you go to the meaning, power, affect framework. Finally, ask the couple what questions they think you should be asking. Give them time to answer, to think. Let them participate in the makeup of the study. This can be most informative.

As always, and as you seem to already recognize, very often it is not the initial question on a topic that gets a subject going. Rather, it is the follow-ups: "What makes you say that? Why? Can you tell me more? How do you feel about what your husband (wife) just said?" That last question is most important. Do play the husband and wife off each other. This is a point I made in my first methodological note. Doing this is not, as I define it, "therapy." It is simply an overt recognition that there are multiperspectives and metaperspectives in family life.

One other point on the substance of the interview: conduct each interview as if you were going to write a case study on each couple. This means that you should get some idea of the history of their relationship. Thus, when the couple tries to provide a historical context to their answers (e.g., "Well, you see, we were married when we were young, so . . .), by all means let them do so. In fact, these are excellent times to ask about their past. The questions then seem natural rather than nosy. When you do depart from the "general idea" to cover some historical information, try to remember where you left off. Then you can say, "Let's see, where were we?" Once again, this is a very nonthreatening conversational style. I can't provide any formal rule on how much background to get. This is something you must feel. There is no need to ask about things that are covered on the background questionnaire [used to collect information on the couples' ages, incomes, etc.] unless you are using the question to introduce something else. . . .

Try to push the second interview to an hour and a half. Continue to diagram the spatial parameters of the interview situation. Pick up on comparisons (e.g., "During the first three months we could do this, but during the second three months . . ."). In other words, we are concerned with longitudinal effects.

THE THIRD INTERVIEW

As you know, this is perhaps the most important of the three interviews. It will be your final opportunity to tap into the couples' experiences.

Begin the interview pretty much as you did the second: "What has happened since I saw you last?" You are, of course, trying to pick up on aspects of the seventh, eighth, and ninth months that make them different from the previous months. Focus initially on the third phase, but do not restrict yourself to this time period. Encourage the couple to give you a retrospective summary of the whole nine months: ask them outright whether they have picked up any differences over the total nine-month period. Again, let them lead you. (I have only had the opportunity to see one second interview transcript—the others are not yet transcribed—but I thought that in this one (couple 4) you did a great job of naturally letting the conversations flow while at the same time getting the couple to respond to the issues we had talked about.)

The couple may want to know early in the interview about what we have found, how the data will be used, etc. Ask them to please hold their questions until the end; say that there will be some time for you to review, once again, the nature of the study, etc.

For the second interview, I talked about the framework of meaning, power, and affect. I still believe these three issues are important and I would encourage you to focus on them after (or during, if appropriate) the couple's preliminary responses to your "What's happened?" questions. (Review the methodological note for the second interview in order to familiarize yourself with the definitions of these terms.)   *Time:* Reading the first set of transcripts as well as some related research convinces me that this is still a potentially important subject. One hypothesis that I am particularly interested in testing is whether the couple begins to view the time schedule which has evolved since the child arrived as something that seems to stand over and above them. In other words, it is not uncommon for people to see routines as "natural" (ontological, God given, inevitable) when in fact they are the ones who set up the routine in the first place. I wonder if this applies to parenthood. A number of couples talked about setting up schedules *for* the kid while others talked about having schedules set up *by* the kid. It will be interesting to compare these two groups' temporal perceptions during the third interview. So be sensitive to the couple's comments on schedules and time for each other and self. If, according to the couple's verbal or nonverbal cues, the issue seems to be important to the couple, then pursue it. This, of course, is a judgment call; it is your sensitivity to the couple's messages that will produce a good interview.

The same criterion that applied during the second interview also applies here: assume that you are going to write a case study on each couple and are interested in the couple you are interviewing as a single case. We'll worry about comparisons after the data are in.

One question that you should throw in is whether the couple intends to have another child, and whether their decision (or non-decision) has been influenced by events during these nine months. While you are posing this question, pursue the theme of how the couples view children in relation to their marriage. In other words, how do they see their children fulfilling or not fulfilling the relationship they have with each other.

Debriefing: Essentially the debriefing will begin when you ask the couple whether there are any issues/questions that they think are important and that they believe you should ask. Given the fact that this is the final interview, many of the couples may begin to ask general questions about the study itself. Do not shut the tape recorder off. While the couple is asking questions about the study, we are getting valuable data about how the couple approached the study. Ask them what they thought about the study, how they would have done it differently, what they liked and disliked. Use their responses to the questions to find out what they were most anxious about, and then reduce that anxiety. Reiterate the fact that their names will not be used. If they ask what the final report will look like, tell them it will probably appear as a series of papers. Some case studies will be presented to give readers a sense of how one or two couples dealt with the experience. Theoretical papers, in which quotes from a variety of couples will be used to illustrate points, will also be written. [At this stage of the research, a book was not planned.]

REFERENCES

ALLAN, G. (1980) "A note on interviewing spouses together." Journal of Marriage and the Family 42 (February): 205-210.

ATKINSON, M. and V. GECAS (1978) "What's been published in family sociology in the past ten years." Paper presented at the National Council on Family Relations, Philadelphia, Pennsylvania.

BELL, C. and H. NEWBY (1976) "Husbands and wives: the dynamics of the deferential dialectic." Pp. 152-168 in D. Barker and S. Allen (eds.) Dependence and Exploitation in Work and Marriage. London: Longman.

BELVILLE, Y. P., O. N. RATHS, and C. J. BELVILLE (1969) "Conjoint marriage therapy with a husband and wife team." American Journal of Orthopsychiatry 39: 473-483.

BENNETT, L. A., K. McAVITY, and S. J. WOLIN (1978) "Couple versus individual interviews: an issue in family research methodology." Paper presented at the annual meetings of the National Council on Family Relations, Philadelphia, Pennsylvania.

BERGER, P. L. (1963) Invitation to Sociology: A Humanistic Perspective. New York: Doubleday/Anchor.

––– and H. KELLNER (1964) "Marriage and the construction of reality." Diogenes 64: 1-25.

BERGER, P. L. and T. LUCKMANN (1966) The Social Construction of Reality: A Treatise in the Sociology of Knowledge. New York: Doubleday/Anchor.

BERK, R. A. and S. F. BERK (1979) Labor and Leisure at Home. Beverly Hills, CA: Sage Publications.

BERNAL, G. and J. BAKER (1979) "Toward a metacommunicational framework of couple interactions." Family Process 18 (September): 292-302.

BERNARD, J. (1975) Women, Wives, Mothers: Values and Options. Chicago: Aldine.

BLAU, P. M. (1964) Exchange and Power in Social Life. New York: John Wiley and Sons.

BLAUNER, R. (1964) Alienation and Freedom: The Factory Worker and His Industry. Chicago: University of Chicago Press.

BLOOD, R. O., Jr., and D. M. WOLFE (1960) Husbands and Wives: The Dynamics of Married Living. New York: The Free Press.

BLUSTEIN, J. (1979) "Child rearing and family interests." Pp. 115-122 in O. O'Neill and W. Ruddick (eds.) Having Children: Philosophical and Legal Reflections on Parenthood. New York: Oxford University Press.

BOTT, E. (1971) Family and Social Network: Roles, Norms, and External Relationships in Ordinary Urban Families. New York: The Free Press.

BRAZELTON, T. B. (1969) Infants and Mothers: Differences in Development. New York: Dell.

BREEN, D. (1975) The Birth of a First Child. London: Tavistock.

BRUYN, S. T. (1966) The Human Perspective in Sociology: The Methodology of Participant Observation. Englewood Cliffs, NJ: Prentice-Hall.

BURR, W. R., G. K. LEIGH, R. D. DAY, and J. CONSTANTINE (1979a) "Symbolic interaction and the family." Pp. 42-111 in W. R. Burr, R. Hill, F. I. Nye, and I. L. Reiss (eds.) Contemporary Theories about the Family, Vol. 2: General Theories/ Theoretical Orientations. New York: The Free Press.

BURR, W. R., R. HILL, F. I. NYE, and I. L. REISS [eds.] (1979b) Contemporary Theories about the Family, Vol. 1: Research-Based Theories. New York: The Free Press.

COLLINS, J. and B. NELSON (1966) "Interviewing the married couple: some research aspects and therapeutic implications." British Journal of Psychiatric Social Work 8: 46-51.

COUCH, E. H. (1969) Joint and Family Interviews in the Treatment of Marital Problems. New York: Family Service Association of America.

COWAN, C. P., P. A. COWAN, L. COIE, and J. D. COIE (1978) "Becoming a family: the impact of a first child's birth on the couple's relationship." Pp. 296-324 in W. B. Miller and L. F. Newman (eds.) The First Child and Family Formation. Chapel Hill: Carolina Population Center, University of North Carolina.

CROMWELL, R. E. and D. H. OLSON [eds.] (1975) Power in Families. Beverly Hills, CA: Sage Publications.

CUBER, J. F. and P. B. HARROFF (1965) Sex and the Significant Americans. Baltimore, MD: Penguin.

DAVENPORT-SLACK, B. and C. H. BOYLAN (1974) "Psychological correlates of childbirth pain." Psychosomatic Medicine 36: 215-223.

DeGRAZIA, S. (1964) Of Time, Work, and Leisure. Garden City, NJ: Doubleday/Anchor.

DOUGLAS, J. D. (1976) Investigative Social Research: Individual and Team Field Research. Beverly Hills, CA: Sage Publications.

DRUCKMAN, D. (1977) "Social-psychological approaches to the study of negotiation." Pp. 15-44 in D. Druckman (ed.) Negotiations: Social-Psychological Perspectives. Beverly Hills, CA: Sage Publications.

DUKE, J. T. (1976) Conflict and Power in Social Life, Provo, UT: Brigham Young University Press.

DYER, E. D. (1963) "Parenthood as crisis: a re-study." Marriage and Family Living 25 (May): 196-201.

EMERSON, R. M. (1976) "Social exchange theory." Pp. 335-362 in A. Inkeles (ed.) Annual Review of Sociology. Palo Alto, CA: Annual Reviews.

——— (1962) "Power-dependence relations." American Sociological Review 27 (February): 31-41.

ENTWISLE, D. R. and S. G. DOERING (1980) The First Birth. Baltimore, MD: The John Hopkins University Press.

FELDMAN, H. (1974) "Change in marriage and parenthood: a methodological design." Pp. 206-226 in E. Peck and J. Senderowitz (eds.) Pronatalism: The Myth of Mom and Apple Pie. New York: Thomas V. Crowell.

FESTINGER, L. (1957) A Theory of Cognitive Dissonance. Evanston, IL: Row, Peterson.

FILSTEAD, W. J. [ed.] (1970) Qualitative Methodology: Firsthand Involvement with the Social World. Chicago: Markham.

FRIEDSON, E. (1976) "The division of labor as social interaction." Social Problems 23 (February): 304-313.

GARFINKEL, H. (1967) Studies in Ethnomethodology. Englewood Cliffs, NJ: Prentice-Hall.

GELLES, R. J. (1975) "Violence and pregnancy: a note on the extent of the problem and needed services." The Family Coordinator 24 (January): 81-86.

GERSON, E. M. (1976) "On 'quality of life.' " American Sociological Review 41 (October): 793-806.

GLASER, B. G. (1978) Theoretical Sensitivity: Advances in the Methodology of Grounded Theory. Mill Valley, CA: The Sociology Press.

——— and A. L. STRAUSS (1967) The Discovery of Grounded Theory. Chicago: Aldine.

GOFFMAN, E. (1971) Relations in Public. New York: Harper & Row.

——— (1961) Encounters: Two Studies in the Sociology of Interaction. Indianapolis: Bobbs-Merrill.

GOULDNER, A. W. (1960) "The norm of reciprocity: a preliminary statement." American Sociological Review 25 (April): 161-178.

HANSEN, D. A. and V. A. JOHNSON (1979) "Rethinking family stress theory: definitional aspects." Pp. 582-603 in W. R. Burr, R. Hill, F. I. Nye, and I. L. Reiss (eds.) Contemporary Theories about the Family, Vol. I: Research-Based Theories. New York: The Free Press.

HAWKINS, J. L. (1968) "Associations between companionship, hostility, and marital satisfaction." Journal of Marriage and the Family 30 (November): 647-650.

HAYS, W. C. (1977) "Theorists and theoretical frameworks identified by family sociologists." Journal of Marriage and the Family 39 (February): 59-65.

HESS, R. D. and G. Handel (1959) Family Worlds. Chicago: University of Chicago Press.

HILL, R. (1978) "Psychosocial consequences of the first birth: a discussion." Pp. 392-401 in W. B. Miller and L. F. Newman (eds.) The First Child and Family Formation. Chapel Hill: Carolina Population Center, University of North Carolina.

——— and J. ALDOUS (1969) "Socialization for marriage and parenthood." Pp. 885-950 in D. A. Goslin (ed.) Handbook of Socialization, Theory and Research. Chicago: Rand McNally.

HOBBS, D. F., Jr. (1968) "Transition to parenthood: a replication and an extension." Journal of Marriage and the Family 30 (August): 413-417.

——— (1965) "Parenthood as crisis: a third study." Journal of Marriage and the Family 27 (August): 367-372.

——— and S. P. COLE (1976) "Transition to parenthood: a decade replication."
Journal of Marriage and the Family 38 (November): 723-731.

HOBBS, D. F., Jr., and J. M. WIMBISH (1977) "Transition to parenthood by black
couples." Journal of Marriage and the Family 39 (November): 677-689.

HOCK, E. (1978) "Working and non-working mothers with infants: perceptions of
their careers, their infants' needs, and satisfaction with mothering." Developmental Psychology 14 (January): 37-43.

———, K. CHRISTMAN, and M. HOCK (1980) "Career-related decisions of mothers
of infants." Family Relations 29 (July): 325-330.

HODGSON, J. W. and R. A. LEWIS (1979) "Pilgrims progress III: a trend analysis of
family theory and methodology." Family Process 18 (June): 163-173.

HOFFMAN, W. (1978) "Effects of the first child on the woman's role." Pp. 340-367
in W. B. Miller and L. F. Newman (eds.) The First Child and Family Formation.
Chapel Hill: Carolina Population Center, University of North Carolina.

——— and J. D. MANIS (1978) "Influences of children on marital interaction and
parental satisfactions and dissatisfactions." Pp. 165-214 in R. M. Lerner and G. B.
Spanier (eds.) Child Influences on Marital and Family Interaction: A Life-Span
Perspective. New York: Academic Press.

HOMANS, G. (1974) Social Behavior: Its Elementary Forms. New York: Harcourt
Brace Jovanovich.

HUGHES, C. C. (1961) "The concept and use of time in the middle years: the St.
Lawrence Island Eskimos." Pp. 91-95 in R. Kleemeier (ed.) Aging and Leisure.
New York: Oxford.

ISRAEL, J. (1971) Alienation from Marx to Modern Sociology: A Macrosociological
Analysis. Boston: Allyn & Bacon.

JACOBY, A. P. (1969) "Transition to parenthood: a reassessment." Journal of
Marriage and the Family 31 (November): 720-727.

JAFFE, S. S. and J. VIERTEL (1979) Becoming Parents: Preparing for the Emotional Changes of First-Time Parenthood. New York: Atheneum.

KANTOR, D. and W. LEHR (1975) Inside the Family. San Francisco: Jossey-Bass.

KUHN, A. (1974) The Logic of Social Systems. San Francisco: Jossey-Bass.

LAMB, M. (1978) "Influences of the child on marital quality and family interaction
during the prenatal, perinatal and infancy periods." Pp. 137-164 in R. M. Lerner
and G. B. Spanier (eds.) Child Influences on Marital and Family Interaction: A
Life-Span Perspective. New York: Academic Press.

LaROSSA, R. (1979) "Sex during pregnancy: a symbolic interactionist analysis."
The Journal of Sex Research 15 (May): 119-128.

——— (1978) "Conjoint marital interviewing as a research strategy." Case Analysis 1
(Fall): 141-150.

——— (1977) Conflict and Power in Marriage: Expecting the First Child. Beverly Hills,
CA: Sage Publications.

———, L. A. BENNETT, and R. J. GELLES (forthcoming) "Ethical dilemmas in
qualitative family research." Journal of Marriage and the Family 43 (May).

LASLETT, B. and R. RAPOPORT (1975) "Collaborative interviewing and interactive
research." Journal of Marriage and the Family 37 (November): 968-977.

LeMASTERS, E. E. (1970) Parents in Modern America. Homewood, IL: The Dorsey
Press.

――― (1957) "Parenthood as crisis." Marriage and Family Living 19 (November): 352-355.

LESLIE, G. R. (1964) "Conjoint therapy in marriage counseling." Journal of Marriage and the Family 26 (February): 65-71.

LEWIS, O. (1959) Five Families. New York: Basic Books.

LOFLAND, J. (1971) Analyzing Social Settings. Belmont, CA: Wadsworth.

――― (1966) Doomsday Cult. Englewood Cliffs, NJ: Prentice-Hall.

MACKEY, W. C. and R. D. DAY (1979) "Some indicators of fathering behaviors in the United States: a crosscultural examination of adult male-child interaction." Journal of Marriage and the Family 41 (May): 287-297.

MARKS, S. R. (1977) "Multiple roles and role strain: some notes on human energy, time, and commitment." American Sociological Review 42 (December) 921-936.

MASLACH, C. (1976) "Burned-out." Human Behavior 59 (September): 16-22.

――― and A. PINES (1977) "The burn-out syndrome in the day care setting." Child Care Quarterly 6 (Summer): 100-113.

McCALL, G. J. and J. L. SIMMONS [eds.] (1969) Issues in Participant Observation: A Text and Reader. Reading, MA: Addison-Wesley.

McLAIN, R. and A. WEIGERT (1979) "Toward a phenomenological sociology of family: a programmatic essay." Pp. 160-205 in W. R. Burr, R. Hill, F. I. Nye, and I. L. Reiss (eds.) Contemporary Theories about the Family, Vol. 2: General Theories/Theoretical Orientations. New York: The Free Press.

MEAD, G. H. (1934) Mind, Self, and Society from the Standpoint of a Social Behaviorist (Edited by C. W. Morris). Chicago: University of Chicago Press.

MEYEROWITZ, J. H. and H. FELDMAN (1966) "Transition to parenthood." Psychiatric Research Report 20 (February): 78-84.

MILLER, B. C. and D. L. SOLLIE (1980) "Normal stresses during the transition to parenthood." Family Relations 29 (October): 459-465.

MILLS, C. W. (1959) The Sociological Imagination. London: Oxford University Press.

――― (1940) "Situated actions and vocabularies of motive." American Sociological Review 5 (December): 904-913.

MORTIMER, J. T. and R. G. SIMMONS (1978) "Adult socialization." Annual Review of Sociology 4: 421-454.

NYE, F. I. (1979) "Choice, exchange, and the family." Pp. 1-41 in W. R. Burr, R. Hill, F. I. Nye, and I. L. Reiss (eds.) Contemporary Theories about the Family, Vol. 2: General Theories/Theoretical Orientations. New York: The Free Press.

――― and A. E. BAYER (1963) "Some recent trends in family research." Social Forces 41 (March): 290-301.

O'CONNOR, P. A. (1975) "A model of power and coalition formation in conjoint marriage counseling." The Family Coordinator 24 (January): 55-63.

OLSEN, M. E. (1968) The Process of Social Organization: Power in Social Systems. New York: Holt, Rinehart & Winston.

OLSON, D. H., D. H. SPRENKLE, and C. RUSSELL (1979) "Circumplex model of marital and family systems: I. Cohesion and adaptability dimensions, family types, and clinical applications." Family Process 18 (March): 3-28.

PARKE, R. D. and D. B. SAWIN (1976) "The father's role in infancy: a re-evaluation." The Family Coordinator 25 (October): 365-371.

PEARLIN, L. I. (1975) "Status inequality and stress in marriage." American Socio-logical Review 40 (June): 344-357.

PLECK, J. H. (1976) "Men's new roles in the family: housework and child care." Working paper. Wellesley, MA: Wellesley College Center for Research on Women.

––– and M. RUSTAD (1980) "Husbands' and wives' time in family work and paid work in the 1975-76 study of time use." Working paper. Wellesley, MA: Wellesley College Center for Research on Women.

POLATNICK, M. (1973) "Why men don't rear children: a power analysis." Berkeley Journal of Sociology 18: 45-86.

RAPOPORT, R. and R. N. RAPOPORT (1976) Dual Career Families Reexamined. New York: Harper & Row.

––– (1975) "Men, women, and equity." The Family Coordinator 24 (October): 421-432.

RAPOPORT, R., R. N. RAPOPORT, and Z. STRELITZ (1977) Fathers, Mothers and Society. New York: Basic Books.

RAUSH, H. L., W. A. BARRY, R. K. HERTEL, and M. A. SWAIN (1974) Communi-cation, Conflict, and Marriage. San Francisco: Jossey-Bass.

RAUSH, H. L., K. A. MARSHALL, and J. M. FEATHERMAN (1970) "Relations at three early stages of marriage as reflected by the use of personal pronouns." Family Process 9 (March): 69-82.

REISS, I. L. and B. MILLER (1974) "A theoretical analysis of heterosexual permis-siveness." University of Minnesota, Family Study Center (Technical Bulletin No. 2), Minneapolis.

ROBINSON, J. P. (1977) How Americans Use Time: A Social-Psychological Analysis of Everyday Behavior. New York: Praeger.

ROSENBLATT, P. C. and S. L. TITUS (1976) "Together and apart in the family." Humanitas 12 (November): 367-379.

ROSSI, A. S. (1977) "A biosocial perspective on parenting." Daedalus 106 (Spring): 1-31.

––– (1969) "Sex equality: the beginnings of ideology." The Humanist 29 (Septem-ber/October): 3-6, 16.

––– (1968) "Transition to parenthood." Journal of Marriage and the Family 30 (February): 26-39.

RUANO, B. J., J. D. BRUCE, and M. M. McDERMOTT (1969) "Pilgrims progress II: recent trends and prospects in family research." Journal of Marriage and the Family 31 (November): 688-698.

RUSSELL, C. (1979) "Circumplex model of family systems: III empirical evaluation with families." Family Process 18 (March): 29-46.

––– (1974) "Transition to parenthood: problems and gratifications." Journal of Marriage and the Family 18 (March): 29-46.

RYDER, R. G. (1973) "Longitudinal data relating marriage satisfaction and having a child." Journal of Marriage and the Family 35 (November): 604-607.

SAFILIOS-ROTHSCHILD, C. (1976) "A macro- and micro-examination of family power and love: an exchange model." Journal of Marriage and the Family 38 (May): 355-362.

SAGER, C. J. (1967) "The conjoint session in marriage therapy." American Journal of Psychoanalysis 27: 139-146.

SATIR, V. (1964) Conjoint Family Therapy. Palo Alto: Science and Behavior Books.

SCANZONI, J. (1972) Sexual Bargaining. Englewood Cliffs, NJ: Prentice-Hall.

SCOTT, M. B. and S. M. LYMAN (1968) "Accounts." American Sociological Review 33 (February): 46-62.

SENN, M. J. and C. H. HARTFORD (1968) The Firstborn: Experiences of Eight American Families. Cambridge, MA: Harvard University Press.

SHAPIRO, D. and F. L. MOTT (1979) "Labor supply behavior of prospective and new mothers." Demography 16 (May): 199-208.

SJOBERG, G. and R. NETT (1968) A Methodology for Social Research. New York: Harper & Row.

SKIDMORE, R. A. and V. S. GARRETT (1955) "The joint interview in marriage counseling." Marriage and Family Living 17 (November): 349-354.

SMITH, V. G. and F. M. ANDERSON (1963) "Conjoint interviews with marriage partners." Marriage and Family Living 25 (May): 184-188.

SOLLIE, D. L. and B. C. MILLER (1980) "The transition to parenthood as a critical time for building family strengths," in N. Stinnett, B. Chesser, J. DeFrain, and P. Knaub (eds.) Family Strengths: Positive Models for Family Life. Omaha: University of Nebraska Press.

SPOCK, B. (1976) Baby and Child Care. New York: Hawthorn.

SPREY, J. (1979) "Conflict theory and the study of marriage and the family." Pp. 130-159 in W. R. Burr, R. Hill, F. I. Nye and I. L. Reiss (eds.) Contemporary Theories about the Family, Vol. 2: General Theories/Theoretical Orientations. New York: The Free Press.

STRAUS, M. A. (1979) "Measuring intrafamily conflict and violence: the conflict tactics (CT) scales." Journal of Marriage and the Family 41 (February): 75-88.

––– R. J. GELLES, and S. K. STEINMETZ (1980) Behind Closed Doors: Violence in the American Family. New York: Doubleday/Anchor.

STRAUSS, A. (1978) Negotiations: Varieties, Contexts, Processes, and Social Order. San Francisco: Jossey-Bass.

STOKES, R. and J. P. HEWITT (1976) "Aligning actions." American Sociological Review 41 (October): 838-849.

SWENSEN, C. H., Jr. (1973) Introduction to Interpersonal Relations. Glenview: Scott, Foresman.

THIBAUT, J. W. and H. H. KELLEY (1959) The Social Psychology of Groups. New York: John Wiley & Sons.

WATSON, A. S. (1963) "The conjoint psychotherapy of marriage partners." American Journal of Orthopsychiatry 33: 912-922.

WATZLAWICK, P., J. BEAVIN, and D. D. JACKSON (1967) Pragmatics of Human Communication: A Study of Interactional Patterns, Pathologies, and Paradoxes. New York: W. W. Norton.

WEBER, M. (1947) The Theory of Social and Economic Organization. New York: The Free Press.

Webster's New Collegiate Dictionary (1977) Springfield, MA: Merriam.

WEISBERG, M. (1964) "Joint interviewing with marital partners." Social Casework 45: 221-229.

WEISS, R. S. (1966) "Alternative approaches in the study of complex situations." Human Organization 25 (Fall): 198-206.

WELLMAN, D. T. (1977) Portraits of White Racism. Cambridge: Cambridge University Press.

WHYTE, W. F. (1955) Street Corner Society. Chicago: University of Chicago Press.

WISEMAN, J. P. and M. S. ARON (1970) Field Projects for Sociology Students. Cambridge, MA: Schenkman.

ZERUBAVEL, E. (1979a) "Private time and public time: the temporal structure of social accessibility and professional commitments." Social Forces 58 (September): 38-58.

――― (1979b) Patterns of Time in Hospital Life: A Sociological Perspective. Chicago: University of Chicago Press.

AUTHOR INDEX

SUBJECT INDEX

Academic life, 179-204
Alienation, 70, 54, 87
Aligning actions
    and change, 88-89, 90-99, 126
    and continuity, 88-90, 126
    and traditionalization process, 88-99
    defined, 86, 125
    legitimacy of, 96-97
    short-term vs. long-term use, 95-96
Aligning actions, types of
    accounts, 86, 164-166, 170-173, 198, 200
    appeals to personal coorientations, 88, 96
    appeals to positional coorientations, 88, 96
    emergence appeals, 87, 96
    excuses, 86-87, 96, 170-173, 198
    justifications, 86-87, 96, 170-173, 198
    motives, 86
    relativity appeals, 87, 96
    remedial interchanges, 86
American Journal of Sociology, 29
American Sociological Review, 29
Androgyny, 85, 89, 180-181, 189
Anticipatory socialization, 231
Attention levels, defined, 49-56, 69
Attitudes vs. behaviors, 19, 20-21, 84-98, 232

Baby care, 230, 232
    and on-the-job training, 66, 111, 126, 198

    and patience, 134, 137, 138, 187-188, 191
    and perceived competence of infant, 26, 63, 66, 197, 199
    compared to air traffic control work, 54
    compared to assembly line work, 54
    compared to hospital work, 46, 72, 211, 212
    first vs. second child, 32, 40, 131, 138-139, 193-194, 226, 239
    helping vs sharing, 27, 57-62, 111-112, 140, 157, 232
    pace of, 54, 105, 107, 182-183
    repetitiveness of, 54, 182-183
    routinization of, 66
    work vs. play, 49-52, 137
Baby power, 108
Babysitting, 46, 57, 107, 138, 187, 210, 215
Bathroom time, 54, 161, 163, 193
Biography reconstruction, 105, 240
Birth
    husband's presence at, 155, 239
    classes, 231, 239
Breast-feeding, 90-91, 116, 160-161, 164-166, 231-232
"Burn-out," 54-55, 215

Case analysis, 39-41, 48, 230-231, 244, 245, 246
Causal proposition, defined, 207-208
Childbirth Education Association (C.E.A.), 27

ABOUT THE AUTHORS

RALPH LaROSSA is a sociologist whose research interests include the transition to parenthood, age and sex stratification, marital violence, and qualitative methods. He is the author of *Conflict and Power in Marriage: Expecting the First Child*, and is currently on the faculty at Georgia State University in Atlanta.

MAUREEN MULLIGAN LaROSSA is a registered nurse who, for the past five years, has been involved in research dealing with the effects of prematurity on child development and mother-infant interaction. She is currently an infant evaluator in the Department of Newborn Medicine at Grady Memorial Hospital in Atlanta.